WHOSE TRUTH MATTERS

JAMES E. CAMPBELL, M.D.

Copyright © 2023 James E. Campbell, M.D.

All rights reserved. No part of this book may be reproduced, stored, or transmitted by any means—whether auditory, graphic, mechanical, or electronic—without written permission of both publisher and author, except in the case of brief excerpts used in critical articles and reviews. Unauthorized reproduction of any part of this work is illegal and is punishable by law.

ISBN: 979-8-88640-598-9 (sc)
ISBN: 979-8-88640-599-6 (hc)
ISBN: 979-8-88640-596-5 (e)

Because of the dynamic nature of the Internet, any web addresses or links contained in this book may have changed since publication and may no longer be valid. The views expressed in this work are solely those of the author and do not necessarily reflect the views of the publisher, and the publisher hereby disclaims any responsibility for them.

One Galleria Blvd., Suite 1900, Metairie, LA 70001
1-888-421-2397

"A wise man is cautious how he becomes
the echo of a commonly received opinion."
French Psychiatrist Philippe Pinel

"We choose truth over facts."

—Joe Biden

What gives elites the right to declare what others say is disinformation—without debate?

—Anonymous

"Truth is so rare that it is delightful to tell it."

—Emily Dickenson

"People who do not believe in facts are dangerous."

—Carson Tucker

"The truth has no defense against a fool determined to believe a lie."

—Mark Twain

"A wise man is cautious how he becomes
the echo of a commonly received opinion."
French Psychiatrist Philippe Pinel

"We choose truth over facts."

—Joe Biden

What gives elites the right to declare what others say is disinformation—without debate?

—Anonymous

"Truth is so rare that it is delightful to tell it."

—Emily Dickenson

"People who do not believe in facts are dangerous."

—Carson Tucker

"The truth has no defense against a fool determined to believe a lie."

—Mark Twain

THE INCONVENIENT TRUTH

The most striking contradiction of our civilization is the fundamental reverence for truth which we profess and the thoroughgoing disregard for it which we practice

—Vilhjalmur Stefansson

CONTENTS

About the Author ix
Opening comments 1
Academia 11
Psychiatry 13
The Left 18
Responsibility 22
Trump Derangement Syndrome 25
Reasoning 26
Finance/Campaign Influence 32
Distorted Thinking 34
Founder's Error 38
Nonsense: Robert John Gula 41
Humor from the Internet 66
Techniques Used by the Left 67
More on Responsibility 74
Blame Thinking 83
Accurate Speech 95
Introduction to Associated Concepts 107
Product or Choice? 111
An Introduction to the Idea of Speaking Accurately 172
About Guns 230
Blaming Kills 236
Appendix I 237
Appendix II 267
Appendix III 270
Appendix IV 272
Acknowledgements 277
Other Books by the Author 278

As one may bring himself to believe almost anything he is inclined to believe, it makes all the difference whether we begin or end with inquiry. "What is truth?"

—Whately

ABOUT THE AUTHOR

James Ernest Campbell, M.D. grew up in Illinois farm country where his two closest companions were a border collie named Peg and an Arabian horse named Razja. He was inscripted into the first grade a year early because the school needed one more student in order to stay open. He graduated co-valedictorian from Warsaw High School and went on to MacMurray College in Jacksonville, Ill. for three years before being accepted by three of the four medical schools where he applied. He chose to go to St. Louis Univ. Medical School in St. Louis Missouri for his medical training. Following that he went to Michael Reese Hospital in Chicago for a one-year straight-medical internship and his basic three-year adult psychiatric residency. In 1971, after completing his military service at Ramey Air Force Base in Puerto Rico, he set up an adult psychiatric practice in Phoenix, Arizona. Nine years later he decided to broaden his practice scope by attending a two-year Child Psychiatry Fellowship at UCLA. Afterwards, he returned to Phoenix where he has been treating children, adolescents and adults.

Dr. Campbell feels fortunate to have had the opportunity to do something he had wanted since the age of six. He concludes that many conflicts can be improved with little effort once we understand how the common institutions we accept as being close to our heart can be double edged swords.

Doctor Campbell does not care whether people are left, or right, politically, as much as he cares about the way they come to frame choices: lying, prejudices, deliberate distortions, blind eye to hypocrisy, no sense of history, destruction of basic principles of decency, tunnel vision, and a disregard for knowledge (truth over fact). He is critical of the lack of an intelligent approach to the problems 'we the people' need to work out our issues.

OPENING COMMENTS

People can be deliberately or unintentionally cruel on different levels. Primo Levy in his book *Survival in Auschwitz* said he was fortunate to have been deported to Auschwitz in 1944 and not earlier (or he likely would not have survived). In Philip Zimbardo's (Stanford Univ.) prison study, where people were clearly in a pretend situation, one-third of the mock guards demonstrated sadistic behavior toward mock prisoners. A scary conclusion of this study is that Americans could get caught in a similar condition the Germans found themselves in during WWII. In America, we projected our fear and anger onto loyal Asian citizens, forcing them to live under substandard conditions, taking possessions away from them, and frequently contributing to the destruction of their sense of value. Today the Democratic contingency of the American family is currently employing those same tactics against the Republican wing of the American family.

When one side of a community is over-represented, and when that side is hostile to the other, the community is exposed to only the interpretation maintained by the majority. In our society today the left has become hostile to all points of view except theirs. There is a pitfall in suggesting solutions to problems only belong to one side of the argument. Most people, especially those in power, like to have solutions: Hitler, Machiavelli, Alexander, Aristotle, Augustus, Aquinas, Lincoln, Marx, Freud, Truman, Norman Vincent Peal, Muhammad and Jesus. The list of course is incomplete because it could include anyone with power, right on down the line to the weakest members of our society. Some solutions have been complete disasters and others have been positively credited.

Our form of government is very unique in the world as it was set up as a covenant, "We the people," and when one side takes the high-ground and declares only they know what is right, the covenant is broken. That is the current condition in the United States.

Norman Vincent Peal's book on *Power of Positive Thinking* was very popular for years, yet I never hear people talking about it. What happened to this idea, why was it so popular and why has it fallen into the hole of oblivion? (This is possibly an inaccurate perception.) Dale Carnegie's book on *How to Stop Worrying and Start Living* is brought up by my patients and is still being read and used.

To understand this, it is helpful to be aware of how our language undergoes transitions with time, and how this transformation influences the understanding we have of not only the solution presented but also of life. Politics can pervert language according to Orwell. Language is also distorted by current usage and present understanding. The left has weaponized our language: "Truth is what matters, not facts." [Said by now President Biden during the democrats debates and also later affirmed by Alexandria Ocasio-Cortez). What the left is apparently communicating here is that what they believe to be the truth carries more weight than facts. This explains why the impeachment effort from the left was dependent on 'my belief, my understanding, my impression" rather than on facts. It explains why the left propaganda machinery was so impressed with the left's impeachment process (since before the election of the President Trump they had been reporting their truth (wishes) day in and day out without regard for FACTS). One does not fault the left on absence of positive thinking. They are very positive they have all the answers.

A possible explanation is that Carnegie's books are written at a low level of abstraction. If you do what he suggests, you will experience the benefit almost immediately. There is less opportunity to distort the process than there is with Reverend Peal's book, which was written at a higher level of abstraction. [What constitutes Positive? Is it possible to be positive, but completely wrong?] The second reason could be how the word 'positive' has, over time, taken on a less 'positive' meaning. Todays left has elevated desire up the ladder of abstraction to **truth**; not to fact. In their game plan they see no reason to be burdened by what people understand (facts) when they can simply replace it with what they desire people to believe, **their truth**. (Their use of the word democracy is an example. They say republicans are trying to destroy democracy—what they do not say is that their use of democracy is the same as Russia ("a democratic, federative, law-based state with a republican form of government" [Wikipedia} we generally describe this as communism) or Chinas (China, according to Politics, "China says it will work with Russia to promote 'real democracy.'") form which has nothing to do with the democracy the U.S. has been practicing for the past 200 years. Because people do not understand the plural definitions, they can get confused. Indeed, republicans are in favor of destroying the democrats form of democracy since it supports the ideas of communism and authoritarianism. Republicans are supporting the American form of democracy. (The American form of democracy is known as a representative democracy government.) [Wikipedia reports "The debate over democracy in China has been a major ideological battleground in Chinese politics since the 19th century. Currently, political scientists do not recognize China as a democracy. Instead, they categorize China as an authoritarian state which has been characterized as a dictatorship.] Another example of redefining a word is the confusing statements by Customs and Border Protection officials that claim the border is secure at the same time millions of illegal aliens are coming across the border. Their definition of secure obviously is different form the meaning of secure that has been used before.) There may be no argument that is higher on the levels of abstraction than "being right." The person who argues they are right claims the highest level of abstraction that exists. It possibly even exceeds the abstraction of God.

People need to familiarize themselves to the concept of *levels of abstraction*. Without some knowledge of the term, it is impossible to understand certain arguments. A quick quote from the internet might be helpful. Levels of abstraction is "The amount of complexity by which a system is viewed or programed. The higher the level the less detail. The lower the level, the more detail." I frame it this way. The lower the level of abstraction the greater is the agreement between observers, the higher the level the less the agreement between observers. The democrats use a high level of abstraction when defining "women" for example. This is why the newest Supreme Court appointee cannot define a woman. Republicans on the other hand use a low level of abstraction to define a woman (2 X chromosomes), Democrats apparently have some high-level abstraction for the word 'secure' not defined but apparently known to democrats. Republicans define 'secure borders' as meaning no entrance without permission. The democrats have created a 'woke' condition similar to a religion. Remember, I said the higher on the level of abstraction the less agreement there is. The National Catholic Register says there are "an estimated 35,496 independent or non-denominational churches according to ARDA. (High level abstraction-low level agreement). Our constitution (not the democrat's version) for the past 200 years has not supported a central government religion, but it appears this is what the democrats are attempting to do, they are just being sneaky and not calling it a religion. It is easier to understand Biden's recent comment when being asked by a news commentator about what his wife thought about him running again. His answer as best I can recall was, "She thinks what we are doing is important." This is obviously not a reference to our economy, our border, our level of safety in our communities, or **our democracy**.

Some people have taken a position on love being the condition necessary to solve most of our problems. I have no conflict with love as a solution, except *it can be* such a high-level abstraction concept it confuses people. Kurt Vonnegut [Kurt Vonnegut: An Autobiographical Collage 1981 Dial Press p.197] says, "…love is a rotten substitute for respect." Does loving the poor and hungry put food into mouths? Would the world be more, or less, worse off, if I hated poor and hungry people so much, I gave what I could to such people to help them get out of their current condition?

An astute reader would say it is obvious the second person does not really hate the people, but hates the condition the people are in. The actual point I am trying to make is not all good feelings are helpful, and not all bad feelings are harmful. In the same way, not all positive thinking is helpful, and not all negative thinking is bad. The left makes factual thinking bad and an inconvenience in a quest for due process and power. It is somewhat understandable where this thinking comes from by looking at our judiciary oath. "The truth, the whole truth and nothing but the truth so help me God!" This of course is a rather inept oath, and the lawyers and judge involved do their best to make certain that stated condition never happens. People generally tell what they believe to be the truth, which is often far from the factual truth. Even facts can be disputed and interpreted differently: take the current non-discussion about the causes of global warming. Why 'non-discussion?' Because the left has declared those who have a different set of facts than their truth is bad and must want to keep the world from their divine protection. No lack of positive thinking there!

Why have I focused on respect and consideration as the more helpful concept? After all, it also has a moderately high-level abstraction definition. It can indeed be a concept residing in the clouds, but the current usage of the word seems tied more to acts, which is a lower-level concept. When my patients,' or their parents, tell me their children are not respectful, they follow it up with a description of behavior the child has done to demonstrate their disrespect. Trump was beat up daily by the left propaganda machinery (LPM) for something he said the left did not like (this is a style of distorted thinking called 'polarized thinking.') At the same time, they were silent about the things he accomplished (this falls under 'filtering'—another form of distorted thinking) for the people: I.e., lowest unemployment for women, minority groups, etc. is low level abstraction. It is there to see. It is a fact. When you reside in 'truth' you can still try and distort what can actually be seen if you look. People can read the transcript of the discussion between Trump and the president of Ukraine (low level abstraction) or listen to what the democrats claim the conversation was about (their level of truth-high level abstraction.) Styles of distorted thinking (SDT) will be discussed in more detail later.

Respect can be used inappropriately and/or with malice. Some delegates to the UN want to make it a capital punishment to show disrespect toward God. At the high level of abstraction [the perfect form as accorded to Plato] this may seem to have some merit, but at the practical low level of abstraction [the behavior resulting from this concept], it has to be recognized as just another way to control, terrorize and subjugate people by the power of those who want total control over others. When the elite left feigns concern for a group of people (immigrants) but acts in a manner that is harmful to another group (American citizens), it is very problematic and suspect. (It also falls under the SDT Fallacy of fairness.) Unfortunately, this is the mechanism the left is using in today's political arena. The democratic left elite has done a great job of weaponize the English language for their political purposes. Each day they create a new definition to justify their tyranny. There is no better example than their labeling the political demonstration at the Capital on Jan 6th an "insurrection."

Even the directive to "Do unto others as you would have others do unto you." has a potential for disrespect. It does not suggest someone wanting to die should go about murdering others. It, likewise, does not mean if you like to be beaten physically, you should go about beating others. We must continuously look for the illusive common-sense interpretation in these directives.

The earlier proclamation, "Do as you wish, as long as it does not harm another," [Wicca] is also subject to interpretations. Unions created to improve working conditions for employees is a plus, but unions created to prevent competition or restrict those outside the union from making a living are not so positive.

My adding, "… under God" when I say the Pledge of Allegiance, is seen by some as being hurtful to them. Some people believe words have a physical force; words appear to them to be hurtful. We have two proverbs addressing this difference: 1) Sticks and stones may break my bones, but words will never hurt me. (From the U.S.) 2) The wounds from sticks and stones will heal, but those from words may never. (From India, I believe.) The American-left wants people to believe words are hurtful, so New York and California create laws to punish people for using certain words. Psychiatrists <u>should</u> understand how that type of behavior belittles people; it does not help them. It is a power play: 'Lets make these crazy laws, get the weak of mind to believe we are protecting them from the boogey man, and we will get more votes and power. Next month we will take something else away from them (free speech, or the second amendment) and they will love us for it.' In the impeachment hearings senators on the left frequently showed empathy to the 'poor abused (usually female, but not always) witnesses who in the face of *all the pressure* on them still *bravely came* forward to give an **opinion** about President Trump's behavior.' I do not think either the senators or the witnesses were aware of just how infantilizing such comments and behavior were. Hopefully, psychiatrists do. This is a form of virtue signaling. This form of thinking is at the root of comments asserting that how I feel about something is more truthful than any facts about the same issue. This "inner light" about what is right comes before God, country, or family. Biden and his political organization likely feel in a Calvinist way that they are part of God's selected. As Biden recently said it, "My wife feels that we are doing something important." The rightness of their acts is repeatedly supported by the self-adulation they constantly impose on themselves. Unfortunately, these self-attributed truths can be quite destructive and dangerous to society. [present situation] This is also why many commentators point out that what the elite left is doing is a religion to them. This religion is supported by the LPM. This is dangerous because they believe only in their own belief system and they are not open to either fact or opposing points of view.

This entire "disinformation" syndrome from the left is merely an attempt to squelch discussions because they are unable to actually support their points of view.

I am encouraging using common sense. I am talking about words as they are used for everyday communication between one person and another. I am not referring to a complicated legal document you may encounter in a court of law. It is no accident these are frequently called "instruments" of the law. They take on a physical characteristic. I have never said we could not be hurt by instruments.

Lies can obviously become hurtful (Intentional, like with Shakespeare's Iago or Shift and Nadler's vendetta, or unintentional, as with Oedipus) at the point where others believe them, or are misled by them, and then someone chooses to act on the lie as if it were true. How insane is it that a whistleblower's concern about a telephone conversation between presidents of two countries could be elevated to such bizarre levels [weeks of hidden secret testimony in the basement of the House of Representatives] even after an official transcript of the conversation being reported on was released for everyone to hear. Why should it matter what a whistleblower thinks they heard, or thought they heard, when we can all hear the same conversation and draw our own conclusions? (low level abstraction) That currently is not acceptable to the left who insist you only hear what they believe (wish) to be true. (high level abstraction) Do we feel we must have someone else tell us what the conversation meant? Does the word bias have meaning to people? Show me a sentence that is so clear that it can not be misunderstood if one wants to see it in a different way. Our education should cover that potential.

I have a couple sayings I put up in my office. One is that "I know what I said, but I have no idea what you heard." Hand in hand with that one,

I frequently suggest to my patient they use "From your reaction, it is apparent to me that what you heard is different from what I intended." Even when people love and like each other they frequently misinterpret what the other has said. How many of you reading this have had parents who were always "On your ass" about something? And they may have even loved you! In their own way of course.

Not only words can be misinterpreted, it can also be our actions. "What have you got to lose?" is a redirection of attention to behavior. It is not a "listen to what I say," but a "Help me and see what we can do together." It is action within the covenant. We the people joining to solve a problem. If you have listened to Trump's rallies, he always makes the comment that "**We** have made the country great again." He does not say "I have made the country great again," which would have been more characteristic of Obama or Biden. (A level of abstraction supported by democrats thinking.)

I try professionally to show people how to work through these complex life quandaries. Situations must take into consideration three factors: our thought, our actions and our feelings. Think of a triangle with each condition at one of the angles. Each one is affected by the other two. So, our thoughts are affected by our behavior and our feelings, our behaviors are influenced by our thoughts and our feelings, and our feelings are influenced by our thoughts and actions. If you apply this understanding to something like Mueller's team of investigators you have to recognize that the feeling and thinking level of his team is going to have a significant effect on actions (midnight raids on individuals for the terrible crime of possibly lying to the investigators), raids on the past president's home by 25-30 FBI over record disputes, and reports (for the first time in reported American judicial history the suspect is supposed to prove his innocence).

Reason with me how actual acts of respect could, and perhaps still may, help to complete the job jump-started 2000 years ago by a Nazarene.

It is an example of irony how it was <u>not</u> the Christian, Richard the Lion-Hearted, who showed the world the meaning of respect, but it was the Sultan Saladin. Richard beheaded, in view of their companions and families, thousands of prisoners he captured. This act of disrespect possibly laid part of the foundation for the current conflict between Christians and Muslims. It is quite possibly the symbolism behind the beheadings we heard about and saw on TV at the hands of ISIS fighters. The Muslim Saladin in comparison, after capturing Jerusalem from the Christians, forbade acts of vengeance against the captured inhabitants, even though they had desecrated sacred Muslim sites. Jerry Nadler and Adam Schiff seem to have Richard's emotional genetics. (If there is such a thing.)

Those considering reparation for slavery in the U.S., should recognize slavery is a human condition started thousands of years before being practiced in the U.S., and it is still being practiced in some parts of the world. If reparation is a consideration my hierarchy would be Native American Indians followed by Japanese displaced during WWII.

The form of government we have in America was established as a covenant: "We the People …" When a significant percentage of the people no longer choose to be a part of "We the People" but instead choose to see those who do not agree with them as bad (neo-fascists) and wrong (deplorables) there is a major breach in the understanding of 'we.' When a country must depend on laws, the interpretations of laws and the enforcement of laws to solve every conflict that arises within it, we have lost the meaning of 'covenant.'

ACADEMIA

The Washington Times reports liberal professors outnumber conservatives nearly 12:1 and the ratio is increasing. Liberal professors of history outnumber conservative 33:1. The latter is attributed to the multi-centralism occurring in the humanities. According to Mr. Kim Holmes author of THE CLOSING OF THE LIBERAL MIND in the area of gender studies "*progressive assumptions* are built into the very idea of the department." The disparity is highest in the most coveted universities (Ivy-league universities where the ration may be 30:1) This one-sided weight in interpretation of history may explain how and why our understanding of certain events in history have become so distorted and mindless.

"Age also plays a role with scholars under thirty-six years old having a liberal: conservative ratio of approx. 23:1. With conservatives being pushed out deliberately, there is no longer a desire to *teach* thinking, but only to *indoctrinate* students to accept a particular point of view." Mr. Holmes predicts, "The American public is going to decline in the ability to self-govern and that's a threat to democracy." Mr. Holmes was assistant Secretary of State under George W. Bush and is executive vice president of the Heritage Foundation.

Coupled with the 90% bias by what is recognized as the "main stream media" (currently the *left's propaganda machine--LPM*) people in the U.S. are being subjected to a demagoguery— "a condition associated with dictators and sleazy politicians or a leader who makes use of popular prejudices and false claims and promises in order to gain power that appeals to the worst nature of people." [Google] Interestingly, these are the words the left uses to label conservatives. [In psychiatry this is called projection: attributing a trait or condition a person has onto another. I will refer to this as looking at the world through a mirror]

A discerning reader will understand there is a circular argument going on in which both sides use the same argument to support their view. I am reminded of a conflict I had in my psychiatric residency as I was trying to get my mind around psychoanalytic principles. It was my concern that when a patient did not agree with the psychoanalyst's interpretation the patient was said to be in 'resistance.' Perhaps I missed it, but I do not recall discussions about what if the analyst was in error and the patient was right. I liked the idea as a first-year resident, but it seemed a little too God-like as I learned more. This may be the underlying force for some psychiatrists to feel they have a right to disregard the APA rules and annotations on ethical behavior and write a book explaining why it was necessary for them to write a book to save the world from Donald J. Trump. I recall one of the criticisms was that he was too grandiose (another projection perhaps?).

With this circular reasoning, how do we attempt to come to a rational conclusion about what is being said? The answer is that you need to look at results. "What have you got to lose?" Ans.: Black unemployment rates fell below 6 percent for the first time, setting a record. [Bureau of Labor Statistics] Look at the lowest level abstractions result (what you can see, feel or hear) to help make up your mind.

PSYCHIATRY

One of my concerns is the forming of what my preceptor Dr. Roy Grinker called "*homoclites*" --those who follow a common rule, their goal is to fit in, do good, and be liked. In other words, the boring members of society who go to work, pay taxes and do what the government tells them to do without making a fuss. When I contemplate the monotonous destructive world of the left, I feel nauseated. If it continues, we will all get to exchange Trump Derangement Syndrome for 'average-itis.'

A good self-esteem is associated with better outcomes in life in general. The advocates for self-esteem (and I am one of them) have frequently made one significant error that has endangered what could be a really helpful concept. The error is that one can not have good self-esteem without having accurate speech. I will discuss this more.

A psychiatrist, Dr. Nassir Ghaemi, suggests "We are all living in a homoclite culture that apotheosizes [to elevate a person to the status of a god—my addition] normal. Just about everyone is in on the act. Just about everyone believes in the myth." This zombie-like characteristic in us may help explain the promotion of Donald J. Trump by Hillary's "Basket of deplorables" who still have enough life in them to recognize someone with a vision: they still have life in their bones and hope in their heart. The revolt against Trump is paralleled by the struggle of mankind against the brain-dead zombies of the TV feature <u>Walking Dead</u>. There are still some life-like organisms in existence attempting to do battle with the mindless manipulations coming from the elite left.

THE DANGEROUS CASE OF DONALD TRUMP: 27 psychiatrists and mental health experts assess the president by Bandy Lee. [Don't you love that title: '…mental health experts…?' Made # 3 on The Top 5 Dumbest Liberal Books of 2017.

"Pres. Trump wasn't in office for 15 minutes before liberals began scheming convoluted ways to have him thrown out [Impeach him]. Their farcical case for using the 25th Amendment rested on a spurious accusation that Pres. Trump was mentally ill — an accusation stemming from the likes of this odious liberal book. Bandy Lee and 27 other quacks bandy around the idea that Pres. Trump has, among other things, extreme narcissism, paranoia, or plain old dementia. After writing such a horrendous liberal book, perhaps Bandy Lee and her merry band of silly shrinks should hit the couch themselves!" [internet comment]

This same group of "mental health experts" seem to have no opinion when their current president attempts to shake hands with unseen individuals, stumbles up the walk way to Airforce One, looks for dead friends at his rallies, and incites division and conflict between Americans.

I read the book and then gave it away to one of my anti-trump acquaintances, so I will spare you a page-by-page rebuttal of the things said. In that we are both lucky. I do question how students of this group might feel. Do they feel privileged to be taught by individuals who surely must talk with God as they bring all their experience and wisdom to evaluate (at a distance) a man they feel is incompetent (he only built over a billion dollars in wealth, defeated 17 politically experienced contenders for the republican nomination and then defeated the second time female presidential candidate and life time politician from the left by outsmarting and out campaigning her, and he did it spending a little more than half of what she spent, and he did it with resistance from the left and the right.) Although he had some controversial [I am not referring to Russia] help along the way most of the people in his campaign acknowledge he made the decisions that mattered.

Another thing the book said was that he was too unpredictable. He was a loose cannon and could/would bring the country to the brink of disaster. I understand that listening to someone is a real inconvenience when you want to be critical of them, but Trump made it very clear in his campaign speeches that he was not going to do what Obama did and tell the enemy what he had planned. It was a part of his intended persona to be as *unpredictable* to the enemy as was possible. Considering the critical left could be his enemy, he was successful there also.

I heard the president apologize, but not on the *left propaganda machine (LPM)*, that he knew he was pushing things a little with "little rocket man; my button is bigger than yours," but he wanted North Korea to have doubts about what he might do. It was a part of his attempt to reign in a bad guy in North Korea. Result: It seems to have done what was intended (at least for a time). The parties were talking. To me it seems better than having missiles flying all over the place which is now happening under Biden. All the talk on the left about impeaching the President must have given countries like North Korea and China the desire to just hold out until some weaker (and perhaps compromised) president comes along. Which does seem to have happened. What a major disservice to the U.S. It appears they got their way with the election of Biden. At this juncture many Americans have serious questions about who is actually running the country.

In 1973 the APA adopted what became Section 7.3 in the Principles of Medical Ethics and Annotations Especially Applicable to Psychiatry. This became known as the *Goldwater Rule*. It states that it is unethical for a psychiatrist to offer a professional opinion about someone's mental status unless he or she has conducted an examination and has been granted proper authorization to make a statement. These individuals writing the book are likely certain they will not face consequences, because most of their psychiatric associates also believe it is fine to break the rules when a conservative is in their sights. Goldwater was a conservative Republican and they got away with it then. I think you can recognize the opinions rendered about Goldwater are like those rendered about Trump.

If you are a Democrat, you will praise your brave teacher for going against the written wisdom of the APA, and if you are a Republican, you might think it is just another example of Orwell's "everyone is equal, but some are more equal than others." On the left, you might think that is just fine, because you belong to that "more equal than others" category. Like the illegal aliens who break the laws of the United States, the contributors to the book apparently feel they have a right to begin their critique by also breaking the rules of their professional society. People generally follow an inner guide.

The participants (all 27) should familiarize themselves with Daniel Kahneman's book THINKING FAST AND SLOW (Recommended by an instructor at UCLA.) or at least PREDICTABLY IRRATIONAL by Dan Ariely to help them understand how much they only think they understand. Looking at THE RELIGIOUS MIND; Why good people are divided by Politics and Religion by Jonathan Haidt might have given them some caution-but I doubt it. Once minds are made up there is little that persuades demagoguery.

Trump's critics, especially psychiatrists, like to label him narcissistic. Looking up criteria for narcissistic, it is first of all a personality disorder. Besides the obvious mythology, the label reflets a person with an inability to listen to others, but only to one's self. Fast forward to Trump winning the election. Why? He listened to the people across the country and understood deep-seated concerns about the country (let's build a wall), about the economy (regulations are killing us) and about the two-tiered justice system (Lock her up). He was in touch with England and Scotland's feelings about Brexit well enough to accurately predict the direction that country was going. That is not the profile of a man who is not listening but is of a man who not only listens but is able to put what he hears clearly forward in his policies. He would likely be very popular with the people if they were allowed by the left to see and identify the things he has done. Instead, the LPM keeps harping on what they want people to believe about him rather than reporting his accomplishments. In addition, his business skills have been attributed to the fact that he paid attention to the people who worked for him from the janitor up.

If your name was Clinton and you looked at the actual reasons you lost the election you would hear such comments as, "Trump listened to the people. He understood the people's concerns. He may not have won the popular vote, but he did win the electoral vote, because he apparently understood the election process better than his long-time-political opponent. [The stats say Clinton won the popular vote—but I am also aware there were places in the country where the number of votes cast were 135% (more than the number of registered voters). These were politically left states. Of course, the left will not acknowledge that fact. [They really don't like facts.]

When Trump was criticized by his enemies as being unpredictable, they were not listening. Obama gave his enemies a timetable they could refer to ahead of the event, so they would see what the President planned. How convenient for them. No wonder he could not stop ISIS. Between telegraphing his intentions and the lawyers how could he win? The people who listened to Trump and not the LPM understood it was all a part of his strategy. The left still has not caught on, or they do not want to catch on. I have a plaque in my office that says, "You can't fix stupid." Guess who was not listening?

Disclaimer: Although I am a psychiatrist, I have not, and will not, suggest a psychiatric diagnosis for anyone I have\or will reference in this book. Stupid is not a psychiatric diagnosis.

THE LEFT

The left took lessons from Obama. One of the biggest accomplishments the LPM learned was to *weaponize the English language.* Trump has the speech of a New York Street fighter. Obama had the speech of the polished academic. Obama and his followers realized the truth of the claim that if you can tell people what to say, you can control them. The news media constantly, even more than with President George W Bush, harped on the things Trump said. It was rather amazing to listen to someone, and then witness the change in his words to what the left would have wanted him to say, followed by consistently claiming he said it. (When he did not say it, the press did.) The examples are numerous, only one will be given. He says of the issues at Charlottesville, Virginia that both sides were at fault (which they were) and that he does not condone white supremacy and that is turned into "Trump supports the KKK and White supremacists' and that lie is perpetrated time after time on the LPM.

Why do I say the Charlottesville comment was true: The city gave a legal pass to an unpopular group to have a rally and perhaps they shouldn't have? A left-wing uninvited mob [Oh, sorry the left says we can't call mobs *mobs*, because they do not like the negative connotation it gives their mobs"] carrying bats and other weapons ascended on the legal rally and chaos ensued. A woman was killed. That can be the conclusion of a mob activity. Would she have been killed if the mob had stayed home? Then with the magic of reframing things the LPM turned it into some terrible thing Trump said. Wow! That makes a twisted pretzel look like a straight edge ruler. The people who made it Trump's fault need to go back to school. Oh, sorry again, that is where this type of understanding is being taught. *Keep your kids at home* and home-school them.

It is a good thing for Obama that he is staying in politics rather than taking up poker. He had so many "tells"; it would never have worked out for him. His enemies likely hated that Trump did not give them information on what he was going to do next: his enemies and the left seem to hate him because he wouldn't tell them in advance what he planned. I guess that is not two groups but only one. I am doing a lot of apologizing and I am not even through the preface. I will try to follow Gibbs' [Mark Harmon NCIS] advice and stop.

I feel sorry for the LPM sometimes? Every day *they still accuse* Trump of lying about something, repeating what they think they identify hundreds of times only to find out they are wrong. (Russian collusion, destroying democracy, quid-pro-quo, etc.) If they had to spend as much time on correcting what they say as they do in telling it incorrectly it would truly be a different world. Because he defies what they say over and over, and what they say is inaccurate over and over, and the fact that what they say is disproved over and over they seem to really hate the man. But this is another projection. They are looking in the mirror again. The real fault is in the lousy reporting. If they were accurately reporting the news, they would not be found to be making up false news so often; then we could appreciate the job they are doing and it would not have to be corrected; they would not have to look so much like the fools they continually show themselves to be. I guess the LPM has a collective strategy that if they throw enough things at the wall someday something might stick, and I guess that could be considered a plan. How often are our lives so pure that digging deep and long enough might not find something we would regret? I believe it is fair to say that the LPM is not interested in reporting the news but rather in making news. Their reward is all the honors they receive for outstanding journalism while getting everything wrong: Russian collusion and Muller's 22month, 32 million dollar "witch hunt" paid for by the American people is one example. Rather than stepping up and doing their time-honored job, they just take the tact that anything different from what they report is *dIsInformatIon*. With that approach they are under no obligation to correct anything they do or say that is in error.

Does D.J.T. love or hate the people? The LPM would like you to believe the latter. You do not have to look very far. I have never heard a politician say "I love you" as often as D.J.T. I think he openly loves the people of this country. He says so, and then he acts to improve lives, as manifested in his taking away multiple burdens on business in the form of restrictions and he has reversed multiple job-destroying regulations. This led to a flourishing economy despite the predictions by the left that he would destroy the stock market and the prosperity of the country. Sorry left; wrong again. The left still wants to give Obama credit for the improved economy, but they have finally stopped talking about it. Contrast Trumps comments with those of the Democratic party during the election. Biden's team had nothing but negative things to say about the country and the people.

Trump was said to be a divisive person but that is not actually true. The people were divided about Trump, but he never identified the American family as composed of "deplorables" as did Hillary Clinton or "neo-fascists" as Joe Biden has done. Trump wanted prosperity for every American, not just black Americans, and he achieved that very well in his 4 years as president. Current political gerrymandering wants us to believe "all lives matter" is racist. That is divisive, stupid and unwarranted trash talk. Some people have the ability to look at everyone, other only have the capability of looking at segments of the whole. It is the later group that are racists not the former. It is also an attempt by the left to look like they have a priority for black Americans. Again, look at the facts. Blacks did better under Trump than they did under Obama or so far under Biden.

President Trump loved this country enough to put people back to work. He loved the people enough not to want them to be taken advantage of by our friends (Canada, Mexico, and Europe) or our enemies (China, Russia, Iran). He did not want the people of the US to be taken advantage of by anyone, even other Americans. He showed it by telling NATO and other allies they needed to step up and contribute a fair share for their defense. Because he disliked NATO? Perhaps; he certainly loves the people of the US. Unlike the man in the fable who shows caring by giving the poor a fish (Obama) Trump showed caring by putting people back to work and getting them a livable income. Biden on the other hand has taken about 7000.00 dollars a year away from families since his election. Both acts can be characterized as caring: the first seems characteristic of the right the second of the left. The injustice is the anger from the left at Trump for not continuing the trend to make people *dependent on the government* for their wellbeing.

RESPONSIBILITY

A good psychiatric principle is to accept responsibility for your own wellbeing. I think we have it wrong when we call firemen, police, etc. "first responders." I am not belittling their crucial importance, but the reality is that they are almost never more then second responders. This error in framing leads to stupid conclusions. The individual involved is always the *first responder*. Ask Anthony Sadler, Alek Skarlatos and Spencer Stone if they should have waited and called the Paris police or fire department for help, before they acted. Ask the Texas Church security if they should have just called the police. Texans solved the problem of a church shooter in five seconds. The LPM said on the air that good guys with guns could not stop bad guys with guns. Wrong again!

Fortunately, our military are taught the principle that they are the first responders. Police who are off duty, but because of training and that little tool of equalization, can truly be first responders. One left-governed state has recently made it illegal for police to carry guns when off duty. There is a reason that states that have allowed open or concealed weapon carry have far fewer gun crimes: the bad guys can no longer identify the "first responders" and that makes it much less safe for them to attack someone. They may be taking on an actual first responder, or two, or three. This is one way the left has successfully weaponized the English language. Congratulations to a congregation that understands the meaning of taking care of themselves. How much good would it have done to have had a sign outside the church saying, "Guns not allowed?" The young man Elisjsha Dicken who interrupted a mall shooting is another example.

When I seen "No Guns" signs on businesses, I really question if I should go into a place run by someone dumb enough to think that the sign will keep criminals out. If I were a person looking to do harm that would be my first stop. A really smart business owner might put up a sign saying "Concealed carry is acceptable within" or "Please, no open carry in this establishment." That would make every criminal uncomfortable.

Unlike the educational bend of the left which wants to blame everyone but themselves, Trump says to China's Xi Jinping that "I do not hold you responsible for the bad deals the leaders of the U.S. have made with you. We are responsible for the choices we have made regarding deals with you." This type of thinking seems to be disliked by the left which has a 75% influence on our young people's thinking. It is the responsibility of the leaders of the U.S. to protect our intellectual property, and our trade secrets. It is not the duty of a foreign government to protect the U.S. from them, or itself. Understanding this principle is a sound academic and psychiatric belief. We repeat this concept over and over in the psychiatrist office. <u>THE SUBTLE ART OF NOT GIVING A F*CK</u> by Mark Manson is a good reminder of that concept.

Most of the press on the left does not seem to understand the concept of *responsibility*. Responsibility is used as I understand it, much more commonly in communications from the right. There are only three things we are responsible for: our own thoughts, feelings and actions. So, opposite to what the left constantly claims on broadcasts like CNN, NBC, MSNBC, and PBS, Donald J Trump is not responsible for their fear, anger, misreporting, or inaccurate predictions on the economy, the division in the country or hurricanes.

The press, presumably and frequently educated in one of the learning institutions with a 75 % left slant on issues, does not understand the word *RESPSONSIBILITY* is an ambiguous word with at least two meanings easily manipulated to create misunderstanding. (Then again perhaps they do; maybe they understand how easy it is to confuse people when they frame issues inaccurately.) The two most common divisions of the word are 'response-ability' and 'assigned- accountability.'

Response-ability entails everything we can do without others help. The numbers of items that fall into that category are mind-bogglingly high, but it does not include other people's thoughts, feelings or actions.

The thousands of times the news makes what the president has done responsible for other people's actions is an outright lie, as is the thousands of times they have indicated he caused some reaction in others.

The second meaning imbedded in the word responsibility is 'assigned-accountability.' This is a convention, custom, practice, habit, tradition, etc. It is something that is made up either on the spot or through time. This is what the left does in the name of responsibility. I will discuss this in more detail later.

TRUMP DERANGEMENT SYNDROME

So, what is *"Trump Derangement Syndrome?"* It is peoples' belief that Trump creates unhappiness; dissatisfaction; fear; bad behaviors; reason to riot; reason not to sleep well at night; confusion about the stock market; air pollution problems; China's stealing of American technology; tension with Europe; unhappiness with the way he says things; obsession with Russia or Russia's involvement with the US elections; belief that he is evil; belief that he is Hitler, Mussolini, or the reincarnation of evil; belief that his policy of wanting borders, or border walls, is immoral; Canada's annoyance at not being able to tax products coming from the US without the US taxing products from Canada; 17 psychiatrists and psychologists feeling their insights about him are so profoundly important he should resign or be impeached from office immediately, their fears of climate change and immoral walls, and everything else their imagination can conger up. From an academic point of reference these are simply things people have chosen to make up about him. For some reason the preponderance of reporters on the left seems to have forgotten, or never learned, the importance of this mechanism of thinking; another case of looking at Trump through a mirror.

Like recognizing who the true 'first responder' is, there should be some understanding that the beliefs we have are our own creation and not the responsibility of the person we are blaming. This is good psychiatry, and a good educational principle. This understanding does not appear to be practiced much by the ELITE Left. A good example of the Trump derangement syndrome was the newspaper story headline claiming Trump was responsible for one of the hurricanes that hit the East coast. Most third graders could recognize that as not true, but the press printing the accusation apparently didn't, or didn't care. This is the same type of fact distortion that we see in the democrats desire to pass wishes off as fact.

REASONING

Another way the left attempts to confuse people is by the use of *inductive reasoning* (IR). Most people think in terms of deductive reasoning (DR) when dealing with day-to-day events. This is the Sherlock Holmes form of thinking. In *deductive reasoning* you start with some fact: The dish is broken; someone was murdered; the dog is missing. Inductive reasoning on the other hand starts with a premise: I think he is beating his wife; I think the husband should always be the primary suspect in a murder; since the dish is broken, it must have been a person who did it; Hilary was supposed to win so Trump must have done something unlawful.

In DR one looks for the evidence and clues that are present and draws a conclusion based on the findings: "Follow the money." In IR one has a premise (I think he is beating his wife, or I want him to be guilty of winning the election illegally) and then an attempt to prove the premise is unleashed. In DR one would first go to the wife and ask if her husband is beating her. This would begin to lay the bases for further investigation. In IR (for example) I might discover that the wife is anemic, so my inductive conclusion might be that she must be losing blood from the beatings she is being given. On Monday mornings if the husband appears to have marks on his knuckles that suggest a trauma, this becomes more proof that he is beating her. Then it is found that they bought a life insurance policy recently. This is seen as further proof that he is intending to kill her. He finds out that he is being investigated, and says I wish you would get over this and let me move on with my life. But guess what, this becomes another proof that he is beating his wife, because if *he didn't do it, he should want there to be more investigations not less*. [That was Adam Schiff comment during the Mueller investigation. Did not suggest this when Biden was being looked at with suspicion.] Trump should support being investigated, or it is proof he is doing something wrong. If readers followed the news on the stations I listed, they could have found nearly all the forms of argument I listed being applied to President Trump but not to Joe Biden. Just in case you were not been watching, I will try to spell it out clearer.

Paul Manafort has done business with the Russians; he has not paid taxes: that proves [by IR] that Trump is in cahoots with the Russians even though this took place before his 6 months association with the Trump campaign. Maybe Trump used poor judgment hiring the guy, but does that prove he has some association with the Russians? If Manafort has the skills to put together a plot with the Russians in 6 months that could win the presidential race for Trump, he would be valuable to someone.

Then there is the issue of the FBI putting someone in the Trump campaign to "protect" them (the campaign) from a Russian influence. To do something like that in the U.S, the Department should have gone to Trump and shared their concerns and asked to have someone there. Remember how they asked the DNC for their computers, so they could see if Russia was infiltrating them, but the DNC said no. Trump was not given that courtesy, because he was being spied on and evidence suggests there were several attempts to set up individuals in his campaign by the FBI. *Different stroke for different folks*! This is IR on the move again: they thought Trump must have done something illegal to have won the election, so let's find out what it was even if we have to ruin the lives of the people who will not support our premise. I think it was Adam Schiff who said that if the President was not guilty, he should welcome more investigation [Why is that same statement not true for Biden?]. This was the same Adam Schiff who told the American people he had proof of the Trumps collusion with the Russians—he has never revealed this evidence to my knowledge, but he did agree to talk with someone pretending to have negative information on Trump at the same time he was condemning Trump's son for something similar. It was uncovered that he may have deliberately misled, by failure to disclose, his connection with individuals involved in the framing of Trump from the beginning. There are reports Schiff and or his staff met and helped draft a "whistle blower" statement accusing Trump of saying unlawful things in a private phone call to the president of Ukraine. Schiff continues his lying without regard for fact. Inductive reasoning at its worse.

There are significant differences between DR and IR. In IR it is necessary that the conclusion follows from the premises. The premise for a reliable inductive argument must be true, or acceptable. The left clearly cannot distinguish "what I want to be true" from what is provable, or likely.

Another area besides the Russian Connection that seems to drive the left crazy is the issue of climate. President Obama says that climate issues are the primary concerns for the United States. He never looked at China, North Korea, or Iran, I guess. Should we be concerned about climate? *Climate* certainly affects us, so why not? On the other hand, getting bent out of shape about it is like the Trump Derangement Syndrome. If you want to detract from trying to make our country a second-rate nation that you need to apologize for, if you want to cover up giving a billion point seven dollars in cash to one of the world's greatest sponsors of world terror, if you want to give an extra billion or two to a country (China) who is building offensive islands in the ocean, highest inflation in nearly 50 years, an open border policy allowing millions of illegals to come into the U.S., highest crime rates experienced in the U.S., government support of the Mexican cartels actions, unequal treatment under the law, failure to uphold the constitution of the U.S., then making climate your center concern would seem to make sense. The problem here is that *confirmation of scientific theories* is also based on inductive reasoning. There are equally valid points of view on both sides of the argument. If you argue that there is going to be an evolution in our climate you will be 100 percent correct—if you agree with evolutionary theory and the evidence recovered from scientific studies. In that theory there has been numerous rather drastic changes in the climate of the world. Do the gasses given off from the cows we eat equal, dwarf or exceed those given off by the dinosaurs? Will a small meteor hitting the earth change the climate more or less than 100 years of running cars with fossil fuel? Does the spill from a Russian pipeline releasing methane gas into the atmosphere equal or even surpass that of driving gas operated cars. Or, will volcanic action alter our climate in ways we might only have had nightmares about? What will a few more atomic bombs tests do to our atmosphere? By getting the North Koreans to stop firing missiles into the air did Trump delay the burning up of the ozone layer more than Al Gore who flies around in his jet discussing climate change and living in his high energy consuming home?

The inductive reasoning the left uses when looking at Trumps relationship with the Russians missed the point. Trump did not need, like most of his opposition, to make villains out of countries that opposes the United States. There are reasons for us to form coalitions with other countries; even ones who behave badly, when it might benefit us. The left's need to blame the other side for the issues is because they do not understand, as Trump did, that we create our own issues. (Biden has created inflation, the consequences of open borders in the U.S., inflation, unnecessary racial tension, and an energy crisis in the U.S. and Europe.) This blaming of other countries does not take into consideration that they are doing what we should be doing: taking care of ourselves. We cannot be the protector of the world, or the savior of the world. In order to be effective in the world we must stay healthy and strong. Biden's energy policy, and Green New Deal, is destroying America prosperity, and will soon destroy our strength.

Staying healthy and strong is the most important thing that we can do to help the world in times of need as we did with Russia and China in the past. This is also a wise policy at an individual level. It seems unwise to follow the liberal point of view that to work with Russia, China and others who compete with us is bad. Maybe the best chance for world peace is to arrive at the conclusion we should not insist we can identify what is best for the citizens of other countries. The left's need to blame prevents us from finding common areas of interest. *Blaming* has prevented the Arabs and the Jews from finding peace for two thousand years. Blaming will keep people at odds and is unwise for the safety of the world and for some reason this seems to be the core of the left's push to power. While dividing nearly everyone, the left blames Trump; another case of looking at Trump through a mirror. It reflects total lack of respect and understanding. Jared Kushner was able to help foster peace deals between Israel and several Arab nations by listening to what their concerns were rather than attempting to impose American solutions on them. The Biden administration is insisting on forcing Elite left ideology on all Americans, has returned to the days of racial inequality (Only black lives matter), has no willingness to do what the majority of Americans want (safe borders supported by 80% of Americans), has tweaked the justice department and the FBI to favor democrats by unjust application of the law, and is provoking Americans with threatening rhetoric apparently hoping to establish fear in people so they will not oppose their unconstitutional behaviors, all the time professing that what they are doing is saving democracy. That is a complete reversal of reality!

Hillary should have won the election, so Trump must have done something wrong, is the inductive reasoning from the left. Comey tells Trump he is not being investigated. Trump fires Comey. The left inductively says Trump fired Comey, so he must be obstructing justice. But wait a minute! How do you obstruct an investigation that you are told is not going on? And what happened to the calls from the left to have Comey fired when he messed up the Clinton investigation? Inductive reasoning takes priority again. If Trump wants him fired it must be a sign that Trump has done something that Comey knows about and, therefore, he wants to get rid of him. Objectively, there is no reason to investigate Trump, but the left cannot accept defeat and must make up reasons to constantly attack him; inductively they create a crime and pin it on him. From a psychiatric perspective that could be called bad sportsmanship, or projection. From an academic position it could be called 'Making something out of nothing.' [A term I learned from the co-author of my first book Dr. Gary Emery.]

Accepting responsibility for your own thoughts, feelings and actions is good policy regardless of whether it is applied personally, in psychiatric practice, or in politics. For some reason the preponderance of those educated by the left seem to have forgotten the importance of this principle when it comes to Trump or the lives of democrats: hence 'the Trump Derangement Syndrome.'

The inductive reasoning on the left has, when looking at Trump's relationship with Russia, missed the point. Trump does not need, like most of his opposition, to make villains out of everyone who opposes the US. The left and some on the right, need to blame the Russians for this or that and it prevented Trump from finding common areas of interest. Trainers of animals are aware that when the animal is acting poorly it is not good to praise them, but when they are doing something even marginally correct it is useful. Having to always push the bad card does nothing but create permanent resentment. Personally, I question if Trump likes Kim Jong-un at all, but he is smart enough to understand you lend a little praise to the soup when things are going in the direction you want. Non-negotiators might not recognize that—I believe Trump does. Where does all our animosity toward Russia lead? The current Biden administration is possibly attempting a régime change in Russia through the war between Ukraine and Russia. Democrats screamed and carried on when Trump was president that he would lead to world to war. Possibly another look into the mirror. There are recent reports that China and Russia are cooperating with joint military exercises. Congratulations left! Perhaps this is what you were after all along: how does it feel when others read your mind?

FINANCE/CAMPAIGN INFLUENCE

Inductive reasoning says that Hillary lost, so Trump must have cheated [perhaps this is a projection caused by knowing one's own party so well.] I am reminded of Sherlock Holmes who would hide things in plain sight, because people have trouble seeing things that are obvious. For example, all the upset about Russian influence has uncovered possible 240,000.00 to 300,000 dollars in Twitter advertisements. Then there is Clinton who spent an estimated 700,000,000.00 to Trump's 400,000,000.00. It is estimated that Sheldon Adelson gave a total of 130,000,000.00 to Republicans and Thomas Steyer gave more than 50,000,000.00. George Soros is estimated to have given 15,000,000.00 to Democratic endeavors, and the Koch brothers spent an estimate of 900,000,000.00 on the 2016 election. The Ford Foundation reported an increase in political spending of 35% since 2014. They estimated that 5,200,000,000.00 would be funded into close races and that it was "mainly coming from a few individuals." So, to put this in some perspective the country of Russia spent the equivalent of $2.40 compared to $9,000.00 contribution from only one family in the US. I understand it is undesirable for countries to try and influence politics in the US, but have we, the US, not been doing the same thing for years? Obama went to Europe to add his support for the Brexit issue. Just flying to England costs the taxpayers. It is estimated that it costs $200,000.00 dollars an hour to fly Air Force One. [Google] Then there is the entire issue of the impact of a news system that is 95% supportive of one side of an issue. A nice summary [Columbia Journalism Review] of the impact of the news media on the election of Trump concludes "Without discounting the role played by malicious Russian hackers and naïve tech executives, we believe that fixing the information ecosystem is at least as much about improving the real news as it is about stopping the fake stuff." Is all the hours of media speculation and accusation proportional to the issue? In psychiatry we call this kind of reaction either a *transference issue* [way too much reaction for what the incident requires], or plain hysteria.

According to TRUE WEST (Feb. 2019 p10) there is an old Vaquero saying: "If voting changed anything, they would make it illegal." Logic would suggest the saying might be more accurate than most would admit; lobbying goes on because it works. That it works seems reflected in the finding that close to 80 percent of former House of Representatives and former Senators become lobbyist: salaries are reported to run from about $88,000.00 to as high as $900,000.00. That is about 7 times higher than what the Russians have been accused of spending to supposedly help Trump win the election (a premise that has been shot down with time and more information). Billionaire Reid Hoffman (Linked-In co-founder) acknowledged he backed disinformation in the Roy Moore election by creating misleading face book pages. He contributed approx. $750,000 to defeating Moore who was defeated by about a 2% margin. Subsequently he apologized.

DISTORTED THINKING

The ELITE left heaps all kind of negatives on Trump. In psychiatry we label that behavior *FILTERING*. It is one of the *"15 Styles of Distorted Thinking* [from the internet] You take the negative details and magnify them while filtering out all positive aspects of a situation." The examples of unfair filtering are so numerous; I do not know where to start: the growth in wealth of the country, the decrease in unemployment, and the progress with North Korea, successful trade agreements are a start." This heaping of negatives on Trump also qualifies as *POLARIZED THINKING* "Things are black or white, good or bad. You must be perfect, or you're a failure. There is no middle ground. If your name is Obama and you are black you deserve the Nobel Peace Prize even if you have done nothing to deserve it. If you are white and you want a border wall to defend the U.S., you are immoral. [Didn't you understand border walls are morally wrong? Or, is wanting border security immoral according to the left? Sorry, I get confused.]

Another applicable style is *OVERGENERALIZATION* "You come to a general conclusion based on a single incident or piece of evidence. If something bad happens once, you expect it to happen over and over. [Trump says during his campaign that Mexicans coming across the border illegally, raped and violated American citizens—an accurate statement. The press reports that Trump is calling **all** Mexicans rapists—an inaccurate statement that is repeated hundreds of times by the LPM.] It is also overgeneralization when Biden makes the statement that Hurricane Ian proves the climate change theories are correct. [Even most grade-schoolers know a single incident of something proves nothing.] There is a rational reason there are flood control measures around Phoenix that have never been needed. The reason is called the 100-year flood cycle. Ian is hopefully in that category for Florida. There have been many one of its kind climate incidents in history. They prove nothing about weather in general.

MIND READING is done on TV Programs like CNN nearly all day long. "Without their saying so, CNN knows what people are feeling and why they act the way they do. They are able to divine how people are feeling …." [I turned on MSNBC this morning and within 2 minutes a presenter declared "Trump loves dictators like Putin, Xi Jinping and Kim Jong-un."] A couple minutes later a reporter said that Mueller is "closing in" and may be coming up with a report soon. Obviously worded to suggest Mueller has something on Trump. At this point that sounds a lot like *EMOTIONAL REASONING*. The investigation had been going on nearly 2 years (when this was written) without evidence of Trump involvement with Russia. MSNBC states there have been 33 indictments, suggesting somehow that incriminates Trump. (This is a type of *ad hominem* called guilt by association.) When Mueller finally provided his report, he could not prove the accusations had links with Trump despite apparent threats and persecution of those he interviewed. When the Mueller report ended (Since this was written Mueller did reveal the findings of his investigation to the dismay of the Left: No collusion with the Russians and no proof of obstruction of justice.) the left ramped up other investigations. First, they tried to say Mueller did find obstruction of justice. When that bombed, they went to *quid pro quo* accusations against the president. That did not fly very well with the public so the verbiage was shifted to 'bribery,' which shifted to "obstruction of congress" and "abuse of power."

NOTE: Throughout this book when I use the term 'left,' please understand it applies to what I hear on the left-oriented television (LPM) and radio media as well as the conservative news media. Most of the radical positions expressed on those media are expressed by very few of the people I meet with personally, or that I see in my office, with only a few exceptions.

CATASTROPHIZING is a frequently used style of the left. "You expect disaster. You notice or hear about a problem and start "what ifs." What if tragedy strikes? What if it happens to you? [One of the most egregious claims by the *experts on the left* was that the Stock Market would collapse if Trump was elected.] Trump's appeal to the Black voter, "What do you have to lose? Black voters have been a predictable vote for the left for a long time. The left was the party that owned slaves (an estimated 95 % of slave owners were democrats), they opposed making black Americans full citizens, in part because they did not want to allow them to possess firearms (Equalizers). Having a higher unemployment rate for black voters was not rewarded by supporting a black President ("By his works you will know him.") but by supporting Mr. Trump.

It is very thought-provoking for someone who has never been very interested in politics to hear the line up of people who feel that they have the answers to everything. I am not certain what gives the average radio or TV personalities the skills to guide, or govern the country, but I guess presidents must start from someplace. I am certain most of the movie homoclites have very little other than negative images to present to normal people. It is rather *GRANDIOSE* when people like Robert DeNiro, Beyoncé, Matt Damon, Jane Fonda, and Will Farrell [There are really a lot of people in this category, and the ones I mention are not special.] come out with all of their hate about the decisions the President is making. Perhaps celebrity nights at the White House or playing presidents on TV and in the movies has given them more understanding, or insights, on how the country should be run than the rest of us have. It truly seems that George Orwell might have had this period in mind when he wrote ANIMAL HOUSE. The celebrities seem to feel that they are more equal than the rest of us. It must really irk them when they find they only have one vote. Then again, we must recognize that those with the money, or press, can buy votes through million-dollar TV advertisement, and political donations. Maybe they really have found a way to be 'more equal' than the rest of us. It is my observation at this point that most of our legislators now vote according to what their doners want and not what the people they are supposed to represent desire. As long at representatives believe, or know, large donors get them elected, I do not see how that will ever stop—but to continue a democracy I believe it needs to be stopped.

Another snippet about me; I have, over the years, been a minor donor to the Republican Party. Enough to keep a membership, but at times I have stepped outside of the party. I voted for Clinton. I thought he was best for the country at the time. I still think he was a pretty smart guy. I was never caught up with his personal issues. It seemed a little hypocritical to focus on his personal flaws, but to ignore them when the name was Kennedy [Just more evidence of the two-tiered system of thinking in Washington] or L.B. Johnson. It seems when an organization wants money, they send out a questionnaire. I almost never give money in the same envelope as the questionnaire. Often, I used to write on the questionnaire "When the party starts supporting what I find important I will support you more." My skepticism of the Republican Party was great enough that I sent contributions only to Trump identified entities and not to the general Republican funds. No way did I, or do I, want to promote the Paul Ryan and Mitt Romney republicans whom I feel had an agendas I am not interested in supporting.

FOUNDER'S ERROR

It occurs to me that the founders of our country may not have imagined a condition where a single individual or company in the US would have a wealth equal to the 7th largest (economic standing) country in the world. Did they envision that one man (Soros) could buy the election of 15-20 congressmen in a single election? Did they envision that after being elected, in order to stay in power, representatives would be indebted to lobbyist's money to get reelected? So, after being elected it is more likely the lobbyist is the person directing legislative decisions, not the people. Did they envision that the unlimited resources of the US government could/would be brought against individuals (citizens of the US) merely for the purpose of attempting to find a crime where none appears to have occurred? Trump, his attorneys, his cabinet, and many of his supports have been targeted by the lefts military arm in the office of the Attorney General of the U.S. Many have faced huge financial burdens simply to demonstrate their innocence. Government money is now being used to hurt or damage given political rivals. Few things can destroy to fabric and meaning of this country as much as that practice.

Our form of government is called a *Federal Democracy*. [Internet definition] The President is the head of the government and is also the head of state in the U.S. The dictionary says that a federal democracy is a liberal political ideology and a form of government in which representative democracy operates under the principals of classical liberalism (Presidential system). One of the key aspects of a democratic culture is the **_concept of a logical opposition, where political competitors may disagree, but they must tolerate one another and acknowledge the legitimate and important roles that each play_**.

Did you get that: **<u>the concept of *a legal opposition*, where political competitors may disagree, *but they must tolerate one another and acknowledge the legitimate and important roles that each play*</u>**. So much for what it is supposed to be, but the left has moved on to a different play book all together. Contrast how Hillary pushed Trump to agree to concede the election if she won with the fact that 3 years later, she and her party are still trying to get the election reversed. The Democrats were calling for impeachment before the President even took office. Perhaps, I have always been more of a libertarian: a person who advocates civil liberty; believes in the doctrine of free will; is fiscally conservative; is a moderate social liberalism advocate, a proponent for individual liberty and responsibility and minimized government; upholds liberty as a core principle, seeks to maximize political freedom and autonomy, emphasizing freedom of choice, voluntary associations and individual judgment.

The real hypocrisy here being that people who believe Biden was not elected honestly are being said to be spreading misinformation and are being told they are acting antidemocratically. They are called names by the left. Despite being the group that said if Trump was innocent he should want more investigation, the left has done everything in its power to block investigation into the last presidential election. The group that never accepted Trumps election say it is unconstitutional to question the election of Joe Biden despite the number of <u>real</u> unlawful behaviors uncovered since the election. It appears to be their <u>real</u> fears that if Trump is reelected there will be investigations into the election and the findings will likely not be to their liking. The left also conveniently forgets all the times they have challenged an election result.

I was watching MSNBC interview a democratic senator. He was saying that he had visited the border and that there was opposition to Trump wanting to build a wall on the border. When asked who was in opposition, he reported it was "people who did not want to be identified." When I watch Fox News, they have interviews with Homan past head of ICE, Police in states affected by the lax immigration policy of the US and others who are on the border protecting the U.S. They seem to be united in their comments of wanting actual borders. **Physical barriers!** The left really must feel that the people are stupid. They want us to leave the security of our borders to drones and electrical notification techniques. They understand full well that means the violators will be within the borders of the US when they are spotted and taken into custody and the only option for the U.S. customs is to tag them and let them loose into the US where only about 10 % will ever resurface for official hearings. Essentially taking all actual enforcement and dumping it. Under Biden's border policies there is no border. Hundreds of thousands of illegals cross the border monthly. The democrats continue to report "**the border is secure**." Obviously, this is another word where the meaning has been changed by the democrats. It appears by secure they mean it is permanently locked open.

Obama, Clinton, and Nancy Pelosi have all said borders are essential for the security of the U.S., but when Trump asked for them everyone who is a democratic politician seemed to have forgotten that **fact** and worked to see that it didn't happen. How can a thinking person believe there is a reason, besides politics, at play on the left?

NONSENSE: ROBERT JOHN GULA

Robert John Gula was educated at Colby College and Harvard University where he taught logic and other subjects. I bought about 50 copies of his book entitled *NONSENSE* and sent 30 of them to a variety of individuals in the Fox family as well as key Senators and other Republicans. To date the only person who has acknowledged receiving a copy was Sean Spicer Former White House Press Secretary. Maybe the others have been too busy promoting their own books. I am not complaining, 1 in 30 is likely good odds of getting a response. What I am disappointed in is the fact that the right is letting the left *weaponize the English language* and, with few exceptions, no one is identifying what is happening. [Better over the past 12 months.] I recognize an error in speech happens on both sides of the isle, but for a group (the left) who controls 85-90 % of our higher education the nonsense spoken and repeated on the air is simply appalling. I have only a medical degree, but I can spot the nonsense in speech that I hear continually on the left without effort. I will attempt to give some examples that are blatant, but there are far more I will be leaving out. Get a copy of NONSENSE by Robert J. Gula.

APPEAL TO PITY This is a favorite of the left. Let's see how many days we can cry about a child being separated from the adult they crossed the border illegally with, knowing full-well that a large number of illegal bad guys pick up and bring children across the border with them, because it gives them priority in the broken immigration process. How about the left showing pictures of children in cages for several weeks blaming Trump [Until the cage pictures were identified as being taken in the Obama Presidency years?] Then there is the outcry for poor Christine Blasey Ford who accused Kavanaugh of attempting to rape her despite no collaboration. The crying here was not limited to Christine, but it became a cry for suspending the rule of law and giving superior consideration for all the ladies in the world that may have been molested or raped. Men were told by the Senator Mazie Hirono from Hawaii to "shut up and step up." The implication being if you are a man, you are not to be believed--AND THIS PERSON IS MAKING LAWS FOR THE U.S.! God help us!

Related is the *APPEAL TO GUILT.* The left really loves this one. The press shows a picture of a child who dies at the border from unknown reasons, but it is immediately tagged as being caused by Trump's policies. Even though Trump inherited the issue from the previous president, who, broke the law thus creating much of the problem (Dreamers). So, the left invites us to believe it is the President's fault every time we see a child, or an adult, who looks hungry or becomes ill after the long journey from their homeland to illegally come to the U.S. [This is a major confusion of response-ability and accountability] It is also a failure to look at who is influencing people to make that illegal trip (Left wing democrats and George Soros have been implicated by the news media) To investigate this would require actual reporting rather than creating the news—a lot more difficult. By the standards used to blame Trump, Biden must be responsible for the thousands of lives lost attempting illegal border crossings, the loss of thousands of lives from the drugs being brought into the U.S. by border crossers, and the destruction of school and economic systems in border states attempting to deal with the influx of uninvited invaders.

In the same vein of thinking there is an *APPEAL TO FEAR.* Regarding the border, the left likes to push the scenario that the right is creating fear in people unnecessarily about illegal immigration. They claimed that Trump was trying to make people fear immigrants, and immigration, unnecessarily. I want borders. I do not fear immigrants as much as I do the legislators who seem to be blinded by hate for Trump. I believe what most of the right fears is the inflow of bad hombres like MS 13 that Nancy chastised the President for calling "inhuman." I fear the human trafficking and harm to illegal immigrants where it is estimated that 80% of female migrants from Central America have been raped. Bidens border policies encourages illegal immigration and are an open invitation for people all over the world to come to the U.S. illegally. Many have died in the process. Many have been raped in the process. Large quantities of drugs are coming in with illegals that are killing Americans. The Mexican cartels are thriving bringing illegals across the border. All these things are the consequences of the Biden and the democrats border policies. They do not appear to care about the consequences until some of the illegals are sent to blue states or sanctuary cities.

A report by Paul Bedard Aug **2018** reports that illegal immigration has led "to 2200 deaths, 118,000 thousand rapes and 138,000 assaults." Said another way, "For the thousands of undocumented immigrants expected to rush the US-Mexico border they will face over one million cases of rape, assault, murder and kidnapping during the journey …. This is all before they even reach the U.S. Did you hear figures like that about other countries? Maybe not: because there is legal immigration in their future. It seemed every day the left and the LPM revealed something related to Trump that people should be afraid of: he was going to start a war with China, he was going to destroy NATO, he is was going to destroy the stock market, he was colluding with Russia, he fired Comey. "Oh My God!." He will get us out of the middle of the conflict with Iran, Russia and Syria (Oh, sorry the left wanted us to stay in those conflicts, so they claim getting out would cause a world uproar and nations would fall apart.) It goes on and on all day on the LPM stations. Have you ever heard the story or the boy who called wolf too often, or the story of Chicken Little? Apparently, no one on the left has taken to heart the wisdom these stories convey. When Biden finally did withdraw from the war in Iraq it was at the expense of the Afghan National Security Forces leading to the takeover of Kabul by the

Taliban. In the process he left seven BILLION in military equipment for the Taliban.

A little closer to home is the *APPEAL TO SINCERITY.* My psychiatric friend in California would say things like "You are too smart not to see how much Trump lies, or surely you can see the errors in his thinking." This is an appeal also to *FLATTERY.* I must say in fairness this is also something that I see the media on the right doing all the time: "The American people are smart enough to see through what the left is doing." I certainly wish that were true, but it really is not. Somehow, the right ignores the fact that more people may have voted for Democrats in the last presidential election than voted for Republicans. The American people are not smart enough to distinguish what the left is doing in part because the news media is not reporting anything but propaganda. Someone must teach them. The politicians on the right need to recognize that the left has weaponized our language, and that until they understand this, they will not understand why the ideas on the left initiate significant problems for the survival of those living in the U.S. The left elite wants to destroy what I grew up believing the U.S. stood for. I do not believe the principles they are putting forward is helping the world as a whole and certainly do not see it improving the wellbeing of the citizens of the US. [E.g., Socialism, anti-Semitic, anti-democratic process, anti-constitution, pro-abortion] A recent poll showed that 27% of democrats saw all negative comment made about a person of color as racist. That means that 27% of democrats apparently believe that everything a person of color says must be accurate and above challenge. Makes me want to stay away from whatever college where they received their education. Even Freud reportedly said, "A cigar can be a cigar."

The *ARGUMENTUM AD POPULUM* "we the people know" simply is not true. If you have watched Jay Leno or Watters go on the streets asking people simple questions about the day to day working of government or business or of holidays, etc. you find the answers are really poor. Or, perhaps you didn't even recognize that the average person off the street can answer little about our country (Who oversees history teachers in this country?) We had better tune in, because I do not know what they are teaching. I experience that 85-90% of the people I see in my office cannot answer the simple question "Who is responsible for that book staying on my desk?" Perhaps the educational contribution to the issue is one Dr. Emery defines in EMERY NEWS Issue 12 July 1994: "Thinking actually makes you stupid—think enough and you won't know anything." Kurt Vonnegut said, "The human brain is too high-powered to have many practical uses in this particular universe." Looking at what is happing in academia would support these opinions.

It seems the democrats must stay up late at night thinking of more outrageous things to complain about. They complain about people dressing in other countries type of clothing, like clothes have a copyright or something, seems preposterous. Doesn't every little boy or girl like to put on a cowboy hat or boots at some time. This kind of petty over-control is nuts. Someone should write a book on the left's hypocrisy. It has been said by some that imitation is the highest form of flattery.

Gula labels Chapter 3 *EMOTIONAL LANGUAGE: PROPAGANDA*. Both parties tend to suggest they have the support of most of the people. The lefts insistence that we ignore who is a legal voter makes it impossible to have proper elections. It is suspect when the left does it because there appears to be areas of government where the president does have majority consensus. (This process of distributing misinformation is what Gula calls the *BANDWAGON*.)

REPETITION: I have already referred to the LPM (left propaganda machine). Gula says "The propagandist says something over and over again." This characteristic is the main reason the media on the left should be labeled a Left Propaganda Machine. The LPM media will report a given comment hundreds of times over weeks in an almost chorus-like manner, using the same key words over and over. [I.e., Stormy Daniels adult films actress a.k.a. Stephanie Clifford, constitutional crisis). This is pure propaganda at the highest level. I would like to see a law that says if you are going to be a propaganda machine you should have to register as a propaganda machine (like a lobbyist), so people who are not smart enough to figure it out will understand it better. The left has used the word "impeach" so often most three-year olds likely understands what it means. Recent reports show the left media discussing impeachment 80+ minutes and the economy 8+ minutes. (This was the case 2 years ago and likely is worse currently.)

CONFIDENCE "The propagandist also speaks confidently." If one listens carefully to the LMP they frame nearly everything in absolute terms. This is another part of what makes the press an actual propagandist machine. I used to say of my x-mother-in-law that she was often wrong, but never in doubt." When I listened to MSNBC and CNN and the other obviously left leaning propagandists, their message was filled with sincerity and confidence, but with what seems to me to be very little data. E.g.: All the rhetoric about the left impeaching President Trump when the prospect seems rather farfetched given they did not have control of the Senate where a 2/3 number of votes was required. At the time of this being written, MSNBC and the left were confident that Trump would back down on the wall.

I saw impeach advertisements where MSNBC told the American people how corrupt President Trump was but there are never details of course. Maybe, they believe they could count on the honorless [my word] republican senators to support them. Another blatant example of this was the democrat's response to Muller's report: in their mind the President was found guilty by the report. I think the error here is that one must be found guilty by the court system, and not by the prosecution team. If the left's approach was adopted by the country there would be no need for judges, juries or the process of law: the prosecution's opinion would be enough. It seems rather egotistical to declare someone has broken the law merely because one does not like the behavior of the other. This seems to be the repeated declaration of the left. What percentage of the 9th Circuit Courts decisions have been over-turned by the Supreme Court? (over 80% of the time) If there were not prejudices even in the law this should not be happening so often. The infiltration of politics into the law is such that decisions of the court are fairly predictable once the president who appointed the judges is known. I do not believe that represents what should happen under the law, but it certainly encourages me to stay as far away from a court as is possible.

NAME CALLING unfortunately is used by both sides of the isle. The left labels the entire right "racists, uncaring, deplorables, fascists, homophobes, infidels, xenophobes, right wing extremists, anti-socialists, right wing-militants, and 10-toothed supporters or Walmart shoppers." More recently we are labeled deplorables and then neo-fascists. The propagandist assigns abusive epithets or uses names that have strong pejorative emotional associations to people or ideas he/she does not like. In his run for president, President Trump effectively used this technique to point out attributes of his opponents more efficiently than they were able to label him. Trump used *STEREOTYPING* more effectively than the left. Unfortunately, the LPM has used this against the right for years: "racists, uncaring, deplorables, fascists, homophobes, infidels, xenophobes, right wing extremists, anti-socialists, deplorables, etc. come out every election cycle.

THE *GLITTERING GENERALITY* is a technique of making "broad, sweeping statements, usually ones with complex and far-reaching ramifications, but it ignores the complexities and the ramifications." [Gula] As I am writing, I am listening to MSNBC reporting on "Trumps buddy Putin." This was one of the left's constantly repeated indictments that had no actual validating evidence. Most of the evidence clearly suggested Trump was harder on the Russians than Obama or other presidents had been with the exception perhaps of Reagan. It is the rhetoric of democrats after the Mueller rendering.

Without a consideration of due process, the democrats declared by fiat that everything they believed was true and accurate, in the same manner of lying that Schiff demonstrated for the past three plus years. A fair person looking at the position the President was backed into by the lying press and democrats might clearly understand his defensive behaviors. He, almost completely alone, moved forward with an agenda to improve the lives of the citizens of the U.S. What was the rating for the congress? Nov 2019 Gallup says it had a 24% approval. The same percentage of people reportedly wanted Trump impeached.

TRANSFER "This technique encourages us to transfer our emotions from one source to another." [Gula] This is where the left shows children in wire cages and uses the image of supposed abuse to stimulate the compassion of the American people to reject the abusive President Trump. The problem of course was that the photographs were taken during the Obama presidency—but that did not matter to the left—they transferred disgust to Trump without a blink or reference to the source of the pictures: Obama.

PLAIN FOLKS The talking point on the left since the midterm election has been that there are 126 constructive, beautiful people (43 women of color) on the left and "hateful white men on the right." This is being portrayed by the left as an example of the anti-woman prejudices of the right. Trump received 41% of the female vote in the presidential election. In a Washington Post article, it was reported that "women who have worked closely with Trump say he was a corporate executive ahead of his time in providing career advancement for women." The LPM will never acknowledge that information.

SNOB APPEAL FBI agent Peter Strzok made a text statement to Lisa Page that "…. I could smell the Trump support…." During Trumps run for the presidency I recall listening to reporters on MSNBC and CNN and other LPM laughing hysterically that Steve Bannon and Kellyanne Conway had joined the Trump Team. This "I am so much better than you are" came through on all the major LPM stations. To this observer it appeared almost every person interviewed from the left exudes an attitude of superiority. Hillary herself called half of those who opposed her "A basket of deplorables" in a presidential election campaign speech. It is clear the Hillary and Joe hate and disrespect much of the U.S. population. The left puts words in the mouth of Trump and his supporters, things that have not been said, and then they ignore what has been said.

Tucker Carlson's guests will say the facts support that illegal immigrants pay taxes, are not involved in criminal activity as much as American citizens and that they are better than American citizens--nothing but the cream of the crop (my words), they kill less people, commit less crime and have less gang affiliation. This *STATISTICS WITHOUT CONTEXT* goes on with almost every guest interviewed. An LA Times report claims "40 percent of all workers in LA County (102 million people) are working for cash; and not paying taxes." This is because they are predominantly illegal immigrants, working without a green card. The Times also reports "95 percent of warrants for murder in Los Angeles are for illegal aliens, 75 percent of people on the most wanted list in LA are illegal aliens, over 2/3 of all births in LA County are to illegal alien Mexicans on Medi-Cal, nearly 35 percent of all inmates in California detention centers are Mexican nationals here illegally, nearly 60 percent of all occupants of HUD properties are illegal" and this is all paid for by the American worker paying taxes. It is also reported that 300,000 illegal aliens in LA County are living in garages," (or perhaps on the street?) "The FBI reports half of all gang members in LA are most likely illegal aliens from south of the border," It is also reported that "less then 2 Percent of illegal aliens are picking our crops, but 29 percent are on welfare, and 29 percent of inmates in federal prison are illegal aliens." This is statistics vs. opinion. The left, like Pointy-haired Boss in a Dilbert comic strip says, "I don't like context" and Asok responds, "It isn't popular." It does not seem popular with the left either. More recently the left has let most of the incarcerated people out of jail regardless of their crime. They are now only interested in having republicans thrown in jail. Currently a father of seven children is facing 11 years in jail for protecting his 7 yo son from an adult assailant.

Propagandists also like to confuse with *LARGE NUMBERS*. Pelosi did not want to fund $1.00 for our national security which would cost (If Trump had gotten what he wanted) approximately 1/10th of 1 percent of the budget. The 1.3 trillion-dollar spending bill in March had little money for border security even though Hillary, Bill and Obama all said it was necessary for American security. Planned Parenthood received around $500,000,000.00 (The majority of this money reportedly will go for abortions which the left feels is morally good, but "not a dollar" for a border wall which the left leadership feels is morally wrong.) If I was Fox News, I would have replayed the Clinton's, Schumer's and Obama's comments about needing the wall on an hourly basis until this issue was resolved.

Another nonsense ploy by the left is *APPEAL TO PITY*. Those poor people from South America need to come to the U.S. Are there people in South America that deserve to come to the US? Absolutely! A point raised by the right is that 80 percent of the populations of the world lives in poverty, 22,000 children die each day due to poverty (UNICEF). It is estimated that half of the world's population—more than 3 billion people live on less than $2.50 a day. The richest 20 percent of people account for ¾ of the world's income.

Where does the US stand on being charitable? According to the Eorlds Giving Index the United Kingdom ranks 8th, India ranked 134th and China 147th. In the US 60 percent of the population has given money to charities (We rank 6th on the EGI). The most generous country per capita is Northern Ireland. Surprising to me, Pakistan is one of the most charitable nations in the world. The country that gave the largest amount of humanitarian aid—a total of 6.6 billion in 2017 was the U.S. The percentage of its gross national income that the US gave for global humanitarian aid was 1.2 percent. Private trusts, foundations and individuals gave 6.5 billion to humanitarian efforts in 2017. It is estimated that in 2015 13.5 % of Americans (43,100,000) lived in poverty. When looking at "near poverty" we are looking at around 100,000,000 people or nearly a third of the population of the U.S. (Wikipedia data). The official poverty rate in the US in 2018 was 12.3 percent. I expect Trump is concerned about poverty everywhere in the world, but his priority is the poverty in the US which he is attempting to do something about by getting people jobs, making it easier for them to find employment, and lowering taxes so they will have more money to do the things they want rather than give money to the government for it to do what it wants. If the policies of the left are followed to a logical conclusion the U.S. will effectively disappear! They do not want prosperity for the average underpaid American, they want them dependent on handouts. Flooding the country with poor immigrants makes it more likely Americans will be back on the federal 'hand out' list. The more people are dependent on government the more likely they are to want a handout leftist government in power. Unfortunately, the Biden policies have cost the average American family over seven thousand dollars this past year. The number of people under the poverty level is increasing, the bread lines have already been getting longer, but Biden would rather help the government of Ukraine more then Americans. He professes to want to help Ukraine with border integrity while encouraging anyone who wants to come to the U.S. illegally.

THE MANUFACTURED PROBLEM—THE BAD GUY, THE SCAPEGOAT and ARRANT DISTORTION. "The propagandist creates or exaggerates a problem, tries to convince you how serious the problem is, and then they appease you by blaming someone for that problem or by suggesting that their proposal will solve the problem." [Gula] The examples of this are numerous, so it is hard to find a starting point. The left blamed Trump for children being separated from parents (handlers, mules, coyotes, etc.) at the border when he enforces a law enacted by congress. [In case no one has read about our type of government that is the job of the executive branch.] They also complain when he did not break the law or refused to disregard the law as Obama did. The left says there is no crisis at the southern border of the U.S.A. when there is and then pretends there is not a personal crisis and abuse of the people illegally crossing the border. There is abuse happening, but it is mainly along the route people have chosen to take to get to the U.S., thanks to the encouragement by individuals on the left who want to create a crisis of drugs, crime and illegals. At the time of this writing, I have listened to 2 days of the impeachment hearings conducted by the House of Representatives. So far, the most serious crime attributed to the President by the handpicked witnesses of Adam Schiff is that the president hurt their feelings by firing them.

The Granddaddy of all manufactured distortions is what the elite left did with the Jan 6 political march on the capital. After watching for nearly a year while the supporters of democrats killed our police, burned our buildings and destroyed thousands of businesses (millions of dollars in damage) without a single investigation, no condemnation from the Whitehouse, and anyone being arrested for their behavior having their bails paid for organizations sponsored by the now vice president of the democratic party. Jan the 6th is singled out as worse than the Japanese attack on Pearl Harbor or the annihilation of Jews by the Germans. The political party in power labeled the political protest an insurrection. They needed to make it sound bad so they could abuse the people involved.

I know the left does not like facts. President Biden when seeking the nomination of his party said "facts do not matter only the truth matters." I hate being a spoiler but the facts seem to be 1. President Trump approved for the national guard to be present but this was not accepted by the Capital police so they were not requested. 2. The statement made by the President Biden that Trump supporters killed four people during the protest is not accurate: One Trump supporter was a female murdered by Capital Police, a second supporter died after

Capital Police pushed a crowd back with teargas and when she fell, she was beaten by a Capital Police officer while she was on the ground until some of the protesters could get her free--too late to save her life. Two other Trump supporters had heart attacks and died shortly after the Capital Police lobed stun-type grenades inappropriately into the crowd very close to the victims. Whether that participated the heart attacks or not has not been clarified. There was a report of another person dying after reportedly being beaten by Trump supporters which turned out to be a natural death unrelated to activities at the capital. So, this "Insurrection" of Jan 6 had no deaths caused by Trump supporters, one or two people murdered by Capital Police, two deaths from heart attacks possibly linked to inappropriate lobing of stun-grenades into the middle of a crowd of people.

The label of insurrectionist is clearly an attempt to make a simple protest about what was clearly believed to be an election tampered with by the democrats appear more ominous. Because of the size of the protest (compared to the 20-30 "peaceful protests" supported by the democrats) there was a need to make it something sinister otherwise it would not look like Biden was supported by a vast number of Americans and he couldn't have claimed an overwhelming support for his election. The only real question remaining is did the administration deliberately withhold the support of the National Guard to participate this atrocity on Trump supporters?

The *ARRANT* DISTORTION that seems most dominant currently was that having a wall is immoral. The left gets up in congressional hearings and rant at the concept of a wall, declaring that Jesus would not want a wall, and that the Vatican does not like that we want a wall. [I haven't discussed hypocrisy yet.] I guess their reading does not include accounts of St. Peter [the keeper of the "keys to the kingdom"] at the "Pearly Gates" screening those who want to enter heaven or the fact that the Vatican is surrounded by walls and guards. In popular culture the pearly gates are generally depicted as wrought-iron gates.

The purpose of the gates (listen up democrats!) is so that "those not fit to enter heaven are denied entrance at the gates and are sent to hell." [Wikipedia] Propaganda is neither right nor wrong, but it is important that we see propaganda for what it is and not allow ourselves to be manipulated by it.

The next bit of nonsense is *EMOTIONAL LANGUAGE*. "When you suggest something, you say something that operates on at least two different levels. Your words make a specific statement, but behind that statement is another more implicit statement." [Gula] Years ago, an associate testified in a nationally important trial regarding Donald Fifield Bolles. When reading the account in the AZ Republic newspaper I was taken aback by the reporter's focus on the doctor taking off his shoes during a break in testifying. Given the wide interest the country had in the trial, I wrote and asked of what importance was the information that he took off his shoes on a break. The written response I got from the paper was that it was the type of things their readers were interested in. I canceled my subscription the same day. I was not interested in being associated with that group of readers. Yesterday, when I was listening to a MSNBC reporter talking about "Trump's buddy Putin" I found myself feeling the same way. That is not reporting; it is propaganda. These constant innuendos on the LPM make it hard to want to see if they have something of interest to report. Watching MSNBC lately is to see a deliberated attempt by a TV show to create a battle among Americans. It seem to have fallen to a level of fostering racism and hate among Americans.

JUXTAPOSITIONING is a favorite of the left. Trump says both sides were at fault in Charlottesville and the left screams and hollers that he is supporting neo-Nazis. No! He said both sides were at fault. After days of inaccurate reporting and multiple corrections being rendered, I am sure the public is still confused about what happened—but that is the goal of emotional language in the first place. The LPM doing their job asks the same question over and over like a disturbed mother-in-law, until the actual communication is completely distorted. Trump wants borders to protect the people of the US from numerous problems related to not having a border: the left juxtapositions this with morality. Trump wants a better relationship with the Russian leader and the left juxtapositions this with being a "buddy of Putin,' being in cahoots, being a traitor, and selling out our country. The crazy combos never seem to stop. The only way I can explain this is that the left listens so much to the LMP they believe it themselves. This is yet another example of looking at Trump through a mirror.

IRRELEVANT DETAIL To me taking off his shoes in the down time of a trial was an irrelevant detail. To someone using inductive reasoning (Taking off his shoes proves that he has gotten a foot infection from his frequent illegal crossings of the Rio Grande River where he goes to get drugs to feed his mother's drug addiction—or some other crazy convoluted premise.) that may make sense to the person using inductive reasoning. Things sometimes are exactly what they are said to be. "I want a wall, a physical barrier, to protect the people of the United States." Perhaps it is the people who never talk straight, or honestly, that cannot accept the President wants a border system to protect the people of the United States. It has been said over and over that the President's base likes what he says and what he means, but his enemies say he lies about everything. From where I sit, I think they wish he did lie. I think they hate it when he says something and then does it, because it blows down the accusations that he did not mean it—the LPM being proven wrong time after time. According to Fox News, he has kept more of his campaign promises than any other president. I must say Joe Biden has kept some of his promises also: keeping the border open, getting rid of fossil fuel power, promoting the destruction of the republican party, demonstrating daily his hatred of Americans, and his intent to engage Russia in hostile actions.

Once the border protection had become more centered the left began the repetitive harping on Trumps claim the Mexican Government would pay for the wall. The left is presenting this as if the President was claiming he was going to get a check from the MX government to pay for the wall. This is a *DIVERSION* technique where people choose to take literally what was said figuratively. The left has never been very good at identifying humor, sarcasm, ridicule, innuendo or parody when it comes from Donald J. Trump. On the campaign his joking, humorous comment about wanting to punch a protestor during one of his rallies was used out of context to justify hate-filled mob violence that shut down one pf his planned rallies in Chicago, antifa's assault on Berkley University, and for the really bad behavior during the Kavanaugh hearings. Trump has said in interviews that he never envisioned the MX government writing a check for the wall, and it is my belief that neither did his followers. I certainly didn't. It appears to me there may be a lot of ways the MX government helps us protect our borders indirectly: Maybe MX will see some advantage of building some of the border on their side.

"When anything goes wrong in the reasoning process, we have a *FALLACY*" [Gula--my emphasis] When Flynn or Cohen were charged with lying to Robert Mueller's team and this was used as proof that Trump did something wrong, we have a fallacy in logic. (Again, it is inductive reasoning—for inductive reasoning to be accurate there must be a high likelihood that the premise is true. If there is no evidence for the premise, it is likely that the inductive reasoning is a fallacy.)

Mitt Romney's personal attack of President Trump falls into the nonsense known as *ABUSIVE AD HOMINEM*. This is where "the personality of someone is criticized or attacked instead of what the person is saying [Gula--or doing-my addition]." Romney also apparently is crediting Trump with "dismay around the world." This is another flaming example of *LOGICAL FALLACIES*. This is like Trump being blamed for Hurricane Florence by the Washington Post (Why do you suppose the Post has not accused Biden of being responsible for hurricane Ian). Hopefully, even a first-year psychiatric resident would know that is nonsense and would be able to identify it as such. Mr. Romney's comments about his party's leader are using another nonsense IRRELEVANCE called *POISONING THE WATER*. Why would an ally do something like that? "When an opponent uses this technique, he casts such aspersions on a person that that person cannot possibly recover and defend himself without making matters worse." [Gula] It seems clear Romney does not want to be much help to the President. Perhaps he earned the characterization "the latest egotistical Republican flake." (NJ.com) If the last word had been capitalized, it would still have made sense. Romney has just declared himself a morally superior being. If he is so damned superior, why didn't he win the election? Trump did!

I enjoy watching Carson Tucker even if he did have some people on the show that just couldn't answer his questions. Carson would ask someone (Richard especially) what they think about a behavior or comment someone made and the response was always "Trump does it too." This is called TU QUOQUE. The statement may be true, but it is irrelevant. It does not answer the question. How can you have a conversation with someone if they will not answer the question? A somewhat more familiar example of nonsense is the NON SEQUITUR. This translates to "it does not follow." Tucker would ask a question and the response was never more than a page from the LPM. The answers were nearly always totally IRRELEVANT. Sometimes, I almost felt sorry for Tucker; I think he really likes to have a conversation with someone. I notice he now longer has Richard coming on his show and his guests do answer his questions now.

Mentioned by Gula is the "I know what I like; do not confuse me with the facts." Each time the right brings up a study and lays out the facts the left accuses them of lying. The head of ICE says we need borders; the left said he was lying. The head of the Border security said we need a physical barrier; the left said they are lying. The left dislikes being confused by the facts so much they have for years, under Obama, refused to do studies, because it is easier to say something is a lie if it has not been studied. Heather MacDonald has said information on illegals is scarce in part "because of sanctuary laws themselves." One of the biggest areas in which this is apparent is gun control. Studies show that in every state that has enacted open or concealed carry for guns serious crimes have decreased. Studies show that for every time a gun is used in a crime or to hurt someone it is used 1000 times for protection or self-defense, but these studies are labeled a lie by the left. The author of <u>IDIOT AMERICA,</u> Charles Pierce, says that the country has reached the point where the person who can yell the loudest, or for the longest, establishes what is right. The left plus the LPM do both things, so the facts are just an inconvenience that they must put up with until it can be shouted into obscurity. Obama, Clinton and Schumer have all said a barrier is needed at the boarder [no comment from the left]. Brazil's president Jair Bolsonaro made it easier for his countrymen to obtain guns and the serious crime rate decreased over 20 percent. Democrats don't talk about these **inconvenient truths**. Maybe that is the term republicans should use to counter the lefts <u>disinformation</u> claims.

The left seems to have an obsession about labeling everything Trump did or said as a lie. The left has perfected the projection of a lie. They began lying about the cause of the civil war and have not stopped since. They lie about their association with the KKK. They lie about mobs not being mobs. They lie about why they want open borders (liberal passion). They lie about attempting to keep blacks from getting an education. They lied about blocking the reconstruction of the South after the war. They lied about involvement in racial terrorism after war. They lie about the establishment of "boss" driven politics (Mayor Daily in Chicago for example) in the cities led by the left. They lie about the reason they want open borders in the U.S. They lie about insurrections, about peaceful protests (the ones killing people and destroying millions of dollars of property) and about the one that did not kill anyone. It makes it very hard to converse with the left.

The left tried to destroy the Union in the civil war. They are trying to destroy the Constitution of the United States; they are trying to destroy the influence of the U.S. worldwide. Recently they have shown their hand by asking to give *voting rights to non-citizens,* and they want, as F.D. Roosevelt did, to expand the Supreme Court (known as 'Packing the court). They lie about a goal of making groups dependent on them for their vote. (Obama kept increasing the number of people on disability.) There were reasons northern democrats got the name "Copperheads." Democrats today are chipping away at reason and replacing it with nonsense. The left lied about slavery "It was better than freedom and better then being employed." The democrats go around pulling down statues to disguise their 'white supremacist' history. The left attacked laws allowing blacks to learn to read and write. The left supports legislating from the courts (rather than by legislators). The left ignores that white supremacy was modeled on the slave holder. Slavery was enforced dependency: the left hopes the new enforced dependency will be the illegal immigrant. The left's claim that slavery was 'like a family' is like the comments about illegal immigrants. The left's support of illegal immigration leads them to believe they will get the illegals support at the voter box. The rights' desire to encourage legal immigration does not give the left leverage, so it does not appeal to them. Educated people who want to take advantage of what the U.S. has provided to its citizens is not seen by the left as people they can make dependent on them, so they are not supportive of the idea of more legal educated immigrants. (Merit immigration) Slavery has been said to compare to Socialism, so it seems logical that unable to have slaves the next best thing for the left is to move to socialism. The left pretended to be the friend of the slave, just like current day left is passing themselves off as a friend to students (free tuition for all), to illegal immigrants (come and we will take care of your medical needs and feed you—just do not forget to come and vote for us as often as you can.) Like Stephen A. Douglas the left today encourages 'diversity' which seems akin to the popular sovereign push of todays abortion rights leaders. (By the way have you ever looked at which race has the most abortions?) The left moved 'free choice logic' from slavery to abortion. A left lie claims President Johnson was responsible for the Civil Rights legislation when in fact it was the republicans in congress who advanced his ideas not the democrats.

Free Choice Logic: On the left free choice, as it related to slavery and as it relates to abortion, cancels out the choice of others (slave-no choice, aborted fetus-no choice). Areas where the left does not appear to favor free choice includes climate control. The left seems to feel that everyone must agree with what they want. I say if you want to affect climate change than do what you can: do not take planes when you can take a train, do not take trains when you can ride a bike or walk, do not eat beef, and do not burn coal in your fire places or cook stoves. Scientists not committed to the left's propaganda report that planting trees could do more for the climate issues than the insane and unworkable suggestions from the left. If you buy what the left is selling, you are giving away your power. If you own a production plant and strive to give it a low footprint in CO emissions—go for it. But I suggest you also look at some of the other things: California, where some of the loudest climate control individuals reside, had multiple forest fires every year because (at least in part) they do not take care of forests properly. Between what forest fires released into the air and the net product of not having the trees to absorb CO, California made a relatively large contribution to the planets over-heating problem if you buy into the *carbon* theory. If you care about the world over heating take care of your forests and plant more trees. No one is standing in the way of those who want to do something to protect the environment. You have choice, use it. If you give in to the left hysteria about climate you are giving away your right to think critically. Don't you wonder why the left is not willing to debate the subject? Convincing thousands of people something dangerous is going to happen if you do not believe me and do as I say, must be one of the oldest cons of civilization. It is the spiel of the medicine-man. The left was proslavery and continues pursuing the same goals, only this time the entire population is the potential slave.

In a democracy we should be able to debate conditions and show the science behind opinions.

Only in a society where it has been determined "Facts don't matter, only the truth matters." is there suppression of various points of view based on science. [Remember science is inductive reasoning.] The problem of course is that the people insisting there is no need to debate are suppressing the fact that their computer projections are not reflecting what is actually happening with climate and they do not want anyone to know. As Abraham Lincoln said in 1887, "You can fool all the people some of the time, you can fool some of the people all the time, but you can't fool all the people all the time.

If you want to give illegal aliens a good home move them in with you. Do not move them in and then tell me I must pay for them (that is not free choice on my part, it is enforced slavery—or as they called it in the old days taxation without representation). If you, as a state, want to give them food, medical care, housing etc. that is your choice, but do not tell me I have to pay for their visit. I do not send you a bill when visitors come to stay with me! If you want to live in a socialist country, I am 100 percent in favor of your right to do so, but I want to live in the greatest country in the world, the US, and I do not want you to take that away from me for your experimentation. Go run your experiment on country-building in some other country. (Actually, it has been tried unsuccessfully in several countries already.) There are a lot of socialist countries that could use some help. I support your right to get an abortion, but I have no idea why I should be required to pay for your choice. It costs me a lot less if women simply are more cautious about not getting pregnant or being responsible if they do.

STRAW MAN When President Trump laid out the reason for needing a physical barrier on the Southern border of the U.S., the left's response was the poor people who are out of work because of the government shutdown need to be put back to work before there can be discussion on border security? I know a government employee: they thought getting paid for not working was kind of an inconvenience, but not much of a problem. For the people dying, being raped, being victimized by the illegal aliens it is more than an inconvenience. The left cannot even stay focused on the problem for 20 minutes, because they are not willing to see it as a problem. [Our border czar says the border is secure.] The children in my practice do not want to accept that they have a problem, so they will not take their medicine. [Chris Magnus is the Commissioner of U.S. Customs and Border Protection. He has 60,000 employees and a budget of fifteen billion—any idea what he is spending it on?] The thinking of course is that if I do not take my medicine, I really don't have a problem. Somehow that does not help either problem go away. It appears to be the democrats approach to the porous border—they don't even want to go see what is occurring at the border. Another one of those areas where it is easier to deny than fix.

Besides the left's expected official consternation of Trumps attempt to solve a problem there were the usual judges, a part of the LPM, along with their "educated assessors" who, through "*fact checkers*", declared that Trump's **opinion** that there was a crisis at the border was not accurate. I guess they have direct contact with God that they can determine unequivocally that an opinion is not accurate—apparently because some workers were not going to get paycheck on time. I guess the opinion of the thousands of victims of illegal alien crimes (including rape and murder) is not important in assessment of a crisis. There is complete disinterest in the 91,799 drug overdoses reported in 2020. Ocasio-Cortez has claimed that without some change in rules regarding climate the world will end in ten years. Do you think this will be subjected to fact-checking from the left? We should be familiar with this hyperbole since Gore made a similar prediction years ago. Where is the fact-checkers when she says the border is like Nazi Germany? Where is the fact-checkers when she says immigrants are forced to drink out of the toilet? Is it improper to suggest the stupidity of their comments might reflect their actual understanding of the problem?

QUOTING SELECTIVELY is another nonsense speech pattern the left uses frequently. Trump, in a direct interview about his statement that he would get Mexico to pay for the border wall, says that he never envisioned that MX was going to write a check to the US for the wall, yet over and over on TV the left kept insisting that Trump was lying to the American people when he said MX would pay for the wall. Most Americans polled (at least Trump supporters) never thought he was saying MX would write a check for the wall, but there were indirect ways they very well might end up sharing the cost of the wall. It would probably be cheaper for them to help the US build a wall than to take care of all the people hanging around border towns trying to get into the US illegally. Is sharing the cost of a wall between two sides unusual? I have done it with two different owners of property next to me over the years. With Trump, and the left should have learned this, it is not finished until he says it is finished. The left keeps reporting on the LPM that Trump wanted a Sea-to-Sea wall. An early statement by him might have suggested that was his intent, but he clarified his statements several times that he is not looking for a 100% border wall. The left of course keeps stating what they want him to have said not what he says. Another repeated lie from the left is that Republicans are in denial that Russia tried to interfere with our election. The denial is not that the Russians tried to interfere with our election, but that Trump was not complicit with Russia's act. No matter how frequently this was gone over they continued to lie about it. More recent information suggests it was actually Hillary who was being aided by Russian efforts.

JUXTAPOSITION is nonsense enjoyed by the left. Trump wants to meet with Putin: Trump is reported by the left to be a puppet of Putin. Trump wants to talk to Putin where the whole world cannot hear what is being said: Trump and Putin are conspiring against the US according to the left. Mrs. Trump wears high healed shoes onto Air Force One: Mrs. Trump does not know how to dress properly for her outing according to the left. Mrs. Trump is not staying in the White House: She can't stand the President according to the left. The President complements Kim Jong-un: President Trump likes dictators and wants to be a dictator so watch out as he is Hitler returned according to the LPM. And this is the group you are choosing to educate your children? I suggest you think it over again. This misinformation makes no sense educationally, psychiatrically or politically.

Juxtapositions have another common form of nonsense: *MIND READING*. [This is also one of the 15 styles of distorted thinking.] All but one of the juxtapositions above requires the superpower of mind reading. The left has no qualms in knowing right out what someone is thinking and why they did something: General Flynn gave 40 years of his life protecting the country [Trump says something like 'can you move your investigation of him along']: Trump was accused of trying to interfere with an investigation according to the LPM, Trump is trying to hide evidence of his wrongdoing according to the LPM, Trump is colluding with Russia and this question is proof according to the LPM inductive type reasoning. I think it is just as likely that Trump wanted to be respectful of the dedication Flynn had shown through his 40 plus years of service to the country. Case closed! At least it should have been.

Gula describes *CONFUSION* and *INCORRECT INFERENCE* "Confusion can result from several sources: from inattention, from imprecise phraseology, from hasty or incorrect inferences, from misinterpretation, from ambiguity, from vagueness, from oversimplification, from the inability to distinguish the relevant from the irrelevant, from the inability to distinguish an emotional appeal from a logical one, and from intentional distortion." (P110) I think there is one other source: meanness. The left has been so successful at weaponizing the English language that they continue to push versions of nonsense to the dawn of understanding and insist they are in the know. Alice in Lewis Carroll's <u>Through the Looking Glass</u> says, "The question is whether you can make words mean so many different things." [The right] "The question is," said Humpty Dumpty, "which is to be master—that's all." [The left] The left is redefining terms we thought we knew a few years ago: racist, male, female, fascist, homophobe, infidel, reactionary, xenophobe, right-wing extremist, anti-socialist, right wing-militant and in California they make it a crime if you use the wrong pronoun. How crazy must assertions get before real people step forward and protest? [Richard Jewell, Duke Lacrosse case, Cambridge police, Rolling Stone UVA story, shooting of Michael Brown, Death of Freddie Gray, Russia collusion hoax, Brett Kavanaugh allegations, Buzzfeed anti-Trump report, Covington High School Incident, and Kyle Rittenhouse incident.]

HUMOR FROM THE INTERNET

I used to think I was just a regular person, but I was born white, which now, whether I like it or not, makes me a racist. I am a fiscal and moral conservative, which by today's standard, makes me a fascist. I am heterosexual which now makes me a homophobe. I am mostly non-union, which makes me a traitor to the working class and an ally of big business. I was christened by my parents (who were married in a church), which now labels me as an infidel. I am older than 65 and retired, which makes me useless. I think and I reason, therefore I doubt much that the mainstream media tells me, which must make me a reactionary. I am proud of my heritage which makes me a xenophobe. I value my safety and that of my family and I appreciate the police and the legal system, which makes me a right-wing extremist. I believe in hard work, fair play, and fair compensation according to each individual's merits, which today makes me an anti-socialist. I (and most of the folks I know), acquired a fair education without student loan debts and little or no debt at graduation, which makes me some kind of an odd underachiever. I believe in the defense and protection of the country for and by all citizens, and I honor those who served in the Armed Forces, which now makes me a right wing-militant. Please help me come to terms with the new me… because I'm just not sure who the hell I am anymore! I would like to thank all my friends for sticking with me through these seemingly abrupt, newfound changes in my life and my thinking! I just can't imagine or understand what's happened to me so quickly! Funny… it's all just taken place over the last 7 or 8 years! And if all this nonsense wasn't enough to deal with NOW, I'M NOT SURE WHICH PUBLIC RESTROOM TO USE……….

TECHNIQUES USED BY THE LEFT

The left feels it can *relabel events* to whatever they like. Most people have seen antifa's attacks on Berkley University, the street attacks on Trump supporters on several occasions, and the hysterical pounding on the doors of the Supreme Court during the Kavanaugh Hearings. The LPM declared against all visual representation that these were not "mob" acts. It must be so, because all the stations [MSNBC, CNN etc.] but Fox seemed to agree these thugs going about destroying property and hitting people were not "a mob." "Do not use the word mob," they said over and over in synchronized speech multiple times. According to the Foundation for Economic Education the cost of the George Floyd riots was **two billion** dollars and there were 25 American deaths associated with the riots. This was the costliest civil disorder event in the U.S. history. The 'insurrection' so called by the left cost 1.5 million of damage. There was one death caused by a capital guard murdering an unarmed woman and another death of a woman beaten by a female Capital police officer—not the four deaths President Biden keeps blaming on Trump supporters.

Let's not forget the *DOUBLE STANDARD*. Clinton creates an e-mail server that she used and from which other countries had access to Top Secret information, but she has received no consequences: General Petraeus was fined $100,000.00 and given a 2-year probational period after pleading guilty to a misdemeanor charge of mishandling classified materials. (He took a computer home with him.) John Brennan lies to Congress, calls President Trump's performance "nothing short of treasonous" and no one seems to care. James Comey leaks information through a friend to the paper with the stated intent to create a special counsel to investigate Trump (costing the U.S.A. taxpayer possibly 40 plus million dollars) and there are no apparent consequences. General Flynn is accused by Muller of lying (several FBI agents said they didn't believe he lied) which led to significant financial cost to him in dealing with Mueller and his team. Papadopoulos was sentenced to 14 days in prison for lying to Mueller's team. There is evidence that Hilary Clinton's election team was behind the Trump-Russian dossier that was tied to the Russians and which was involved in getting 4 FISA warrants to spy on Flynn and others in the Trump campaign. Mueller claimed he didn't even know what this was all about. He never investigated the issue. New evidence is emerging that areas he claimed not to have investigated, where areas he actually did investigate, but when it was clear it would lead in a direction away from a Trump involvement with Russia, it was buried. Is there an enquiry into Clinton's Foundation for receiving millions of dollars in donations from the Russians while she was Secretary of State and conducting business with Russia that led to Russia getting control of a percentage (20 %) of the U.S. uranium deposits? On the other hand, there has not been any crime identified nor evidence that Trump participated in something illegal, but he and his campaign personnel have been under surveillance since the FBI imbedded agents into his campaign. The double standard is so immensely problematic; I can only scratch the surface. Who has asked why an American official would broker 20 percent of our uranium to Russia? Don't they point nuclear weapons at the U.S? Do we need the money that bad? Are the people in charge of our government trying to destroy this country? I guess I suggested that was happening, quite a few pages ago. And the latest event is the Biden FBI raiding the home of President Trump.

A day could be spent looking at *CIRCULAR REASONING* from the left: "When an argument uses one of its premises as a conclusion, that argument is said to be circular. It proves nothing; it merely restates one of its premises under the guise of proving that premise." [Gula] Trump was not supposed to win the election; Trump must have cheated; Flynn lied to the FBI; Trump must have cheated: Papadopoulos is accused of lying to the FBI: Trump must have cheated; Trump's lawyer is going to jail for several reasons; Trump must have cheated; Manafort helped Trump in his election and he is going to jail: Trump must have cheated. Cohen is a liar; Trump must have cheated. On-and-on the cycle goes, and where it stops no one knows.

One type of *INFERENCE* is when "people misinterpret words or statements, assume more than they have a right to assume, inappropriately read between the lines, infer a cause-and-effect relationship when there is none, and generalize from insufficient data." [Gula] This summarizes the Charlottesville coverage and the impeachment hoax. What a hatchet job those are. They are not examples of critical accurate reporting. This is the case with the report about numerous comments made by Trump on the campaign. When I talk with my friends on the left, I say I will talk with them about what Trump said, but I will not discuss reports by the LPM. LPM reporting is dishonest; conclusions and editorials are not separated from what they portray as news. Even though to know everything they profess they would have to have a direct line to a higher power than themselves, it does not seem to bother them at all. I guess, therefore, this is the reason they are referred to frequently as the 'elite.' This was also the intent of the Mueller testimony. The entire show on the democratic side was inference.

I heard a lot about how Trump's desire to protect our borders was like the behavior of Hitler. Gula discusses *ERRONEOUS COMARISON*: The comparison of Trump and Hitler becomes thin after declaring both are men. Both did well in school. Historian Gavril D. Rosenfeld wrote these words in his study of how the Nazi past has become a recurring theme in contemporary culture—"to the point of almost becoming trivial." (theconversation.com). Godwin's Law holds that the longer an online discussion progresses, the likelier someone will eventually be compared to Hitler. Even Obama was caught up in that comparison. We now have the left comparing a generally peaceful protest of nearly a million Trump supporters with **the 9/11 attack, WWII, and the bombing of Pearl Harbor.** All I can say is, "Give me a break," or in Biden's own words, "Come on Man!"

EVASION is rather rampant in the LPM. When President Trump gave a talk to the American people about the need for a barrier on the border to protect the US from murderers, drug smugglers, and sex traffickers all the left wanted the conversation to be about government workers not getting a paycheck. This is an example of evasion. The response to the President's request for funds to secure the border was nonsense! Actually; non-existent.

Chapter 14 of Gula's book NONSENSE has to do with arguments. It is a great chapter and I highly recommend reading it. I have personally found that most arguments are errors in framing. *Errors in framing* have to do with the speech pattern framing the issue. Take for instance the way the argument about funds for border security were being taunted. The left said that it is the fault of the right; the right said it was the fault of the left. The error here is that both sides do not want to accept responsibility for whether the government shutdown continued or not. To argue about who is responsible is NONSENSE. Both sides were, because both sides could do something to fix the problem. Other than trying to get political points the issue really did not exist. For a border barrier to be built there must be money from somewhere, however, so that issue remained for some time until Trumps team found a way around the do-nothing congress.

The left likes the idea of an open border with illegals coming into the country, so they like security by drones and electronics that let the border agents watch the immigrants come into the country where they can only round them up, give them a number and send them into the interior of the country were there is a 90 percent likelihood they will never be seen again. While the country continues to struggle over illegal aliens and immigration practices the population of illegals continues to increase. Currently estimated at 20,000,000 the left is happy to see that number keep climbing, because they see the illegals as potential left voters and cheaper labor costs. The impact on the social fabric of our society has taken a major beating under Biden governance.

It appears President Obama wanted to destroy the U.S. and create a new order in the world in which the US was not a leader but merely a member. Given the elitist attitude of the left this seems contra-intuitive. Dale Lindsborg of the <u>Washington Post</u> is credited with reporting the following from a Sept 7, 2008 televised "Meet the Press."

The then Senator Obama was asked about his stance on the American flag. General Bill Gann, USAF (ret.) asked Obama to explain why he doesn't follow protocol when the National Anthem is played. The General stated to Obama that "according to the United States Code, Title 36, Chapter 10, sec. 171… During the rendition of the National Anthem, when the flag is displayed, all present (except those in uniforms) are expected to stand at attention facing the flag with the right hand over the heart, or, at the very least, Stand and Face it". Senator Obama replied, "As I've said about the flag pin, I do not want to be perceived as taking sides. There are a lot of people in the world to whom the American flag is a symbol of oppression… The anthem itself conveys a war-like message. You know, the bombs bursting in air and all that sort of thing." He continued: "The National Anthem should be 'swapped' for something less parochial and less bellicose. I like the song 'I'd Like To Teach the World To Sing.' If that were our anthem, then, I might salute it. In my opinion, we should consider reinventing our National Anthem as well as 'redesign' our flag to better offer our enemies hope and love. It's my intention, if elected, to disarm America to the level of acceptance to our Middle East Brethren. If we, as a Nation of warring people, conduct ourselves like the nations of Islam, where peace prevails, perhaps a state or period of mutual accord could exist between our governments. When I become President, I will seek a pact of agreement to end hostilities between those who have been at war or in a state of enmity, and a freedom from disquieting oppressive thoughts. We as a Nation, have placed upon the nations of Islam, an unfair injustice which is why my wife disrespects the flag and she and I have attended several flag burning ceremonies in the past. Of course, now, I have found myself about to become the President of the United States and I have put my hatred aside. I will use my power to bring change to this Nation and offer the people a new path. My wife and I look forward to becoming our Country's First black Family. Indeed, Change is about to overwhelm the United States of America."

So, it could not be much clearer: Obama hates/hated the people of America and the United States of America and what it stands for and Trump loves Americans and the United States of America and what it has always stood for. Obama's hate for the country seems to have rubbed off on once good Americans. His hatred is imbedded in the left's intolerance for historical figures, our constitution, our laws, and freedom of speech. They appear to have more concern for power than people. Can you imagine what the FBI, CIA and the other ten agencies in the U.S. that are supposed to protect this country would have done if Trump had said exactly the same things as Obama, but substituted 'Russia' for our 'Middle East Brethren?' The FBI and the Attorney General of the U.S. have clearly demonstrated political biases.

A lot of hoopla was been made about Trumps questioning court decisions, especially the 9th Circuit Court judges, suggesting bias in their decisions. Chief Justice John Roberts joined in criticizing the president for his comments saying judges did not let their own feeling determine how they ruled cases. He should have waited a couple weeks to do that; because shortly after he made the comments Associate Justice John Paul Stevens admitted in an interview with the *New York Times* that his extreme anti gun bias did play a role in his decision-making regarding second amendment rulings. It is sad but the left seems myopic when it comes to issues of prejudice. The composition of Robert Mueller's team is another example. Examples are quite frequent.

It seems Judge Roberts might be experiencing a similar issue. It seems obvious the left desires judges to make laws through judge's rulings. I do not believe that was the intent of the founding fathers. The left is also aware of this but apparently do not care if it is left leaning judges making up the law.

MORE ON RESPONSIBILITY

I would like to turn to another concept that was touched on in the <u>NONSENSE</u> book, but which I feel plays a much greater role in the confusion people have daily than most of the 'nonsense' that people speak. Responsibility is a word that has two meanings and unscrupulous people use this ambiguity to deliberately create confusion. The majority-education-system on the left does not appear to want to correct this error in speech and/or grammar. Understanding this concept is very helpful at a mental health level also.

RESPONSIBILITY as used in daily conversations--does not distinguish which of the two meanings is intended:

meaning 1. response-ability;
meaning 2. assigned accountability.

Characteristics of **RESPONSE-ABILITY** are:
Choice (without choice there is no responsibility)
Constantly in flux
Cannot be shared (can overlap) *
Cannot be transferred

Influenced by: Internal factors such as strength, Attention, IQ and External factors such as equipment, Time and Distance. This is low level abstraction: with a high level of agreement

Three (3) things we have response-ability for are our own thoughts, feelings, and actions

Characteristics of ***ASSIGNED-ACCOUNTABILITY*** are
  Compliance
  May be fixed
  May be shared
  Can be transferred

In this form there is not much influence from internal or external factors. Exception; Law has some exceptions under the concept of diminished capacity. Accountability is a convention: It is basically made up as we go along! This has high level abstraction: often with low-level agreement.

Three (3) things we are commonly held accountable for:
Other's thoughts, feelings, and actions. The left does this constantly.

*Probably the most confusing, and most arguably inaccurate concept under 'response-ability' as I have defined it is saying that it cannot be shared. My deconstruction of this is that as a doctor, firefighter or other specialist we cannot really share what we can do as an individual. If we look at events not requiring accumulation (i.e.: electing someone to office), 'response-ability' is an individual trait, but the ability to get elected is an accumulative one where a person might argue getting it done is a shared activity. Like individuals in a Circus a voter in an election is still an individuals doing what they can do as individuals.

There are several consequences this definition should bring to attention rather quickly. One is that we have response-ability for an uncountable number of choices in our lives. If we tried to be 'responsible' for all the conditions we potentially could do something about, we would likely never make it out of our bedroom, or house. Events, or conditions, that we become aware of that we can do something about are now our responsibility.

It is interesting to see the reaction of people when I ask them, "Who is responsible for the paper weight (that I just laid on my desk) staying on my desk?" The typical high-level abstraction answers include: "nobody, gravity, whoever put it there, whoever cleans up the room, whoever bought it, you are…." I will then ask one of those present if they can take it off the desk, and once they do, I enquire as to whether their original answer is still seen as complete or accurate. In characteristic Socratic manner people finally arrive at the answer that all of us in the room are responsible for it staying on the desk, since we all can remove it from the desk (**ability**), and we are all **aware** that it is on the desk, and we all have a **choice** to remove it, or not. The difficulty in arriving at an accurate answer is impeded by several cognitive struggles.

One error people make is to assume acknowledging responsibility is admitting having done something wrong. The concept, and the word itself, is often associated with doing something bad. ("Trump is responsible for keeping the government shut down." Those on the left say it and add in their minds 'Another basis to impeach the president'; those on the right think, "thank God for a person with the courage to stick up for something badly needed to protect the people.") In fact, the labeling of good or bad has nothing to do with whether we are responsible, or not. That is like adding frosting to a cake. Just something that has been added that may make it more, or less, likable. People in my office are hesitant to say that "You am responsible," even when that is the way they feel, because they do not want to <u>accuse me</u>—which of course is exactly what they would generally be doing. I have spelled out above the characteristics of responsibility (response-ability and assigned-accountability) and will try not do it again except to say that using these concepts interchangeably is tantamount to lying. It is what lawyers do to win court battles; it is what politicians do to win elections. It is lying. It is deceitful. It is utter nonsense; it is another way to weaponize the English language.

We do not have responsibility (response-ability) if we don't have choice. We need to learn to be comfortable with the idea that there are a lot of things in life that I could perhaps do something about if I had the time, money, knowledge, strength, etc. It is ok to choose not to do something. We must prioritize our choices. Responsibility used as blame is a redundancy: "You are capable of doing something, so I am holding you accountable for it."

Don't you love the way the left stands up and says, "President Trump you did not do what you said you would do, you lied, you had a majority in both houses of congress and you didn't do what you said you would." Fact: A majority in congress does not assure a bill will pass and the left understands that. Having the majority may sound nice but the number of votes needed in congress for many proposals to pass is 60 votes, and for those of you who don't follow such things that was 9 more votes than there were republican senators, 7 more than the republicans had at the time of this writing. So, the reality is that President Trump is not responsible for either getting a bill to pass (It is not his choice), or not getting a bill to pass. Bills are passed by the congress, not by the president. Those who like to blame and point the finger may say he is responsible, but he really isn't. It is just another lie. Why don't the fact *checkers* do their work here?

A new door possibly opens: if the law allows the President to declare an emergency, and he is lawfully able to do something without passage of a bill by congress, then he does have responsibility for whether the task gets done or not. Accountability should reflect some continuity of premise. "President Trump is responsible for hurricane Florence" [paraphrased from the Washington Post] has got to raise some question of validity in even the dumbest academician on the left. If he really possessed that Superpower the left would want to be more cautious about calling him names. Again, why don't the fact checkers do their work here? President Biden labels 70 million Americans neo-fascists. Does that make it true? President Biden calls nearly a million Americans insurrectionists. (No guns, no killing, no intent to harm any legislator) Does that make it true? Democrats do what they do to gain more power. Does labeling this political demonstration an insurrection give them more power. Of course! Otherwise they would not make such outlandish accusations.

Once we comprehend the concept of responsibility, we can begin to put it to work to understand other really screwed up ideas. Most parents do not recognize their children are "delusional" (Not in a mental health diagnosis way, but in fact they have multiple beliefs that are completely inaccurate which they are not willing to alter.) Delusional children grow up to be delusional adults, if they never come to the realization that their beliefs are nonsense and inaccurate. Piaget demonstrated the child's ability over time to understanding concepts like volume, distances, etc. We see young children do not understand ideas like death, or lethal. One concept I do not believe Piaget looked at was children's propensity to learn blaming behaviors from the adult world. Part of the problem in studying this concept is that the vast majority of the children's parents would be greatly offended, because it would put them in the spotlight.

A series of cognitive frames (events) in the raising of children during formative years assures conflicts will follow them. The *left educational system* does not seem to like teaching this awareness.

The Event: Children are self-taught by experiences (interactions with the physical world) to frame events in blame language. The interactions occurring between the human organism and the physical world are *cause and effect* in nature. If you fall, you often experience pain caused by the impact of ground and body. If you run into something you may feel pain from the impact to the body. If someone hits you accidentally, or on purpose, the tissue damage may be painful. If you step on a nail the injury to tissues causes pain. When explaining these physical events, it is accurate speech to use blame language: "Ouch, that hurt me!" The nature of cause and effect is that the event is accurately seen as creating/ generating/ causing the outcome.

The Error: Parents, teachers and people in general fail to help children understand how the physical and psychological worlds are different.

This failure is related to the perpetual nature of the problem, not from malice. Events occurring in the psychological world are not cause and effect related in the same way they are in the physical world. I want a new toy and am told I can't have it. I feel bad. This is sequential ordering of an event; it is not cause and effect. I want to go play with my friends and am told I can't. I feel bad. My brother won't let me play with his new Christmas present. I feel bad. Someone at school calls me a name. I feel bad and maybe angry. I think my mother does not love me. I feel bad. Again, this is *sequential ordering of events and not cause and effect.*

Explaining these events using cause and effect language is an inaccurate over-generalization of cause and effect thinking. The bad feelings in these examples have no causal connection to the event.

Consequence: Believing there is a connection between the event and our feelings, or actions, is an error in reasoning leading to a major error in our understanding of the event. The events listed are merely something to focus our thoughts on. Non-physical events in life create the same mental process that the Rorschach does in psychological testing. It has only the meaning the person's thinking places on it. The Emperor Augustus Caesar of Rome reportedly said, "Others hurt us only to the degree that we believe they have." This is a clear example that even a 1000 years ago there was recognition of the importance of *thought* in our experience.

The belief system that evolves from this inaccurate application of what we learn about the physical world onto the psychological world contributes to the *inaccurate impressions* we form about our world. Failing to understand this difference creates inaccurate perceptions in the child and, unfortunately, many adults.

The Event: Thoughts are the replacement for cause in the psychological realm. The only *cause and effect* operating in the psychological world is between what we tell ourselves about the event and the feelings or behaviors those thoughts generate. If I think others *cause my unhappiness,*

I avoid them, or strike back. If I think others *make me happy,* I find reasons to spend more time with them, and I feel warm and cozy when with them. One of the reasons people confuse this in their thinking is that there are *feelings* generated by our thinking (our mind) and there are feelings generated by the physical body. When we use the word *feelings* these two experiences become interchangeable, but they really aren't. We need more accurate words.

As we begin to better understand epigenetics in the creation of our response to external events and stimuli, this problem may begin to be more understandable. Infants crawling on a glass floor will hesitate, or stop, at what appears to them to be a hole. I doubt most researchers believe the baby is contemplating the possibility of a fall into the hole, but some type of message is being transmitted that warns them off. For the followers of "Intelligent Emotions" this might be their best example. I am more inclined to see this as a genetic, or epigenetic expression, or what we used to label as instinct.

I was listening to a car salesman tell me how his car was so smart that if the car sensed it was in danger of hitting something it set itself up in what he called a 'pre-stop condition' that allowed the braking mechanism to work faster, if needed. I believe this is like the highly trained martial artist who on some alerting event may not appear to do anything, but internally is readying his body for all out action. The body's reaction might be the same in both an untrained and trained person, but the expression of the feeling might be completely different because of the combination of body memory and mental training.

If we are allergic to bee stings and our body pumps out adrenalin when we hear a buzz, the flight response is possibly a life-saving reaction. For the non-allergic child who hears the buzz and then runs unthinkingly into traffic, the response itself may be a cause of injury, or death. It can be difficult to separate these different types of feelings, because they are both implemented by the same neurological system.

Children mimic the *inaccurate speech of the society* they grow up in. Our educational system does a very good job of teaching children to speak correctly. When we listen to individuals from other countries struggle to speak English, it is often quite humorous; we usually recognize the incorrectness and adjust in our minds what the person is attempting to tell us. This type of error rarely causes consequences of importance. The song says, "He made me love him, I didn't want to do it." This is not understood by people to be a completely inaccurate statement: a really stupid statement in fact!

The Error: Others do not make us… The words imply others create our love for them. This is not true. It sounds romantic, I guess. It sells a lot of books and valentines. Others do not make us love them. Our own mental processing creates our attraction to others. The danger here is that the person, who believes someone else created the loving feeling, will also then feel that the other person created the hate they may later have for the same person when things go wrong. People do not accept, thanks to common and inaccurate word construction, responsibility for their own feelings. This is a major error. Our educational system has failed us.

The Event: The well-meaning, but frustrated, parent tells their son, "Stop making your sister feel bad and give her what she wants."

The Consequence: From this exchange the son learns that he makes/creates his sister's unpleasant feelings. He learns he is 'responsible' for other's feelings. The sister learns she is not 'responsible' for her feelings, but that others are. She also learns that others need to change when she doesn't like something. The fired ambassador believed Trump made her feel bad so the left congressional caucus tries to make it an impeachable offense. When we look at ways children receive this message (conversations, books, news, songs, movies, etc.) it is easy to see how they develop this inaccurate set of beliefs: what others do or say causes my thoughts, feelings and actions; what I do or say causes other's thoughts, feelings and actions; others are responsible for my thoughts, feelings and actions; I am responsible for other's thoughts, feelings and actions. To the degree that one believes this belief system, it creates problems for them all the remainder of their life. When individuals buy into it there is often a progression to crimes such as assault and murder or suicide. This belief system enforced by society leads to creating crimes without the perpetrator even knowing how they got there. When governments buy into this craziness, they want to fine people for saying words they don't like such as 'illegal alien' in NY or for calling someone the wrong pronoun in California. This is infantilization on hormones. It is an attempt to micromanage someone's speech. Control! Control! Control! Is the goal. It is a good way to destroy a person's mental health. As usual the democrats, and the republicans who support them in these areas, have not clearly thought through what they are doing.

BLAME THINKING

The traditional opinions related to blame thinking are known as <u>*a blame system of thinking*</u>**: I call it System 1 or S1** for short. The reason I label it such is that it is one of the first important and influential belief systems in people's lives.

Teaching children (people in general) to accept the beliefs related to this way of thinking sets them up to be vulnerable to things like bullying. Adults and children need to learn to speak accurately. System one is an example of language gone wrong. Countries who prohibit girls from going to school do so at least in part because men know knowledge is power and they wish to keep it for themselves. States that charge Americans money for saying the wrong pronoun or charging someone for calling a person by their accurate name are doing it for the same reason—to gain power. Don't be misled into thinking it is because they care about your feelings. They most certainly do not. They care neither about your feeling nor your mental health. Speaking directly is the only way to intimacy, which may be why Trump has as much support as he has from Republicans and is disliked by Democrats. Republicans like being up close and friendly, the left talks a game of caring but demonstrates only hostility and hatred.

Two other attributes of the human experience also play a significant role in creating undesirable outcomes: 1) the desire (maybe *need* fits better) to be right, and 2) the overlooked builder of our internal frame of reference--our speech. Our speech not only conveys what we believe, but it acts as a conveyer of concepts from one person to another. If I learn to speak like my father, I am likely to incorporate his beliefs as well. This may generate either a positive, or a negative outcome. This is why the left wants to control how you speak. The person who controls how you speak controls you.

The bully recognizes intuitively that others give them power. The misunderstanding parents and others have about the way the psychological world works (seeing a cause-and-effect relationship where there is only sequential ordering of events) creates a child and an adult who will be vulnerable/susceptible to the negative influence others exert.

The defense against being bullied is to recognize the opinion of others is not important. This is a concept with two sharp edges (I just heard a couple of you gasp.):

Edge one: We want our children to be liked by others, but because people do not take responsibility for their own feelings (inaccurate thinking), we have to help our children understand others may get upset with them when they do not buy into being responsible for the other person's feelings. The problem here is that the people most likely to do this are the parents. This is what the parent was taught as a child, and it is a part of the damaging cycle that is created. This is a manipulative process we shouldn't want our children to incorporate.

Edge two: At the same time, we need to teach them that other people do not understand about not being responsible for others feelings, so if they do what is correct, they may still get complaints. They need to learn patience in developing relationships. (Friends may not like how they behave because they are not able to manipulate them.) Unfortunately, adults are just as prone to be manipulated as children.

Whether it is politically correct, or not, we need to help our children understand they are not responsible for other peoples' thoughts, feelings and actions--if we want them to survive in the world and be healthy. In life, we are our own *first responders*. This is another trap both right and left have fallen into. The left has weaponized this to mean, "Don't find ways to protect yourself, let the officials do it." The right on the other hand says, "Responders are almost always the second group of people to be on the scene, and you need to recognize how to deal with situations firsthand. The conscious individual at the scene is always the *first responder.*

Insisting others are responsible for their own feelings and actions is not being mean, it is being accurate!

On the surface this *error of blaming* in speech may not seem like an earth-shattering revelation that could account for much of the mental distress people have. But, it should, because until it is recognized and taken into account when determining the mental health and fate of others, whether in the psychiatrist's office, in the courts of law, or the court of public opinion, it is a major player and a major determinant in how a life is going to play out. The people of the U.S. have not yet come to the realization that they indirectly groom individuals (often their own children) to become law breakers.

It is accurate to insist each person is responsible for their own thoughts, feelings and actions. Failure to do so often creates criminals!

Consequence

It is total insanity when people become so afraid of litigation, or complaints, that they cannot complement someone, or say what they feel. This is the worst type of fearful interaction imaginable. This is political correctness used as a mallet against others. It is the desire to punish anyone who speaks poorly about God. This is creating fear and subservience. This is the democrat play book: keep the black community angry at the white community; keep women angry at the men; show immigrants preference over citizens.

Our interpretations can create a problem.

It has been suggested that the use of the atomic bomb on Japan was predicated on our misinterpretation of a single word in the communications exchanged between Japan and the United States toward the end of the war. When interpretations are inaccurate it can cause a lot of negative consequences, especially when the parties turn to the legal venue, or drop bombs. Basically, it is the rules/beliefs that we follow that determine our experience in life (whether practiced only by us or by society as a whole). The elite democrats make as their reality what they want their reality to be, then they initiate an impeachment on the bases of what they want people to believe, not on the reality of what is accurate. How often do they have to step in the same cow paddy before they get awareness of how it smells? Jared Kushner in his book <u>Breaking History</u> discussed how much of the progress made during the Trump presidency came from moving away from the 'usual' rules in making deals.

The rules we live by create our experience in life!

Belief systems act like invisible rules in the background of nearly all interactions going on between people (even at the level of countries). It is a major player even when we are not dealing with each other directly. The consequences of not understanding this can be devastating to the individual and to society. Just what is this belief system professed by the democrats? "We believe in truth not in facts." Truth is higher on the ladder of abstraction than is facts. The higher on the ladder the less consensus there is. Facts can be worked with, looked at, checked and replicated. Truth remains in Plato's perfect world of perfect forms. After all, don't we refer to them as the 'elite' left? No one I know has ever accused them of being the practical left; the accurate left; or the fair left.

Case

Mary yells at her child whom she perceives as being too noisy, "Be quiet you are driving me crazy!"

Consequence

What goes on in the head of the child who hears this comment? If she has learned to be in the blame system (S1) she sees herself as making mother unhappy, and she sees her mother as making her unhappy. She may also have a surge of feeling power over mother. This is a power the oppositional defiant child cultivates. Not uncommonly she might become vindictive (making even more noise) toward the adult she believes is causing her pain, or who is seen as limiting her enjoyment. Or, depending on her thinking process, she might withdraw, feeling the sting of her mother's words. The words becoming her inner voice later down the road.

If this type of comment is frequent, it is likely to generate self-esteem issues in the child. These comments are also detrimental to the exchanges made by adults. Although I am using children to explain the process, it is just as relevant in describing adult interactions, and just as damaging. Another possible response to the comment is to become defensive and want to argue. "Why are you always picking on me? When Billy plays out here you don't yell at him. I don't make any more noise than he does." So, in all but the most fortunate, or enlightened families, both the children and the adults of the family are processing things through S1 thinking. If the parents blame the children for the way they "are made to feel," it is a model for the child to blame the parent for the way "they are made to feel." This inaccurate thinking feeds on itself like a California forest fire. The more blame there is from one quarter, the greater is the blame that comes from others. (Think political.)

The Case: Ainslie, in the same predicament as Mary, asks her child if she would like to help her prepare the meal she is making for the family. She starts by telling her about what she has done so far and what is needed to finish the job.

The Case: Robert is a real estate agent struggling with the failure of not being able to close a deal. His new wife noticing his down demeanor asks, "What's wrong?" The response she gets is "Nothing!" as he rapidly storms off to another room. Ainslie has learned over her life to stay out of the S1 trap, so her response to her curt and obviously frustrated husband is different from the family he grew up in. There he would have been attacked for his rudeness and put on the defensive. (Does that remind you of groups you encounter?) She goes into the kitchen and fixes his favorite drink. Then she brings the drink and her calmness into the bedroom where he is emerging from the shower. Looking him in the eye she smiles and offers him the drink saying, "Honey, it is pretty obvious you experienced something unpleasant today, if you would like to share what it is, I am all ears, if you just want some time to yourself, dinner will be ready in about twenty minutes. I love you." Robert's self-esteem should increase, because he had sense enough to marry this woman.

Resolving the issues created by system one *mistakes* requires three steps.

Step 1: Our first act must be to either stop giving away our power or get it back. When we frame something in the "You made me …" vernacular, we are metaphorically giving away our power. "You made me," says "I am giving you my power and now you are responsible for how I end up feeling." "*YOU MAKE….*" says "I am giving you all my power, and I will be holding you accountable for everything." It is no wonder the left fights so determinedly to get back power; it is constantly giving power away in blaming.

The Case:

John was struggling with a law concept his friend Bob appeared to easily understand. When Bob chuckled, either from amusement or his own anxiety at his friend's challenge, he was told "You are really pissing me off." Bruce who was listening in said, "You are an irritable bastard today." [For some reason, that didn't help the situation.] Bob responded, "My chuckle was about all the times I have been up against the wall thinking I would never figure something out only to have the answer fly in like a spooked bat once I let my mind relax. I suggest we give it a few minutes and then, if you still want my help, we will take another shot at it."

Bob obviously chose not to get pushed into a reaction to his friend's blame statement and instead he chose to defuse the situation (by sharing his own experiences), help John relax (by changing the subject) and provided him with some useful self-building techniques (by reflecting on how often before things had worked out).

The Consequence:

When we give away our power through blaming, we feel helpless. Blame thinking frames the issue (Bob's laugh) as the cause of the bad feeling. The laugh really has no power until John places a meaning on it. He apparently saw it as a put down, and he responded in a somewhat threatening manner. Studies have shown that if this conversation were taking place in the Deep South there is a much higher likelihood it might turn out as a physical confrontation than if it were an event between individuals in the north. This has to do with the ways people construct and then feel a need to protect their honor.

The Solution:

The act of *keeping our power* is one of *reframing the problem*. In blaming, we see the problem as always residing outside of us. That infers others must then solve the issue by bringing about some change. When we keep or take back our power, we are making a concession that perhaps the solution to the problem resides in us. That is a position of *personal power*. This was the personal power displayed in J Kushner's approach to the challenges he was given.

The Case:

Ainslie recognized her husband's issues were not about her, and she did not make herself the center of the issue. She did not try to take the problem away from him (a mistake a lot of men make when dealing with concerns their wives present to them). She offered to listen to him if he wanted (a wise man would certainly take her up on the offer). Her response was respectful in that by not offering a solution she was saying indirectly that she had confidence he would be able to work the problem out. It would be disrespectful for her to imply he *needed* to talk it over with her. That suggests she feels he is not capable of finding a solution to the problem. This is one reason why women get angry with men who try to solve problems they present. Changing our perspective from believing it is what lies outside of us, to a willingness to look for the solution to the problem inside us, is a major reframing event. It is also a significant life altering event.

The Case:

Frank was an angry man. He had been an angry child and an even angrier adolescent. He said he did not just get angry, but he raged nearly every day of his life that he could recall. His wife was on the verge of calling it quits. She loved him, but his constant explosions were becoming a deal breaker. He had gone to a doctor and was told he was bipolar and needed to be on Lithium, Depakote and Zyprexa to get his anger under control. He sought a second opinion.

The second opinion examiner found none of the criteria for bipolar DO present (The diagnosis was apparently made on the presence of anger alone) and he gave Frank three options: 1) he could practice staying out of blame which would get rid of the problem of anger, 2) he could go on one of forty-two different medications (antidepressants, mood stabilizers and anti-seizure medications) which would bring down the intensity of the anger feelings as long as he stayed on them, and 3) he could use a combination of one and two if he felt he could not give up blaming right away.

Frank chose to give up blaming, with some fear his wife would not like the idea of his not being put on medication for his perceived psychiatric problem. He was a good learner and at his one and three months follow up, he reported he had not had even one anger episode since discussing the cause (blaming). He said he realized almost as we talked about it that he was always seeing something other than him as the cause of his feeling, that was the way things had been framed in his childhood and he simply thought that was the way things worked. (This is *the cycle* that must be broken. This is the never-ending Hillary Clinton narrative of why she lost.)

When we give away our power metaphorically, it contributes to a whole host of problems, but the two that are most apparent are failure to develop either self-esteem, or trust. Giving away our power creates low self-esteem and distrust.

The Case:

Michael had never been able to get beyond the dating level in a relationship with a girl. The girls accused him of being afraid of commitment. The first relationship he had with a girl lasted about 9 months, he believed he was deeply in love with her and she went off to college in another town and his heart was broken (as he described it). He vowed not to let anyone hurt him that way again. So, he kept his distance expecting to have the girls leave him, and his self-fulfilling prophecy kept occurring. Fear of commitment is generally a *fear of being hurt*. It was pointed out to Michael that the anguish he felt was not caused by the girlfriends leaving, but by his interpretation of why she left. Psychological events are not painful. Our interpretation of events, however, often makes them painful.

Step 1: He initially resisted the idea, but it finally made sense to him. He had given her his personal power and when he felt bad about her leaving, he had felt she caused the feeling. Framing it that way led him to try and manipulate others into becoming dependent on him, (like the democrats do) so that they would not leave him. The result however was that he was overbearing (hopefully more democrats and independents will come to understand this) and the ladies soon moved on. His inability to control others led him to believe he could not trust others. He began to pull away as he created a script about women being untrustworthy.

All his failures were not doing much to benefit his self-esteem. Once he understood that his negative script about women and his self-esteem issues were related to the error in the way he framed his relationships, he began to see people more realistically and his relationships began to develop into something more lasting and more intense. He had one last issue related to his feelings. He believed he was becoming dependent on his lady friends again for his good feeling. He believed that *feeling dependent* was a bad thing, and he should try and get rid of the feeling. It was pointed out to him that he might have made an error in the way he framed dependency issues.

It had been his point of view that dependency was a bad thing and he should avoid it at all costs. He seemed to relax when it was explained to him that the common usage of the word was negative, but that dependency was not always a bad thing. People who believe like Frank, once they begin to develop dependent feelings about others will want to strive for more independency. This was what Frank was doing and he was already experiencing the negative outcome—more emotional isolation.

The opposite of dependency may be better understood, not as independence, but as *healthy dependency*. Healthy dependency acknowledges that others can provide something for us that we cannot create by ourselves. Unhealthy dependency wants others to do something for us that we should do for ourselves. Healthy dependency is like going to bed with someone knowing that each of you will do everything possible to keep the other one safe.

In withdrawing people are saying, I am not failing, the world around me has failed, and I really do not want more to do with it. This pushes the child/adult into loneliness, isolation and fosters the sense of futility. "I have tried and tried, and I can't do anything to make it better."

A child 12-15 years old decides that life is too hard for them and that death would be better. Is this Depression? The condition often gets diagnosed as a depression. Children, like adults, get caught up in the belief that others are responsible for their feelings. The more they see that as true the more helpless and hopeless they feel. Great is the despair that sets in. Giving others our power leaves us without power. An unpleasant experience in politics as well as in person. Some individuals will do what they can to get, or get back, power. The lefts' frantic behaviors would suggest the truth of this statement. They do not want to come out of their protected cage and address the issues raised, they would rather try and win the argument by identity politics, or by declaring those who do not see things the way they do are bad or immoral.

If children have not been educated to see it otherwise, they see themselves as causing their parents (and other peoples) reaction to them. So, if the parent does not seem to like them, they feel they have created that condition; if the parent is mean to them, they feel they have created that condition; if the parent rejects them, they feel they created that situation; if the parent gets a divorce, they feel they created that situation, and if a parent drops out of the family, they feel they have created that event. The result is that the child carries a lot of shame and guilt about what is happening in their family. It seems the left's educational track is to foster this point of view.

Step 2: Identify blame language! The second step necessary to get rid of S1 inaccurate thinking is to learn to identify *blame language*. It seems this is the most difficult of the three steps for people. Most everyone recognizes comments like, "You make me mad. You hurt my feelings. You made me love you," are blame statements. There are a lot of comments people struggle with seeing as blame statements: "I can't tell them that, it will hurt their feelings," or, "Because she said that, I felt really bad." In today's political climate, anytime someone says something the person does not like they call them "racist." "Racist" is just another way of articulating that I do not like what you are saying. It is like, "You are not being fair."

Blame statements take place in three areas [emotions] "You/He/She/It/They make me …. mad/glad/sad/happy/ frustrated/ angry/feel bad/etc.;" [cognitions] "You …. made me love you/hate you/adore you/ trust you/believe in you/etc.;" [actions] "You …. Made me marry you/divorce you/steal from you/lie to you/beat you/drink/eat too much/etc."

If you cannot recognize blame language you will not be able to make the third step work.

Step 3: Remove blame language from your speech.

I challenge my patients to look for blame language everywhere: on the news, when reading a book or when listening to music lyrics. Some TV shows have a lot of blame language, and others do not. I have been aware of only one blame comment coming from the Mark Harmon's NCIS team in all the years it has been on TV. Harry's Law on the other hand frequently had blame comments in the dialogue. This attribute does not make a show better or worse, just more mature or immature in what is presented. If you really want to see S1 at warp speed, watch the daily soap operas or listen to one of the LPM on TV.

ACCURATE SPEECH

The solution to the problems created by S1 inaccurate thinking is simply that we need to start early in life teaching children to speak accurately, as well as correctly. *Accurate speech* is different from *correct speech*. Children say hundreds of thousands of things that are inaccurate speech, and they are never corrected. We have a repetitive error in our speech when it relates to the psychological aspects of our world. We frame sequential ordering of events in cause-and-effect language and that is inaccurate. This inaccuracy of assessment causes a person to believe something that is not true which then leads to inappropriate actions. These actions often lead to people being put in jail. Often the person going to jail does not even understand why they have been incarcerated. "He was making me mad; I just hit him over the head to make him stop; why are you putting me in jail?" Inaccurate speech creates inaccurate beliefs which lead to inaccurate actions.

Certain political groups go out of their way to foster this problem and make people more vulnerable to life. Fining people because they use the wrong pronoun, rather than teaching people how to respond correctly to someone using the wrong pronoun, is not helpful in developing a healthy society, but just makes more healthy people criminals. To fine someone for a type of speech is an attempt to control speech. It is a very bad thing to do in a free society. It is stupid and it infantilizes people. We need to back down our punitive vengefulness until we do a better job of helping people frame life more accurately. To punish people for the products of a sustained inaccurate belief system originating in childhood and contributed to by almost all of us, and which is rarely ever addressed, is a blight on our educational system and our legal system. Listen up educators on the left. You must recognize blame language in order to remove it from your speech.

A recent Scientific American MIND magazine had an article titled (approximately) "You Believe Your Own Lies" and that is exactly what the belief that others are responsible for our thoughts, feelings and actions is. It is a lie we tell ourselves, and that other people tell us, that we too frequently believe. People do not even see that it is a lie. It is also a lie that we are responsible for other's thoughts, feelings and actions. It is such a common belief that when unexamined, people just accept it. Don't: it is a lie. I feel sorry for the left because I believe they believe their own lies. I am aware the left feels the same way about the conservatives.

Blaming (in the psychological world) is inaccurate framing (a lie).

One external pressure helping people move out of S1 thinking is a good job. Individuals in high functioning businesses usually do not rise to the top of the management ladder unless they understand that their job is to perform to the satisfaction of higher management. Blamers are not likely to reach that pinnacle except in politics and in education. S1 is a blame system. It is not a desirable trait for obtaining a good job. As ironic as it may seem, most individuals who master the trait of not blaming others in the work environment, seldom bring that skill home with them. They drop it off at the door, and frequently begin blaming the wife, the kids, the dog, or the cat for the things they do not like upon returning home. [Remember the Saturday Evening Post cover March 20, 1954—cost 15 cents.]

This occurs because S1 thinking was the belief system we were creating when we formed our first close relationships: with our parents, with our siblings, with our best friends, with our first boy/girlfriends and possibly with our first husbands/wives. It is an immediately available default position in our thinking because of our prior experiences.

Why do some people get out of the blame system of thinking and others don't? Some children are lucky to have parents who are not blamers, or they have parents who recognize the damage blaming can do, so they help their children learn to frame things differently. Some just come to recognize it themselves. When this occurs, it is generally an intuitive process, and not really one built on understanding S1. Parents generally believe their actions are helping children become more accountable and, eventually, more responsible adults even when their actions are doing the opposite. Trumps comment to the leader of China that he did not hold him responsible (blame him) for the U.S. allowing him to steal from us is an example of understanding the principle I am discussing.

What are some of the common ramifications/products of staying in the blame system, S1? Look at the left. Look at the current educational system.

The Consequences:

When studying drug, or alcohol addictions, it is a common medical lore that people stop developing emotionally at the time the addiction takes off. If we look carefully at the emotional level of development when drug dependencies occur, we find people are still in S1 thinking. People are not so much fixed at an age as they are fixed in a specific system of thinking (S1). System 1 generates a lot of unpleasant experiences for people, many of whom use drugs, alcohol, etc. to take away the misery associated with it.

The characteristic attributed to individuals who develop alcohol problems is called "*field dependency.*" This is a rather technical sounding phrase that implies the same thing as S1. People who are "field dependent" are individuals who are in greater reaction to what is going on outside of the brain (in the environment) than what is going on inside their brain. So, the "field dependent" person sees events as causing the way they feel and what they do. It is not really some attribute of alcoholism; it is just childhood thinking being manifested along with alcoholism. Believing Trump is causing all their insanity is another example from the left of Trump derangement syndrome and is an error in thinking.

Self-esteem: Typically, when I ask someone immersed in S1 thinking what pleases them the answer I get is, "I don't know." There are a lot of products from S1 thinking, but the most devastating one is the damage it does to self-esteem. When an individual gets out of S1 and takes back power, self-esteem begins to improve immediately.

The courts punish children and adults for believing what society teaches them to believe.

The courts want to put 15 and 16-year-old children away like they were adults for offenses they may have committed. These children are locked mentally into S1 thinking. They are not finding a way out of the failure system they have been stuck in for the first years of life, but they continue to approach life in the same way over and over. [You know about the attitude that if you just try harder, you can be whatever you want—crazy! Despite what the democrats say men cannot become women.] They blame others for their predicament, and they are blamed by others for their failure to function in society. The more they fail, the more anger they express, and the more confused they are. They get angrier trying to make this belief system work. It doesn't. Then they withdraw or do something that puts them in jail.

In societies where victims constantly see others as causing the bad feelings they experience; it is not much of a reach to see why society wants the maximum sentencing--even when it involves our children and our mentally challenged. The occasional person who can stand up to the tide of blame sticks out like a clown in church. The news people marvel at, "How can they do that; they are so brave." I do not want to take away from those individuals, but the comments are baloney. The person is not brave, they are smart. A non-blamer recognizes that forgiveness is a gift to one's self, not to the other person. To forgive is smart, not brave.

Inaccurately framing the way the world works helps create criminals, democrats, college professors and lawyers. This is another place where the law frequently gets it totally messed up. Children rarely have the understanding that others are not responsible for their thoughts, feelings and actions, and a high percentage of criminals have no more understanding of this than children. In other words, if it were looked at factually, we would see that the level of understanding about the correct way to frame life is completely missing in lots of adults. With our experience in the world at large, it would seem this defect would be better recognized. Countries that want to perpetuate vendettas go to great lengths to prevent the people they control from getting an education. Better education (not like the one getting taught in the USA) is a way one can begin to comprehend what is inaccurately framed. The more education is kept away from people, the more people can be convinced others are responsible for their dismal existence (This is called blame). Why do countries hate the U.S.—because their people can be convinced by their leaders that we are responsible for their misery (S1 blame thinking). Why do so many people in the U.S. seem to hate each other—because our left controlled educational system is teaching blaming as the way to address conflict? "You are wrong, just shut up." Educational systems that want to shut people up, stop debate, and insist things are only one way, ARE NOT EDUCATIONAL SYSTEMS! THEY ARE PROPAGANDA SYSTEMS! IF YOU ARE UNABLE TO DISCUSS THE SUBJECT, YOU HAVE NO INFORMATION ON THE SUBJECT to discuss.

What the person in this state of mind is not recognizing is that they have been framing the world in an inaccurate manner. If a person believes that 2+2=5 they have an inaccurate frame of thinking, or a mistaken impression. Depending on the math questions presented to them they may not fail completely, but they are not likely to do well overall. In a similar way the belief that others are responsible for my thoughts, feelings and actions, and I am responsible for others thoughts, feelings and actions, is not a good frame in dealing with life, and it is not going to contribute to a good outcome, any more than 2+2=5 is going to help with getting a good math grade. In life, like in math, if you do not frame the problems accurately, you can't get an accurate answer.

The Case:

William is a 15-year-old oppositional boy. He was admitted to the hospital's behavioral health unit on three occasions. Each time he was diagnosed bipolar and put on several numbing medications which he stopped as soon as he was released because of the side effects. His parents are concerned he will end up in jail the next time he acts out.

Assessment of William reveals he meets the criteria for Attention Deficit and Oppositional Defiant DO (ODD). He is given medication to deal with the medical condition (ADD) and his parents are taught that William is much more alert than his peers. He should never be lied to as he will immediately identify a lie and confront them with this information. This confrontation is what is seen as ODD. The parents need to learn to speak accurately when talking to him. They should never tell him he can't do something, if he can, because he will need to show them their error. They are encouraged to take pleasure in their son's abilities. [This is a new frame for them.] Treating his ADD and learning to talk honestly to him greatly improves his behavior over the next couple weeks.

Symptom vs. Product

There is another place where issues are framed inaccurately. Symptoms are generally thought of as indicators: I.e., Five to six "symptoms" of hyperactivity are adequate to assume that attention deficit is present, provided they are of significant intensity. In the psychological world it may be more beneficial to see symptoms (indicators) as different from products (outcomes).

Indicators vs. Outcomes: What is the significance of "symptoms" being products? The biggest thing is that understanding this means you do not have to work on them to get rid of them. You don't have to waste energy; you can conserve it. If you choose to stay indoors when the weather is zero outside you won't feel cold. If you do not put your hand on a hot burner, you do not get burned. If you do not stay in S1 inaccurate thinking you do not experience the products that are related to S1. (A list of common S1 products is provided below.) As soon as the person chooses to frame life in S2 (the understanding that we each create our own thoughts, feelings and actions and others create their own thoughts, feelings and actions), nature provides an entirely different set of products for us. It does not seem to be understood by people that nature manifests the products; we are, merely, allowed to make certain choices upstream from the products, so we either encounter them or do not encounter them.

An assembly line pumps off products. If all the products coming off the assembly line are broken there are two primary choices that can be made. We can either keep attempting to fix the products (this is like therapy interminable) or we can fix the assembly line. If we fix the assembly line, we will be creating a set of new products and in time the old products will simply disappear. The products related to S1 are unpleasant. Perhaps not as much so as putting your hand on a hot burner, but it is my impression the pain related to S1 thinking is there for the same reason that we get burned. Mother Nature does not want us to put our hands on burners, and she does not want us to stay in S1 thinking.

Getting out of S1 thinking creates self-healing of the products associated with it.

"Yes" answers are generally products of S1 thinking

HURT:

Do you let your feelings get hurt easily?

Are you defensive in arguments?

Do you keep replaying in your mind situations you have been in?

Do you try to maintain a distance from others to protect yourself from being hurt?

DISSATISFACTION:

Are you frequently dissatisfied with your life?

Do you feel dissatisfied with the people you associate with?

Are you dissatisfied with where you are in your career or life in general?

Do you lack faith in your abilities?

DISAPPROVAL:

Are you critical of yourself?

Are you critical of others?

Are you critical of situations you find yourself in?

Are you suspicious of other's intent toward you?

JEALOUSY:

Do you feel your partners (or associates) do things to deliberately upset you?

Do you frequently worry about what your partner is doing and whether they are faithful?

Are you envious of the success of others?

Do you feel that you would be happier if others did what you wanted them to do?

FRUSTRATION:

Do you feel others keep you from accomplishing what you need to get done?

Do others move too slowly for you?

Are you easily frustrated by what others do?

When you are feeling overwhelmed do your thoughts turn to suicide as a solution?

When you feel frustrated do you turn to anger to intimidate others?

WAITING:

Are you frequently waiting for other people to make a decision before you proceed with your plan?

Do others stand between you and your goals in an irritating manner?

Do you try to find the **right action** before acting?

Do you keep thinking about previous decisions you have made?

WITHDRAWAL:

Do you tend to withdraw from situations and activities when under pressure?

Do you put up walls in relationships?

Do you often turn off feelings in order to be comfortable around others?

AGGRESSION/ANGER:

Do you have a short fuse?

Do you throw tantrums?

Is anger a problem you deal with at home or at work?

When angry have you hurt or considered hurting someone?

Do others see you as an angry person?

HELPLESSNESS:

Do you feel you cannot solve the problems you encounter?

Do you feel dependent on others for solutions to your problems?

Do you frequently think that you are not smart enough, not strong enough or wise enough?

HOPELESSNESS:

Do you feel others are unable to help you solve your problems?

Do you feel your efforts to solve problems are useless?

Do you find life is void of meaning?

DEMORALIZATION:

At times, do you feel no one can help you solve your problems?

At times, do you feel your problems have no solution?

Have you pulled away from other people because you do not trust them?

RESENTMENT:

Do you get angry at others when you believe they could solve your problems if they wanted to?

Do you feel others get the breaks that belong to you?

Is there anyone you feel strong resentment toward-someone you feel has harmed you?

SENSE OF FAILURE:

Do you frequently feel you have failed to resolve your personal problems?

Do others criticize you for what they see as failures on your part?

Do you avoid new challenges out of fear of failing?

Do you feel it is justified when others belittle you for what you do or how you think?

DEPRESSION:

Are you unhappy with yourself a lot of the time?

Are you unhappy with others a lot of the time?

Are you unhappy with situations a lot of the time?

COMMUNICATION FAILURE:

Do you tell people what you think they want to hear?

Do you worry about making others unhappy?

Are you uncomfortable with others being upset with what you tell them?

Do you feel that others do not understand you?

INTIMACY ISSUES:

Do you feel others can hurt you emotionally?

Do you sometimes create a problem in a relationship when people get too close?

Do you feel unlovable?

Do you keep your thoughts to yourself and not share them with others?

SENSE OF SELF:

Are you frequently unsure of yourself?

Do you get down on yourself frequently?

Do you have trouble believing in yourself?

Can you answer the question, "What makes me happy?"

Do you wish you had greater confidence in your abilities?

Do you depend on others to keep your life in order?

STAY OUT OF BLAMING AND ALL THESE PRODUCTS GENERALLY DISAPPEAR.

INTRODUCTION TO ASSOCIATED CONCEPTS

There are several associated concepts I believe we frequently misunderstand.

Manipulation: Direct speech is replaced by manipulation in S1.

Some of the manipulative behaviors people use to get others to do what they want are *feeling* hurt, *showing* disapproval, *showing* dissatisfaction, *being* jealous, *expressing* anger, *withdrawing*, and *being* depressed. When the situation defines these as manipulations, it removes the need to ever work on them. They go away automatically once the person learns to communicate directly. When we encourage one set of people to be responsible for other's thoughts, feelings and actions we're encouraging personal slavery. (P.S.: I am not implying there cannot be biological depressions.)

What are the main reasons people try through manipulation, rather than directly, to get what they want? One reason is they have had disappointments so they have little expectations that directness will work. Second, they don't want to hurt the other people's feelings (S1 thinking). Even though the success rate in getting what they want is nearly zero; they continue to spend their life trying to do what they think others want them to do. They remain grounded in the S1 thinking; eternally the optimist, they are not willing to let go of S1 ideation and do something else.

Life framed inaccurately causes therapy/struggle interminable. Therapies that allow individuals to continue to frame life inaccurately contribute to the concept of never-ending therapy. A patient once told me that he felt he had gained more understanding of his issues in one 30-minute session with me than he had gotten in 2.5 years of psychoanalysis.

I was trained in a predominantly psychoanalytic setting (Michael Reese in Chicago) and I am appreciative of what I learned there. I considered doing a psychoanalytic training program, but the training schedule would have meant making three trips a week from Phoenix to California: not economically feasible for me at the time. I am rather happy I didn't go that direction as the amount of therapy necessary to help most people has become less than 3-5 sessions. I enjoy seeing what people can do for themselves once they find the way to properly frame issues.

A life framed accurately makes more sense to the person living it. **When we get out of system one, we realize we do not have control over the products created by our belief system.** This may go against everything a counselor, therapist, social worker, psychologist or a psychiatrist has learned in their training. The products of our belief system are commonly seen as symptoms of a psychiatric disorder. The belief system creates the symptoms which are then assembled to make up the psychiatric diagnosis. S1 thinking produces multiple psychological products. The process (the way symptoms are created) is not identified as a psychiatric disorder, but some of the products are depression, anxiety, and helplessness. To understand this better think of a common recipe used in the kitchen. The cook does not control what product is created; he/she only has choices about the ingredients that are used. If they use the proper ingredients in the proper amounts to create a cake, they will get a cake. That is determined not by the cook, but by nature.

Working on products does not make the products go away! Certain approaches may make some products of S1 better for a time. If one does not want S1 products the best thing to do is to get out of S1 thinking. When we do that, nature removes S1 products and we are given a completely different palette to work from.

When you put your hand on a hot burner, you will be burned. The burn is a product of putting your hand on the burner. You don't control the product; most of us cannot put our hand on the hot burner and not get burned. Nature does not generally give us control over products. In the same way that the Diagnostic and Statistical Manual can generate multiple diagnosis through several hundred combinations of symptoms, nature may not always produce the same product each time. They both have the same frame running, but the impact on lives may add up differently. If all the symptoms occurred all the time in an illness, it would certainly simplify what we call a diagnosis, but that does not happen very often.

What is missing in our current approach to mental illness and politics is the realization that belief systems may be the source of multiple problems which, in the past, have been seen as caused by something else: parenting, mothers (never fathers of course), accidents, Trump, etc. The types of therapy which constantly pursues what these *primary causes* might be are missing the overall perspective of the mental condition. The problem is that there has not been recognition of the cardinal nature of S1 thinking in the formation of problems people experience. This is equally true when dealing with the political arena.

INTRODUCTON TO THE CONCEPT OF *HOW WE CREATE PSYCHIATRIC AND POLITICAL PROBLEMS*

WOULDN'T IT BE A BLAST TO DISCOVER (**REALIZE**) WE ARE CREATING PSYCHIATRIC AND POLITICAL PROBLEMS SIMPLY BECAUSE WE DO NOT SPEAK ACCURATLY?

The Case:

Joe had a great deal of anger at his parents. He spent three years talking to his therapist on a weekly basis, and he went to anger management classes after being arrested for fighting. Over time his anger subsided.

Scott had a great deal of anger at his parents. He was shown in the first appointment how his thinking as a child was inaccurately framed (S1) and how that inaccuracy distorted his perceptions of what had happened to him up to this point. He was shown that when appropriately framed the actual events had very little, or nothing, to do with his feeling. He was educated to understand that anger and blaming are two words for the same mental condition and when blaming is stopped the anger experience disappears. A follow-up appointment in 30 days revealed he was no longer experiencing anger.

Having anger and then being asked to talk about all the incidents when anger was present in order to get rid of it is a little like walking in a shoe with a rock in it. It is nonsense! Get rid of it! People are angry because they blame. The same events in life will not get the same mental outcome, if they are framed differently. This is an error demonstrated on almost all cop shows: "The suspect didn't act the way we think he should have if he was innocent." The left demonstrates a grotesque amount of anger and sees it as being caused by something Trump does or does not do. This is an error in framing. Trump has no responsibility for how the left sees him. He has no more responsibility for the left's feelings than he does for NATO's feelings, or Schumer's feelings, or Nancy Pelosi's feelings, or Maxine Water's feelings, or the hot dog vender at Home Depot's feelings and especially for hurricanes. These accusations are all manipulations. They are **nonsense.**

I once engaged superficially with a psychologist friend who told me directly, "I can't date you, because I cannot find any way to manipulate you. I don't think I can be in a relationship with someone I can't manipulate." I don't know if she realized how refreshing her acknowledgement was.

In general, people are often confused about the products created by their choices.

PRODUCT OR CHOICE?

Parents will tell children they are choosing a punishment when they do not do what has been requested. This is not correct. The child is choosing to do a specific behavior. The punishment is something that has been added by the parent, the judge, or whoever. Neither children, nor adults, often choose consequence. If we take off our clothes and run outside in zero-degree weather, it is generally not to get cold. We are not making a choice to be cold; we are making the choices to take off our clothes and to go outside. The product of that act is to get cold. If we put our hand on a hot burner the consequence is to be burned. It is not necessarily what the person had in mind (Like the cowboy who jumped into the cactus said, "It seemed like a good idea at the time.") The point here is that nature creates products, and we don't have the ability to change them. We need to separate products from the costs imposed by others. Understanding that the products of S1 will disappear when we get out of S1 thinking allows the person to witness all the products associated with S1 thinking disappear without having to work on them.

We make the best decision we can at the time the decision is made. The left has decided, like a parent, to punish Trump whenever he does something they do not like. With the complicity of the media, every act the President does that they don't like they make up some false charge and it gets repeated for days or weeks until it is found to be nonsense and it is dropped for another accusation. If this behavior was done to a child, it would be considered child abuse. Done to the President of the U.S. it is egotistical and stupid, and it interferes with the functioning of the Government. President Trump fortunately showed the nation how to stand up to bullies.

Physical damage vs. mental damage. Mental damage occurs when the accuracy of our thinking is compromised. Just as with the first step in AA where a person must accept they have a disorder, in the case of the struggling person, they must be willing to look at their role in creating the damage they have experienced; at the same time, they need to leave open the possibility that with proper understanding they can alter their experience for the future. They must be willing to initiate the first step which is to accept that they have a role in the creation of their own thoughts, feelings and actions by keeping, or taking back power. People must come to understand they are *the* first responders. The left, through constant projection of their own traits onto others, seem oblivious of the products they are creating for themselves and those in their party. They do not "ride 20 feet ahead" as her horse trainer kept advising my wife to practice. The left seems to ignore consequences of their choices. [Inflation, huge price increase in gas, uncontrollable crime, tent cities in their towns]

Another benefit of getting out of blame is that we can realize the benefit of actions like forgiveness and acceptance. In the same way that forgiveness is smart, acceptance is also smart. *Acceptance* does not mean resignation or giving up. Acceptance as I use the word is a grounding in the reality of what is (My parent is dead. My parents have divorced. My dog is going to die.) We don't have to like the things that happen in our life, but if we do not accept them, we join the emotionally wounded. The people who don't practice acceptance are the perpetually challenged members of society. They are in nearly constant pain about something. When we get into acceptance (grounded in the reality of what is) we do not have to give up our choices. It is important to understand this is not an act of giving up. It is an act of letting go of pain. Donald J Trump/ Joe Biden is the President! Get over it! Accept it!

Non-acceptance creates challenges in life. I may not distinguish what the painful event is that someone holds on to, but they do. It is an event seen as someone doing something to them: a parent had the gall to die, a father divorced their mother. Trump beat Hillary in the election. It doesn't matter much what the event was (It is not necessary to look for the needle in this haystack), what matters is that the event is seen as having power over feelings (And often thoughts and actions). People sincerely feel that the event is the cause of their anger, depression, anxiety, withdrawal from others, and the use of drugs or alcohol (to sooth the pain of course) or the need on college campus for safe rooms for students to cry and be coddled after a president is elected whom they did not like. This is the thinking of the S1 child, even if the person is 80 years old who is doing it. It also seems to be the predominant belief system of the political left and the left educational system. The error in thinking here is that it is not the event but need for something to be different from how it is perceived that generates pain. This is another time when two words pain (psychological) and need are the same thing. So, when we get rid of need pain goes away.

Inaccurate framing of responsibility can cause problems. Parents frequently try to help children become more responsible, which on the surface, would appear to be a movement in the proper direction. Unfortunately, the errors in understanding 'responsibility' compounds the problem rather than helping to resolve it. Parents often see children as being responsible only when they do what they are told. This is not responsibility; it is compliance. Children frequently have the better working concept of responsibility; they do not acknowledge having responsibility without having choice. The left seems to have a similar mentality, 'If you aren't doing what I think you should, you are not being a responsible President." "If you do not vote democratic you are not a real black person." When I watch CNN and other LMP stations I am amazed at all the people who feel they could run the country. I only hope there are enough people out there who recognize the insanity of such verbalizations as, "Men should just shut up and step up" to keep the country healthy.

Choice is critical to the concept of responsibility. Responsibility is directly proportional to our awareness, our capability and the choices available to us.

Psychological injury: This is a coat of various colors. A child physically abused, may suffer less emotionally, than a child not liked by a parent who takes good care of them. One abandoned child turns to drugs and alcohol to appease themselves; another becomes CEO of a large corporation. One lady claims post traumatic distress, because her boss asked her out to dinner one day; another is gang raped and shows no psychological scars. The patient with an identifiable depression, appearing to be in a lot of distress, has a sudden disappearance of symptoms after the lawsuit is decided in their favor. How can we understand this type of experience? It is related to WHAT PEOPLE TELL THEMSELVES.

What do you think the college students, who finds it necessary to have a room they can go to in order to depressurize from the trauma they are experiencing from D.J. Trump being elected President, are thinking? It obviously must be something traumatic. Later these same students are likely part of the violent protest blocking conservative speakers from coming to the campus to give a talk. [Isn't there something wrong with this picture?] If one is not in the blame system, the products of that system are not produced. The overall message of this behavior is somehow that the bad feeling was created by Trump being elected President. This is nothing but propaganda and distortion of reality intended to create hate, fear and division.

Anger management: There are courses, usually mandated by the courts, called *'anger management.'* They run between 3 and 9 months. My quickest **cure** of a major anger problem is between 6-9 seconds. I have never figured out why people would want to learn how to manage anger, a process taking 3-9 months (I doubt that is enough time), when they can receive all the information they need to get rid of anger forever in 3-15 seconds. Anger management should only be offered to people who choose not to get rid of anger in their lives, or who demonstrate an inability to get out of blaming. [In my opinion there is one psychiatric patient group that demonstrates this inability, They are called borderline personality disorder]

Diagnosis (i.e., Bipolar) based on the presence of anger should be reconfigured. Anger, or irritable mood, is listed as criteria for bipolar disorder. My experience is that anger, or irritability, can have a presence or be absent in all psychiatric disorders (including bipolar). The field is still trying to find out what the cause of anger is in each disorder. I know what the seed of anger is: it is blaming. Mild blaming is irritability, blaming is anger, and severe blaming is rage. These are all words that describe various stages of the same cognitive state. The only logical explanation as to why anger is seen as intrinsic to bipolar disorder is because this group of individuals has some similar characteristics to the Borderline Personality DO.

When it is accepted that anger is a *synonym for blaming*, and when blaming is stopped, anger is rarely if ever, experienced again. It does not matter what the events were that were associated with the anger. It doesn't matter if there is one event or several, when people stop blaming others the anger experience disappears. Wake up people! The left and other manipulators of course do not want you to understand this principal. And they are teaching our children! Anger is a manipulation; it is not needed except by power-hungry individuals. Colleges are teaching children to give away power to events for their own aggrandizement. President Bidens, "Come on people" spoken in anger is nothing but manipulation. Another inconvenient truth.

Legal issues: I hate to tell the lawyers (they probably aren't reading this in the first place) but cause and effect in the psychological world has very little to do with the event. In the psychological world someone says, "That is a really pretty dress you are wearing today." The person who hears the statement goes through a process of self-talk, and out of this thought process the response may be: 1) a smile and a thank you, 2) no response or indifference to the person's comment, 3) anger, 4) filing a harassment suit, 5) making an attempt to get the person fired, 6) or other imaginable responses. This is not a cause-and-effect event; it is a sequential ordering of events. The statement made has no causal relationship to the feelings, or acts, the other person generates. The problem is that in discussing these types of events people use cause-and-effect language, and the use of cause-and-effect language creates an inaccurate frame, and an inaccurate frame creates an inaccurate belief system that can go on to create all kinds of mischief (often legal mischief). This is the circle of blame continuing. This is what the left is doing when they want to get someone arrested for using the wrong pronoun. This is what the woman who gets infuriated over a complement from a co-worker is doing, or what Comey did when the President asked if the investigation of Flynn could not be speeded up. His response says more about him than it does about the President.

Misuse of language creates an inaccurate frame; inaccurate belief systems cause all kinds of problems. I mentioned lawyers before; some make a living persuading juries that there is some cause-and-effect relationship between a comment made and the other person's experience. There really isn't any. Even in extreme cases the reality is the same. I have had wives who have divorced husbands, because they looked at a pornographic magazine. Pretty extreme? Not in the person's mind who took that action. I had a parent report that the police tried to file a sexual assault charge against their 5-year-old son for putting his hand on the backside of a female peer. The prosecution was pushing to have the child labeled a sex offender. Pretty over the top? I thought so.

Because people *are taught* to believe *others are responsible* (called *blaming*) for their experience people inaccurately hold others accountable for the wrong things. Currently, people in the U.S.A. hold others "responsible" for their feelings and actions. This is thought of as being politically correct. It is so ingrained in our culture to such an extent that some people are not receptive to getting out of S1. Ironically, the individuals I find most entrenched in S1 are often the very religious. They equilibrate this with "turning the other cheek." Nothing could be further from being accurate. Everytown reports that "in an average month 52 American women are shot to death by an intimate partner." This is defined as a gun issue: it is not. It is an issue of blame and lack of respect. According to Huffpost 5900 Native Americans 12 years and older report being sexually assulted each year. Victimsofcrime.org reports that 1 in 5 girls and 1 in 20 boys is a victim of sexual abuse. They also report that 20 % of adult females and 5-10% of adult males recall a childhood sexual abuse event. (The 2010 censes showed 74.2 million people below the age of 18 year in the country) This is a problem of lack of respect and it should stay in the statutes as a criminal behavior when it exceeds a normal childhood interaction.

Teachers to the rescue: Teachers could teach basics (accurate speech) that would in turn help children move to a healthier way of dealing with life. This approach is simple; it could be implemented without expense except to educate the educators. It is something that should be happening in the educational system anyhow, because it is an intrinsic part of the education process. What needs to happen is that there should be more attention paid to the accuracy of speech as well as to the correctness of speech. Unfortunately, the left has a major role in the educational process and in the weaponization of our language; I suspect it is seen as more helpful to them to distort and weaponize speech even though it is very detrimental to society as a whole.

Correctness has to do with the grammatical construction of the sentence. Teachers do a great job in this area. They do not pay enough attention to the accuracy of the sentence itself. What good is it to make a correct sentence if the sentence itself is inaccurate/nonsense?

Some people intentionally mislead others for profit, or amusement. Certain constructions (syntactic ambiguity or double entendre) can lead to a humorous outcome. I am not concerned about this; I am concerned about the things people say in daily conversations that lead to a completely erroneous belief that is not understood by the person to be inaccurate. These sentences all have a common origin: they are all statements about mental or psychological aspects of our world. They are all statements about sequential ordering of events that are framed as cause-and-effect events. This is an inaccurate framing and it confuses reality. This confusion in framing seeds more confusion and it goes on indefinitely.

Most of us would not want our children going around speaking incorrectly making a fool of themselves; yet, we allow ourselves and our children to say inaccurate things without guidance at all. This mistake has far more negative consequences than an error in syntax. Newspapers use this error in people's understanding to attempt to make history instead of reporting news.

If schools would do as I have recommended there would not be the predicted insufficiency of psychiatrists, and those of us in practice could focus on actual mental illness.

Summary: The solution to the problems outlined above is a simple one that could be implemented in our schools for, what I am certain, would be a huge savings of the dollars spent on mental health issues.

QUESTIONS I WOULD LIKE ANSWERED

There are things I would appreciate the left and the academic community would explain to me: and some observations I have made.

- MY QUESTION IS JUST HOW MORAL IS IT TO SUPPORT BREAKING THE IMMIGRATION LAWS OF THE U.S. AND BRINGING ON THE KIND OF ABUSE TO PEOPLE THAT THAT POLICY ENCOURAGES? [*THE*

LEFT APPEARS TO BE A PARTY OF MANIPULATION AND DECEIT TO ENCOURAGE ILLEGAL IMMIGRATION AND AT THE SAME TIME TO REFUSING TO SECURE OUR BORDERS] Today the number of illegals is over 2.5 million known and approximately 300,000 "got aways."

- The big metropolitan areas of the U.S. seem to want to act independently of the country in general by establishing Sanctuary Cities, and Sanctuary States, where they want to pay for all the illegal aliens' medical needs, birthing costs, and supportive services after they come into the country. I am in favor of states having more rights and being given the opportunity to solve the country's challenges. WHAT I DO NOT UNDERSTAND IS HOW THEY CAN DO THAT AND DRAW MONEY OUT OF THE NATIONAL FUNDING. I CARE, BUT I CONCEDE THAT IF CALIFORNIA WANTS TO TAKE CARE OF ILLEGALS THE COUNTRY SHOULD LET THEM—AS LONG AS THEY DON'T TAKE MONEY FROM A GOVERNMENT THAT HAS NOT APPROVED THE ACTION. WHY SHOULD I HAVE TO PAY FOR CALIFORNIA'S EXPERIMENT? My wife and I agree that we may never plan a visit to California's big cities again. Even their beaches are not enough incentive. *THE LEFT ELITE APPARENTLY SUPPORTS STATES DOING WHATEVER THEY WANT AS LONG AS THE DIRECTION IS TO BREAK THE LAWS OF THE U.S. GOVERNMENT AND IS SUPPORTIVE OF ILLEGAL IMMIGRATION. Surprise!* Recent events suggest Sanctuary cities and states are not all that happy when illegal aliens are bussed to their states.

- I was pretty much wowed during the Kavanaugh hearings by a group of female senators advocating that women should be believed and that men should just shut up. MY QUESTION IS WHY ISN'T EVERY AMERICAN SCARED TO DEATH

WITH THAT KIND OF POLICY BEING ADVOCATED BY MEMBERS OF CONGRESS? I don't think I have ever heard a sane person mutter such nonsense before. It was shocking. What was even more concerning was that no one has suggested that person is not competent to be a member of the U.S. congress. *THE LEFT ELITE APPEARS TO BE THE PARTY SUPPORTING RACISM when they advocate DO NOT LISTEN TO MEN, ESPECIALLY WHITE MEN, or call a voting group DEPLORABLES.*

- I WOULD APPRECIATE IT IF SOMEONE COULD EXPLAIN TO ME HOW A MATERIAL MATTER LIKE A BARRIER, FENCE OR WALL IS IMMORAL OR MORAL. The answer of course is that no one can because inorganic items have no moral or immoral characteristic. Morality suggests a choice, but inanimate items have no choice. So, what is the argument of the academician and the left? If one assumes God is one level of morality above Jesus, there is reference of God keeping undesirable and unwanted people out of heaven with a wall guarded by St. Peter. Those weeping and mashing teeth about the wall really seem quite ingenuous. The elite seem to have a rather high percentage of living arrangements behind a wall. A wall like the Berlin wall which was created to keep non-criminal individuals locked into a condition of lack of freedom might be considered an immoral way to use a wall. Putting a wall around one's property [Benjamin Franklin in Poor Richard's Almanac said, "Love your neighbor, yet don't pull down the hedge" became the proverb attributed to Robert Frost "Good fences make good neighbors."] has for a hundred years been touted as a sensible act. Most people with common sense in most of the Cosmopolitans run by the left would be wise to have fences and to lock doors and perhaps have a resource to protect themselves and property. *THE LEFT ELITE SEEMS TO BE THE PARTY INCAPABLE OF UNDERSTANDING*

THE BENEFIT OF A BARRIER BETWEEN WANTED AND UNWANTED--EXCEPT AROUND THEIR OWN HOMES. Currently the left insists that the border is "secure." I would infer from the fact they are letting in millions of uninvited aliens that means it is secured open.

- HOW DOES CALIFORNIA PROP 47S REDUCED PENALTIES PROTECT THE AVERAGE BUSINESSMAN IN CALIFORNIA? (CBS/AP) This Prop made theft below $750 a misdemeanor. Shoplifting jumped by 25 to 50% the first year. This does not seem like much protection for the shop owner trying to make a legal income. *THE LEFT ELITE SEEMS CLEARLY TO SUPPORT ILLEGAL OVER LEGAL AND IMMIGRANTS OVER CITIZENS.* Time has confirmed this policy invites more crime and is causing business to leave cities and states that think this way.

- No one condones school shootings, BUT WHY DOES THE LEFT CONTINUALLY DISTORT AND LIE ABOUT THE FACTS? An article in Government Uncovered titled "NPR FINDS MOST SCHOOL SHOOTINGS IN FED REPORT DIDN'T ACTUALLY OCCUR." The federal report listed 235 shootings in one year (2015-2016). When each school listed was contacted by NPR the stats changed to a confirmed 11 reported incidents. One incident is obviously unwanted, but there can be no accident in the intent of the inaccurate reporting. *THE LEFT ELITE CLEARLY HAVE NO HESITATION TO IGNORE, OR LIE, ABOUT ISSUES THEY WANT TO PROMOTE.* The lefts insane push to take guns away from law abiding citizens, is not likely to deter school shooters who are looking for a safe place like schools (unprotected places) to kill others.

- PERSPECTIVE IS NOT MUCH APPRECIATED. We live in a large country. The Feb 2018 estimation of population in the U.S. was 327.16 million. Everytown reports 100 Americans are killed daily with guns (36,500) Suicides cut that figure to 22,274. 47,950 are estimated to have died in 2017 of opioid OD. (This is much higher with all the immigration issues.) In adults, alcohol related deaths were 88,000 [CDC/niaa.gov], obesity is estimated to have killed 111,900; and tobacco related deaths were 480,000 [cdc.gov]. Motor vehicle deaths of children was estimated at 3,669 followed by gun deaths. Perspective is not appreciated on the left. The number of deaths caused by drugs brought into the country by illegals is something that our legislatures could do something about but they are not. While they push their gun restrictions, they invite people to come into the country with their people killing drugs.

- HOW IS DESTROYING STATUES OF HISTORICAL FIGURES IN THE U.S. DIFFERENT FROM THE DESTRUCTION BY CHINA OF ART AND ANTIQUITIES IN TIBET OR THE DESTRUCTION BY ISIS OF ART AND CULTURAL ITEMS IN IRAQ AND SYRIA? Like China and Isis, it appears to be an act of trying to destroy history. What is the value of history? It is not to honor various people of history, although that is sometimes done, but to remind us of the good and bad decisions people of power have made in the past. It is a picture along the road of our travels in life, some good and some bad. MORE CONFUSING TO ME IS WHY GOOD PEOPLE STAND BY AND ALLOW THIS BEHAVIOR TO OCCUR WITHOUT CONSEQUENCES. ARE WE A NATION OF LAWS, OR THUGS, OR MERELY WIMPS? People trying to somehow correct history seem to ignore the things in history that do not play well to their dogma: The first slave owner in America was a black Angolan who achieved his own freedom and thereafter became a property owner who owned slaves in Virginia. Those who want the U.S. to initiate reparations for slavery seem rather myopic since the practice of slavery emerged with the societies not formed around hunter-gatherer populations as far back as 3500 BC in Mesopotamia. Why stop with the U.S.? *THE LEFT ELITE SEEMS TO BE THE PARTY SUPPORTING DESTRUCTION OF HISTORY THEY DO NOT LIKE AND THE RIGHT SEEMS TO BE TOO WEAK TO RESIST THE MOB ACTIONS.* It is interesting that the left never mentions it was democrats who composed 95% of all slave owners. Blacks of the "Black Lives Matter" group never confirm that blacks brought to the U.S. were slaves in their own country before being exported to this country. (Not intended as an excuse only as information.) It will not be accepted of course but this is just one more example of the left's violence and hatred of this country.

- IN WHAT WAY IS A RIOT NOT A RIOT or A MOB NOT A MOB? The spectacle on TV of individuals on the left punching reporters, setting fire to cars and throwing fire bottles at schools, bringing bats and chains to lawfully scheduled rallies and the left media saying, "Don't use the word mob, these are not mobs" seems really distorted. Apparently, it is working, because I never hear that the people doing these unlawful acts being charged or put in jail. I recognize it could be happening and the left is not reporting it, but we should be hearing about it. Watching the failure of police to intervene when individuals are being assaulted is hard to witness. WHY ARE THESE NON-RIOT, NON-MOB creeps not being put in jail? ARE THE POLICE BUYING WHAT THE LEFT ELITE IS SELLING: THIS IS NOT A MOB?! Why did the now Vice President help raise money to free the rioters? The left's elite, holier than thou, coordinated, propaganda smear attack directed at Catholic high school kids, some of whom were wearing 'Make America Great Again' caps is just one more example of meanness. Just another media lie from the left! Under the left's way of changing the meaning of words. Perhaps Trump should have built a wall and when he was finished named it a fence? *CLEARLY THE LEFT IS THE PARTY THAT SUPPORTS MOB BEHAVIOR AND EVEN GOES OUT OF ITS WAY TO PROTECT IT.* On 7-29-19 the President was reported to be considering putting Antifa on the list of terrorists. What a sensible act that would have been. Let's not just make America Great again let's make it safe again. The left labels mobs as 'not mobs', riots as 'not riots,' and political protests as insurrection. Why do we let them get away with it? Antifa is now using threat of violence to get conservative speeches canceled in parts of the country. Police in these cities are allowing this type of behavior. Obviously, they are in support of the Antifa agenda. So sad!

- WHY IS CONGRESS NOT INTERESTED IN THE COST TO THE AVERAGE AMERIAN FOR THE FOLLOWING: money being given to countries that hate us and try to stab us in the back whenever possible, countries unfairly taking advantage of us in trade, wars that have nothing to do with our national security, peace-keeping missions that protect others without others paying a fair share for the protection, medical care for illegals, educational expenses for illegals, welfare expenses for illegals, court and attorney costs for dealing with illegals, interest on debts partially created by taking care of illegals, regulations that cost taxpayers billions of dollars, money allocated to support countries who buy oil from our arch enemy Russia--making it richer, while we spend money to protect them from guess who: Russia, and why do we give countries money to not produce illegal drugs that end up still being sold to Americans? *THE LEFT ELITE APPEARS TO BE THE PARTY WILLING TO SPEND ANY AMOUNT OF YOUR MONEY FOR SUPPORT OF THEIR IDEAS AND POWER.* The democrats have found a new charity, and while Americans are under siege from individuals all over the world, Biden is sending billions of dollars to Ukraine to keep Russia out of their country. Wish he cared as much about Americans!

- WHY ARE AFRICAN AMERICANS TYPICALLY DEMOCRATS? From most appearances the left has supported ideas that keep blacks and Latino's poor. [illegal immigration being one of them] I question if this is a specialized form of Stockholm Syndrome (Wikipedia) "a condition that causes hostages to develop a psychological alliance with captors as a survival strategy during captivity." Is this a reach? Of course! But given the fact that 90-95 percent of all slave holders were democrats, [The left might remember the violence Carolyn Bryant's family imposed on Emmitt Till a 14 year old black boy], it is the left that supports open borders allowing undocumented aliens to come to the country suppressing both job potential and job income, it just does not seem to make much sense. As I suggested at the beginning of this book, do not listen to the rhetoric but look at the action. Who was getting jobs for African Americans, Latinos and women, and who was getting them higher wages? And if you look a little further down the road, who wants to take that all away from them? *IT APPEARS TO BE THE ELITE LEFT'S POLICY TO KEEP BLACK AND LATINOS AS LOW ON THE ECONOMIC SCALE, AND AS DEPENDANT ON GOVERNMENT, AS POSSIBLE; AN OUTCOME OF MORE PEOPLE (IMMIGRANTS) LOOKING FOR THE SAME JOBS COULD BE SEEN AS A CONTINUATION OF THE SLAVE MENTALITY PERVASIVE ON THE LEFT.*

- The left keeps making references to people on the right (Trump) being connected to the Klu Klux Klan. Do blacks on the left realize that as recent as 1924 the KKK controlled the democratic National Convention? Do they know that Franklin Roosevelt's first appointment to the Supreme Court was a lawyer for the clan? [In case you do not remember, Franklin Roosevelt was a democrat] (Life, Liberty, and Levin) Democrats continually accuse the right of the things they are doing. There is not much mystery in why the left seems entangled with the Chinese: neither of them likes to play by the rules. *THE LEFT ELITE IS CLEARLY THE PARTY OF ASSOCIATIONS WITH THE KLAN. THEY ARE MISTAKING THEIR REFLECTION IN A MIRROR FOR THE OTHER SIDE.*

- 'TOXIC MASCULIINITY' IS A CONCEPT BEING SUPPORTED BY THE LEFT, SO, APPARENTLY, MASCULINITY AND COMPETENCE ARE NOT BEING SUPPORTED. WHAT HAPPENED? When Obama was elected, I don't recall hearing about the need to have a 1000-student march to protest him (Michigan State), or a need to have "Speed Advising" where students could debrief emotional responses and concerns about the president-elect. I guess republican children are just stronger emotionally. Watkins Health Center at the University of Kansas helped stressed students by bringing in therapy pups for stressful times, the Women's Political caucus at Pace University established programming to help alleviate anxiety because communities "need to inhabit safe spaces," Boston University "released a self-care guide for students who feel emotionally impacted by recent events," (USA Today) and Fox reports: "Around the nation, students are turning to tools of toddlers as a bizarre form of therapy in the wake of Donald Trump's election last week. Colleges and universities are encouraging students to cry, cuddle with puppies and sip hot chocolate to sooth fragile psyches, an approach some critics say would be funny if it weren't so alarming." As a psychiatrist I try and help people who make something out of nothing to learn to make nothing out of something. [Gary Emery PhD's concept] It saves a tremendous amount of energy. WHAT ARE THESE EDUCATORS THINKING? *THE LEFT ELITE IS CLEARLY THE PARTY THAT INFANTALIZES OTHERS: DO COLLEGE STUDENTS REALLY NEED A CRYING ROOM TO DEAL WITH THE ELECTION OF A*

PRESIDENT? PERHAPS ON THE LEFT THEY DO. I would suggest we need a lot more psychiatrists, but then I remember most psychiatrists unfortunately likely support this behavior on the left. The inconvenient truth here is that teachers are indoctrinating students to be afraid of conservative principles.

- IF THERE IS A LAW ON THE BOOKS OF THE FEDERAL GOVERNMENT THAT SAYS STATES ARE SUPPOSED TO TURN OVER TO ICE ILLEGAL CRIMINALS AND THE STATES DO NOT TURN THEM OVER ON PURPOSE AND THAT CRIMINAL GOES ON TO KILL AN AMERICAN CITIZEN WHY IS THE GOVERNANCE OF THOSE STATES NOT LIABLE FOR THAT DEATH? Do government officials of states not take an oath to uphold the constitution of the United States? Do states not have a duty to protect, or is that only for doctors? Do government officials have a special backroom oath where they agree to protect foreigners over citizens of the U.S? What about the police departments, do they have the right to refuse to help groups of people [like conservatives or Trump supporters]? Does the country need to start having police for conservatives and police for the left? Maybe we can establish a police force for blacks and one for Hispanics, and one for Asians, and one for Europeans. *THE LEFT ELITE IS THE PARTY CLEARLY SUPPORTING ILLEGAL OVER THE LEGAL AND IS CLEARLY THE PARTY DIVIDING THE COUNTRY.* Why are people who do not take their oaths seriously allowed to hold their office?

- When the left supports the suggestion taxes should be raised to 70-80 percent of one's income, when they support Nancy Pelosi's desire to put a Windfall Tax on all stock market profits (including retirement funds, 401K and Mutual Funds), when she wants to use what she can confiscate from American workers to help the 20 million illegal immigrants, and she wants to work toward a goal of equalizing income in our country (or is it the world?) IS SHE NOT ADVOCATING FOR US TO BECOME A COMMUNIST COUNTRY? I will be advocating for California to secede from the union, if they promise to take Nancy Pelosi (estimated worth 29.3 million in 2015--most of it since becoming a legislator) and Maxine Waters (estimated worth 10 million) with them. Our country was founded in part as a revolt against taxation without representation. *THE POLICYs OF THE LEFT ELITE SEEMS TO NO LONGER REPRESENT THE INDIVIDUALS MAKING MONEY AND PAYING TAXES, BUT ONLY THE COLLECTIVE POWER THAT CAN BE MASSED BY EXPLOITING THE INDIVIDUAL.* ISN'T THIS WHAT WAS CALLED SLAVERY IN THE PAST? It is now a toss up as to which is worse, taxing us at a high level, or spending more than we can afford.

- WHY HAVE CONGRESSIONAL HEARINGS WHEN THE LEFT CONGRESSIONAL LEADERS HAVE NO INTENT IN GIVING THE NOMINEE CONSIDERATION? I don't understand why Congress holds hearings on the Supreme Court nominees and wastes all that time, when all the left has already decided that they were not going to vote for a republican regardless of qualifications. This does not show due process, but only total disregard for the process. The left had protests made up with everything but the name filled in before a name was announced. This is not government at work. *THE LEFT IS THE PARTY WANTING TO TEAR DOWN THE GOVERNMENT OF THE U.S.* For our form of government to work there is the implicit acceptance that each side has something legitimate to contribute to the process. *THE PARTY OF THE LEFT CLEARLY FEELS IT IS HAS NO OBLIGATION TO BE RESPECTFUL OF THE OTHER SIDE.*

- JUST HOW IS A CANDIDATE FOR PRESIDENT DEEMED A THREAT TO THE COUNTRY FOR SAYING HE WOULD LIKE TO HAVE A CLOSER RELATIONSHIP WITH ANOTHER COUNTRY'S LEADER? A recent report suggests that the investigation of candidate Trump was initiated by the FBI after Trump said during his campaign that he would like a better relationship with Russia. (This was reported as a cause to investigate Trump, but Hillary's resetting of the button with Russia was not.) *THE PARTY OF THE LEFT CLEARLY WANTS TO HAVE THE ABILITY TO CRITICIZE EVERYTHING, ANYTHING, ANYWHERE, ANYTIME EVEN IF IT IS NOTHING. THE PARTY OF THE LEFT IS THE DEFINITION OF SELFISH. THE PARTY OF THE LEFT CLEARLY DOES NOT WANT THINGS TO BE BETTER BETWEEN OUR COUNTRY AND OTHER COUNTRIES. THE PARTY OF THE LEFT IS THE PARTY SUSTAINING CONFLICT WITH OTHER NATIONS.*

- ARE YOU AWARE THAT AT LEAST 3 OTHER TIMES IN OUR HISTORY ACCUSATIONS OF BEING INVOLVED WITH RUSSIA HAVE BEEN BROUGHT AGAINST POLITICALLY PROMINANT PEOPLE? WALLACE IN 1940, KING IN THE 60s AND MCGOVERN IN 72 were all accused of involvement with or being communist by the FBI. (John Kiriakou-guest on Life Liberty and Levin-former CIA agent) *THE LEFT IS THE PARTY OF ACCUSATIONS, MIS-DIRECTION, LYING, DECEIT, AND DIRTY TRICKS*

- HOW IS IT LEGAL FOR THE FBI TO INSERT ITSELF INTO A CAMPAIGN "TO PROTECT THE CAMPAIGN FROM FOREIGN INFLUENCE" WITHOUT TELLING THE CAMPAIGN LEADERS WHAT IT IS DOING? *THE LEFT IS THE PARTY OF ACCUSATIONS, MIS-DIRECTION, LYING, DECEIT, AND DIRTY TRICKS*

- WHY SHOULD A PRESIDENT LEAVE TOP SECRET CLEARANCES IN THE HANDS OF PEOPLE WHO OPENLY OPPOSE THEM? *THE LEFT IS A PARTY THAT SOMETIMES SHOWS NO COMMON SENSE.*

- HOW IS SUPPORTING TROOP WITHDRAWAL FROM A COUNTRY, RESIGNATION OF CHIEF OF STAFF, PARTIAL GOVERNMENT SHUTDOWN, AND/OR BEING INVESTIGATED FOR NO APPARENT CRIME A GROUNDS FOR IMPEACHMENT? *THE LEFT IS THE PARTY THAT CAN CONNECT TOTALLY UNCONNECTED EVENTS AND PRETEND THEY ARE RELATED. THE LEFT IS THE PARTY THAT FAVORS INDUCTIVE REASONING OVER DEDUCTIVE REASONING. The left seems to love inductive reasoning.*

- IS THERE A MEDICATION FOR THE TRUMP DERANGEMENT SYNDROME? PERSONALLY, I THINK ECT IS LIKELY THE MOST IDEAL TREATMENT. [since the left cannot identify a joke, I would like to label this a JOKE] *THE LEFT IS THE PARTY FULL OF RIDICULE BUT SEEMINGLY IS INCAPBABLE OF UNDERSTANDING A JOKE.*

- IS THERE A TREATMENT FOR THE IMPEACHMENT OBSESSION? Prozac might be tried. [another JOKE] It is really something to have to point out a joke to the group of people controlling 80-90% of our educational system. *THE LEFT IS SO INTENT ON STEALING POWER THEY USE ANY PRETENSE—EVEN A JOKE.*

- IS THE LEFT AWARE THAT THE BIBLE REFERENCES BUILDING WALLS 245 TIMES--SOME WALLS AS HIGH AS 387 FEET TALL AND 78 FEET THICK? Walls were used to protect cities from unauthorized entrance. Nehemiah felt that God directed him to build a wall around Jerusalem [Steve Shirley] King Solomon also built walls around his cities. The Bible affirms God is not opposed to protecting with walls. There are references in the Bible of God being a "wall" or "hedge" of protection. Another left hysteria shot down. Pope Francis, who lives behind a fantastic wall system and is also protected by bodyguards, much like the elite on the left, uses walls, but apparently does not approve of them being used by others. The left calling walls immoral looks pretty much like another made up lie. Sixty-five countries have recently completed or are building walls across the world. Forty-five other countries have proposals to build walls. Since 2015 approximately 800 miles of barriers have been built in Europe. *THE LEFT ELITE IS THE PARTY OF ACCUSATIONS, MISINFORMATION, LYING, EMOTIONAL REASONING, UNFOUNDED ANGER EPISODES, DISTORTING OF FACT and so much more.* And guess what, the U.S. is helping some of the countries build their walls.

- Identified propaganda terms used by the left: IMPEACH 45, STORMY DANIELS, RACIST, MESSOGONIST, TOXIC MASCULINITY, WHITE SUPREMICIST, RAISE THE TAXES, OPEN THE BORDERS, NO VOTER FRAUD, WALLS ARE IMMORAL, DO NOT CALL MOBS 'MOBS,' TRUMP'S AN AUTHORITARIAN ANTI IMMIGRANT STRONGMAN IN THE NATION'S HIGHEST OFFICE, TRUMP IS LIKE HITLER, U.S. IS WICKED IF IT DOESN'T ACCEPT ANYONE WHO WANTS TO COME TO THE U.S., SUGGESTING ANYONE WHO WANTS TO COME TO THE U.S. SHOULDN'T--MAKES YOU A RACIST, DRUGS ONLY COME IN AT BORDER CHECK POINTS, BEING MORALLY RIGHT IS MORE IMPORTANT THAN BEING FACTUAL, GUNS ARE BAD, MS-13 ARE GOOD AMERICANS, IF TRUMP IS

INNOCENT HE SHOULD WANT THE MUELLER PROBE TO KEEP RUNNING, FAMILY IS NOT THAT IMPORTANT, BEING WHITE OR MASCULINE IS EVIL, GET IN THEIR FACES, WANTING BORDER WALLS IS RACIST, IF YOU ARE WHITE YOU ARE RACIST, IF YOU ARE A TRUMP SUPPORTER YOU ARE RACIST, IF YOU ARE A TRUMP SUPPORTER YOU ARE DEPLORABLE, GUILT BY ASSOCIATION IS ACCEPTABLE, IF YOU ARE WHITE OR MALE JUST SHUT UP, WOMEN ARE RIGHT EVEN IF THEY ARE NOT, LONG INVESTIGATIONS ARE GOOD UNLESS YOUR NAME IS CLINTON OR BIDEN, IF YOU TALK TO A WORLD LEADER AND WE DO NOT HEAR WHAT YOU SAID YOU ARE A TRAITOR TO THE U.S., IF YOU SUGGEST YOU WOULD LIKE A BETTER RELATIONSHIP WITH RUSSIA YOU ARE A TRAITOR TO THE U.S., IF THE U.S. HAS THE LOWEST UNEMPLOYMENT ON RECORD IT IS BECAUSE OF OBAMA, TAX SAVINGS FOR THE MIDDLE CLASS ARE PEANUTS, ALL EMMIGRANTS ARE BETTER THAN CITIZENS, DO NOT REQUIRE IMMIGRANTS TO FOLLOW THE SAME LAWS AS AMERICANS, IMMIGRANTS TAKE PRIORITY OVER CITIZENS FOR HEALTH CARE AND OTHER FREE SERVICES, BELIEVE THE FBI, HOMELAND SECURITY AND THE CIA WHETHER THEY LIE OR NOT, YOU SHOULD BELIEVE WOMEN WHETHER THEY LIE OR NOT, TELL YOUR ENEMIES YOUR PLANS SO YOU DONT HURT FEELINGS, IF YOU TALK TO AN ENEMY YOU ARE A TRAITOR, YOU SHOULD BE GRATEFUL IF THE FBI INFILTRATES YOUR CAMPAIGN UNINVITED, PEOPLE WANTING TO CROSS THE BORDER ARE FINE POTENTIAL LEFT VOTERS, THE PEOPLE ARE DUMB ENOUGH TO BUY WHAT WE SELL ON THE LEFT, GUNS KILL PEOPLE are a few of the identified propaganda terms used by the left: Witch hunt, identify politics, coercive liberalism, irrational left, fair and reciprocal trade, make America great again, 300 Americans are killed every week from heroin--80% of which comes from south of the border, in past 24 months there have been 100,000 assaults, 30,000 sex crimes, 4000 homicides, walls work which is why the left doesn't want them, the double standard in law should not be tolerated in the U.S., do not reveal what might hurt you to the enemies, praising an enemy does not mean you have to like them or that you are their puppet, 127 border police have lost lives protecting our southern border from all the good people who want to come here illegally.

- OVER THE YEARS, HOW MANY FOREIGN ELECTIONS HAVE WE TRIED TO INFLUENCE? I have no problem wanting to keep Russia out of our elections, but I find the response of the left to be far greater than the situation deserves. In psychiatry, as I have said before, we call this a transference reaction. This basically means the reaction is way out of proportion to the event. Given the dozens of ways individuals and groups affect our elections, all the uproar over Russia sounds like a DIVERSION or RED HERRING. Try talking to the left about voter fraud and they will hear nothing of it, even when Judicial Watch wins a case after showing that there were more votes cast than there were eligible voters (even if 100 % voted). *Investor's Business Daily* reported "Los Angeles County, whose more than 10 million people make it the nation's most populous county, had 12 % more registered voters than live ones, some 707,475 votes. That's a huge number of possible votes in an election. But Murdock notes, "California's San Diego County earns the enchilada grande. Its 138 % registration translates into 810,966 ghost voters." Of course, the left denies these figures are accurate. Perhaps Hillary did not win the popular vote if you don't count the ghost voters. *THE LEFT IS THE*

PARTY OF COVERUP. Tim Fitton of Judicial Watch says, "Its clear from what we have already learned that the Obama administration freely used our tax dollars for political purposes, including support of Soros operations." It also used the FBI and CIA and other branches of government to impede the Trump presidency. *THE LEFT ELITE IS THE PARTY OF THE DEEP STATE.* This issue has become so blatant the FBI is no longer trusted by a large portion of Americans and the office of the Attorney General is seen as serving the democratic party not the American people.

- DOES THE LEFT REALLY NOT SEE THEIR ROLE IN DIVIDING THE COUNTRY? THEY CERTAINLY TRY TO MAKE IT SEEM LIKE AN ACCOMPLISHMENT OF TRUMP. The stupidity of making war with your own president should not awaken images of Hitler, but of the Civil War. When the losing side of an election in the U.S. wages a personal vendetta on the elected President, it should remind the people of the destructive nature of a divided country. "Get in their face let them know they are not wanted!" (Thank you Maxine.) In the country where I was raised it would have been recommended that the person saying it should be "hung out to dry." There is something seriously wrong with them and with the spineless republicans who do not address the problem. [That's not a psychiatric diagnosis, it is a personal observation.] *THE PARTY OF THE LEFT ELITE IS THE PARTY OF DIVISION IN THE COUNTRY. THE PARTY OF THE LEFT IS THE PARTY OF HATE. THE PARTY OF THE LEFT IS THE PARTY OF NAME CALLING* The left campaign to do away with tradition, religion, familiarity, family and decency and accuses the right of dividing the country. Wow! These are the things that hold a society together. To Hillary a quarter of the country are deplorables, and to Biden half the country are neo-fascists. But they claimed Trump was the divider. "Come on man!"

- WHAT IS THE LEFT'S OBSESSION TO GET RID OF PEOPLE'S RIGHT TO PROTECT THEMSELVES ALL ABOUT? Whether we are talking about building physical barriers on the southern border or the right to have firearms, the left seems to be against it. This obsession started when the country was divided over slavery. The left did not want the black Americans to possess firearms, bluntly, because it was not as easy to control or kill them when they were armed. It was the republicans that pushed for the black community to have that right, and it changed the complexion of the south drastically. The left pushes that guns kill. Guns kill in the same manner that cars kill, or knives kill. About 2,000 children under the age of 16 years die in traffic collisions every year. [Wikipedia] According to The Daily Caller knives killed five times more people in 2016 than rifles; hammers and feet kill more people than rifles. An FBI report said 1,604 people were killed by knives and cutting instruments and 374 were killed by rifles in 2016. The left hates facts! ("Facts don't matter just the truth matters.") The Federalist makes the following point: "gun bans, and strict gun control do not prevent gun violence, Take, for example, Illinois and California. In 2013 there were 5782 murders by handgun in the U.S. According to FBI data, 20 percent of those—1157 of the 5782 handgun murders—happened in Illinois and California, which have the toughest state gun control regimes in the entire country. Even though California and Illinois contain about 16 percent of the nation's population, those two states are responsible for over 20 percent of the nation's handgun murders. SO, WHERE IS THE LEFT'S HYSTERIA ABOUT KNIVES, HAMMERS, FEET, AND CARS? A study published in 2013 by the Violence Policy Center using five years of nationwide statistics (2007- 2011) compiled by the Federal Bureau of Investigation found that defensive gun use occurs an average of 67,740 times per year. [Forbes] That is the low-end estimate. The high-end estimate is up to 4.7 million times per year. Another 1995 study by Kleck and Gertz estimated that between 2.1 and 2.2 million 'defensive gun use' events occur in the U.S each year. [Wikipedia] Of course the left claims all the studies are false. *THE LEFT ELITE IS THE PARTY EMBRACING THE AGGRESSOR, THE MURDERER AND THE CRIMINAL.*

- I am told that the left used to be the party for free speech. "WHY IS THE LEFT TRYING TO SUPPRESS FREE SPEECH? I can only think of one reason why a political group would want to shut down free speech: they cannot support their point of view. If I feel I have a winning point of view, why would I not want to openly debate it? Perhaps, I would rather govern a society of homoclites. I tell the parents of oppositional defiant children that their children are thinkers. That their goal as children is to challenge the adult perspective on life, and that we need more children and adults like that because they are becoming a rare commodity in our society. Oppositional children are more difficult to raise and parent, but they are great kids, not bad kids. The educational system on the left appears to want to indoctrinate your children not debate with them. CONSIDER HOME SCHOOLING YOUR CHILDREN! *THE LEFT ELITE IS THE PARTY OF "SHUT UP AND STEP UP."*

- WHAT IS THE MESSAGE BEING SENT BY ORGANIZATIONS CUTTING TIES WITH NRA: AVIS, DELTA, INTERPRISE, ALLIED, BUDGET, HERTZ, FIRST NATIONAL BANK OF OMAHA, NATIONAL, MET LIFE, BEST WESTERN, UNITED PARAMOUNT RX, ALAMO? According to First Principles, The National Rifle Association (NRA) "promotes the shooting sports and works to protect the right to keep and bear arms. True to its founding purpose, the association continues to emphasize its role as a training and educational organization." Did I miss something? Has the NRA been indicted for some crime? I experience the NRA as an organization that informs and teaches about the history of guns in protecting the country and about men in the service of our country. They also provide courses to teach young people how to handle firearms safely. IS THAT THE HORRIBLE THING THESE GROUPS ARE AGAINST? Oh, I have not forgotten that the NRA supports our constitution which says, in opposition to the desire of the left, that I may keep a gun in my possession for protection. The NRA, to the best of my awareness, does not say they support the 23.31 abortions per 1000 women (15-44 year old), or the more than 1 million abortions performed in 2008 in the top 25 states. The NRA also does not support the 125,000 abortions per day. [Wikipedia] The NRA is concerned however with the estimated 3.7 million burglaries occurring in the U.S. each year from 2003-2007. "A household member was present in roughly 1 million burglaries and became victims of violence in 265,560 burglaries." [FBI data] Guess which state has the most bank robberies? It's the state with the most severe gun restrictions. *THE LEFT IS THE PARTY OF 'YOU ARE NOT ALLOWED TO PROTECT YOURSELF OR WHAT IS YOURS.' THE LEFT IS THE PARTY OF 'MAKE YOURSELF A VICTIM'. THE LEFT IS THE PARTY OF 'KEEP THE GUNS IN THE HANDS OF THE BAD GUYS'. THE LEFT IS THE PARTY THAT 'CANNOT DISTINGUSH BETWEEN GUNS KILL PEOPLE AND BAD GUYS KILL PEOPLE'. THE LEFT ELITE IS THE PARTY OF 'LETS REGISTER EVERYONE'S GUNS' (TRIED AND THEN GIVEN UP IN CANADA BECAUSE THERE WAS NOT ONE INCIDENT OF FINDING A CRIMINAL THROUGH USE OF A REGISTERED GUN). Is it fair to say that* AVIS, DELTA, INTERPRISE, ALLIED, BUDGET, HERTZ, FIRST NATIONAL BANK OF OMAHA, NATIONAL, MET LIFE, BEST WESTERN, UNITED PARAMOUNT

RX, ALAMO are all against the constitution of the U.S.? Is it fair to say they are all against people protecting themselves against violence? Is it fair to say they are against a sport that millions of Americans enjoy? Is it fair to say they oppose gun education? Is it fair to say they are against children and adults being trained to properly use guns so they are not the victim of an accident? I wish someone would tell me what they think the NRA has done that they are so against. They just seem like "fall in place dopes" supporting whatever the left wants.

- There are a few studies suggesting that illegal immigrants commit fewer or less serious, crimes than citizens of the U.S. With the way the left suppresses data they do not agree with, I am not certain that information is reliable, and I admit being a little skeptical of data on such an issue from the Univ. of Wisconsin. *THE PARTY OF THE LEFT SUPPORTS ILLEGALITY. THE PARTY OF THE ELITE LEFT SUPPORTS SELECTIVELY CHOOSING THE LAWS IT LIKES AND WANTS TO ENFORCE.*

- DOES THE AVERAGE DEMOCRAT REALLY SUPPORT THE GOAL OF NANCY PELOSI TO "WORK TOWARD THE GOAL OF EQUALIZING INCOME IN OUR COUNTRY?" I think I studied this idea when reading Marx. *THE PARTY OF THE LEFT ELITE SEEMS TO FAVOR A COMMUNIST OR SOCIALIST FORM OF GOVERNMENT OVER A CAPITALIST SYSTEM OF GOVERNMENT.* Nancy has an estimated worth of 120 million Dollars and a salary of 223,000 dollars. Is she ready to give it away to the illegals to support her equity programs? It needs to be understood when the left sends out a message that the republicans are against democracy, they are only telling a half truth. (Similar to their half-truth ploy about republicans and climate) Republicans are not against the democracy established 200 years ago in the U.S.

Republicans are against the type of democracy established in China and Russia which the left has adopted. B. Sanders was open about his ties to Russian Democracy. These are communist countries with titles of democracy that are nothing like what the U.S. had until Biden came on board. Why do you think we have not been hearing much from him? Could it be because he is getting from Biden's presidency everything he wanted?

- When asked how she (Nancy Pelosi) would spend the tax dollars she wants to collect from everyone she reportedly replied, "We need to raise the standard of living of our poor, unemployed and minorities. For example, we have an estimated 15.5 million [closer to 22 million studies show] illegal immigrants in our country who need our help along with millions of unemployed minorities." Nancy approaches this by handing out benefits [from your tax dollars] and Trump did it by employing more people and getting them more money (higher wages) for their work. THIS SEEMS LIKE A PRIMARY DIFFERENCE BETWEEN A DEMOCRAT AND A REPUBLICAN. *THE PARTY OF THE LEFT WANTS TO PUT YOUR MONEY IN THE HANDS OF A GOVERNMENT THEY RUN AND NOT IN YOUR HANDS. THE PARTY OF THE ELITE LEFT LIES ABOUT WHAT THEIR TRUE PLAN IS. IT APPEARS TO WANT TO MAKE PEOPLE MORE DEPENDENT ON GOVERNMENT HANDOUTS.* With all the Americans who need better paying jobs, just what is the advantage to them of allowing millions of illegal aliens into the country to compete with them for a livable wage?

- One of America's greatest successes has been the assimilation of diverse groups into one people. The left and others do not seem to understand that assimilation of other groups into our way of life is what has kept the country strong. They talk about diversity like they are the same. Bringing people in too fast does not increase assimilation but prevents it from occurring. *THE PARTY OF THE ELITE LEFT IS ANTI-ASSIMILATION: REPLACING ASSIMILATION WITH 'FLOODING THE MARKET.'*

- *THE ELITE LEFT IS THE PARTY OF UNEQUAL TREATMENT UNDER THE LAW!* If you are Hillary Clinton, you can destroy your e-mails while under investigation and directed by congress not to, the people you work for can get immunity from the government before answering questions, you can be exonerated before you even testify. If you are Trump the FBI can infiltrate your campaign without an invite, a special prosecutor can be assigned to find a crime you MIGHT have committed (now two more special counsels have been assigned by the Biden DOJ to investigate Trump), the people who have worked for you can expect nighttime raids from the FBI with guns, helicopters, boats and armored cars swarming your residence, even though you have been cooperative (not destroying materials, like Hillary) from the start and of course they may raid of your home even if you are the immediate past President. If you are on Trump's team anticipate that the Special Prosecutor will *'accidentally'* lose e-mails from your accusers and political enemies. Where did equality under the law go? Another example of an inconvenient truth.

- *THE ELITE LEFT IS THE PARTY THAT LIES ABOUT LYING.* Participants in psychiatry, law or education should be versed on the mechanism of memory. It is known and accepted by memory researchers that memory is not a static item but is something that naturally evolves. [THE RIVER of CONSCIOUSNESS by Oliver Sacks: The Fallibility of Memory chapter] The more times a memory is accessed the more likely it is to change. This is not lying; it is simply that a memory is not static because our speech regarding a memory is not fixed. Even better is the finding that sometimes people will totally recall the same event differently. My wife and I have a completely different memory about when we first talked about getting married. When attorneys try to impeach someone for remembering something differently at a different point in time, it is a game with villainous intent. EVERYONE SHOULD UNDERSTAND MEMORY IS NOT A FIXED THING UNLESS YOU HAVE AN EIDETIC MEMORY WHICH ONLY A SMALL PERCENTAGE OF PEOPLE HAVE, or you are talking about music. To pretend a person is lying when there is a difference in recall from one time point to the next is a great big lie perpetrated on the individual by a legal team. It is a disgrace that attorneys do this to the unexpected, and it works in a court of law where we testify to tell the truth and nothing but the truth (attorneys should have to make the same testimony). It appears Flynn was the victim of this type of trap.

- THE ELITE LEFT IS THE PARTY OF LIES AND DISTORTIONS. My friend (?) and psychiatrist in LA made me aware of a report on lies Trump had (according to the fact checker) told. I read through the report. The lies, as reported in the propaganda media, included a statement from JAN. 23 "Between 3 million and 5 million illegal votes caused me to lose the popular vote." The fact checker claimed "There's no evidence of illegal voting. THERE IS A LOT OF EVIDENCE OF ILLEGAL VOTING WHICH I HAVE ALREADY POINTED OUT. I DO NOT KNOW IF IT CAN BE PROVED TO HAVE BEEN THE REASON FOR THE LOSS OF POPULAR VOTE, BUT THE LONGER IT IS LOOKED INTO THE MORE EVIDENCE THERE IS OF ILLEGAL VOTING. A large percentage of the items listed as lies from Trump don't hold the muster of time: like his claim of being spied on by the FBI. (Turns out to be true) It is also interesting to look closely at the "fact checkers" on the left;

frequently what they are reporting is opinion disguised as fact. Fact checkers are another invention of the left reportedly with some origination from China.

- HOW CAN YOU SERIOUSLY READ A NEWSPAPER CLAIMING "YES, YOU CAN BLAME PRESIDENT TRUMP FOR HURRICANE FLORENCE" FOR ANYTHING BUT COMEDIC VALUE? THEY DID REVISE THE STATEMENT TO, "NO, THE PRESIDENT DID NOT CREATE HURRICANE FLORENCE ALL BY HIMSELF." This truly goes from weird to weirder. *THE ELITE LEFT IS THE PARTY OF LOUSY JOURNALISM, BUT GREAT PROPAGANDA AND UNENDING NONSENSE.* It is too bad Trump Derangement Syndrome has affected journalistic abilities to such a large extent. Refer to <u>UNFREEDOM OF THE PRESS</u> BY MARK R. LEVIN

- WHY DOES THE LEFT ELITE LIE SO MUCH ABOUT WHO IS RESPONSIBLE FOR THINGS? The legislature enacts a law about immigration. Without legal justification for doing so, Obama ignores the law. Trump being president has the duty to enforce the laws enacted by the legislature. [Obama had the same duty but ignored his responsibility.] When Trump enforces the law as written by the legislature the press makes him out to be a dictator; I think he was accused of being one by the left—why, because he tried to enforce the law the legislature passed. When he did his duty of office the LMP machine called him every name possible. Trump was not responsible for the law. He was responsible and accountable to the legislature for enforcing the law. If the legislature didn't like the law they passed, they should have entertained another law. Instead, the legislators went on the war path giving all kinds of speeches about how horrible a President he was for doing what they legislated him to do. *THE LEFT IS A PARTY THAT REALLY*

MESSES UP UNDERSTANDING THE THREE BRANCHES OF OUR GOVERNMENT AND WHO IS RESPONSIBLE FOR WHAT. Instead of being out drumming up discontent the law makers should possibly have been in the office doing what they were sent to Washington DC to do: create legislation to deal with problems. I guess that would have not propelled them as high on the 'next president" list.

- So, the President enforces the laws the congress passes, and the obvious deficiencies of the law become quite apparent. Children were separated from the people who illegally brought them to the U.S. The intrinsic problem being that children were brought in by non-relatives to take advantage of the broken immigration laws. The left goes epileptic and accuses the president of all kinds of things he did not create. To stop the hemorrhage the President had to back away from enforcing laws. *THE LEFT IS THE PARTY PUSHING FOR ILLEGAL SOLUTIONS TO PROBLEMS. THE LEFT IS THE PARTY NOT PERFORMING THEIR DUTY TO LEGISLATE SOLUTIONS. THE LEFT IS THE PARTY VACATIONING IN PUERTO RICO WHILE THE PRESIDENT IS IN THE WHITE HOUSE WORKING ON SOLUTIONS TO THE SECURITY OF OUR BORDER AND COUNTRY.* WHY DOES THE LEFT ELITE GET AWAY WITH ADVOCATING THEIR DUTY TO THEIR CONSTITUENCY? Is this what the average person on the left wants, or is it just the elite left's desire?

- Another diversion technique the left uses is to selectively enforce laws. If you listen to the LPM you would think NRA is against all 'gun law.' That couldn't be further from the truth. The NRA has fought "for decades for tough enforcement of existing laws against violent criminals, drug dealers and gangs with guns. Instead of calling for full, tough enforcement of existing laws to take violent predators off our streets, the political elites cry for more laws that effect only the law-abiding. From gun bans, to ammunitions bans, to special taxes on lawful gun owners, to every licensing and national registration scheme they can conjure, their siren calls for more gun control is backed and shouted from the rooftops by most in the national media." (LPM) [Wayne LaPierre March American Rifleman] In other words they do not enforce the current laws so they can keep screaming for more laws.

- WHY CAN THE ELITE LEFT NOT SEE ACTUAL RESPONSIBILITY WHEN IT IS IN THEIR FACE? A person, or family, in South America decides to come to the U.S. illegally. They make a choice (necessary to have responsibility) to do this. The members of the left who go to foreign countries and raise the hopes of people that they will be accepted into the U.S. illegally are encouraging an illegal act but aren't responsible for the person's decision to make the trip. They may be responsible for committing a crime. Things that happen on the way to the U.S. are not the responsibility of the U.S. Likewise the U.S. is not responsible for the dismal conditions of the country people are coming from. (That has been suggested by numerous individuals on the left, but it is also not accurate.) Lack of borders encourages people to come to the U.S. illegally. The security of the border is mainly the responsibility of the legislative branch of our government. Congress has the choice, and the capability (the second requirement for responsibility), to do something, or not to do something. If they do not do their job the rules may make it possible for the President to declare an emergency and build the border with funds he could direct. Responsibility is a product of awareness, capability and choice. One of the real questions is why is the anemic republican members of the house and senate not making an effort to confront this situation?

- A psychiatrist recognizes that when there is ambivalence, or ambiguity in a situation there will always be people who will pull in the direction they want. Open borders create ambiguity. Remember a successful Liberal Democracy is based on respect between oppositional parties. [Totally absent in the present political climate). This is very destructive for the safety of the Republic. *THE LEFT IS THE PARTY THREATENING THE SURVIVAL OF THE FEDERAL REPUBLIC. WHETHER THE LEFT RESPECTS THE PRESIDENT, OR NOT, THEIR DISRESPECT FOR THE OFFICE OF THE PRESIDENT IS APALLING AND POSSIBLY DANGEROUS.* THEY CONTINUE ACTS TO CANCEL DEMOCRACY ALL THE TIME CLAIMING IT IS THE REPUBLICANS. THE ELITE LEFT HAS TAKEN THEIR GRUDGE OF THE PRESIDENT GLOBALLY. That is like one of a marital partnership taking the marital problem to the entire family, or city. If you believe solving problems with China and North Korea are good for America, what is being done is very destructive.

- THE ELITE LEFT IS THE PARTY THAT DISRESPCTS THE LAW AND LAW ENFORCEMENT. The left wants to get rid of ICE. The left is negative on police enforcement. The left wants to defy federal legislation. The left bad-mouths the efforts of the police to keep the country, or the cities safe. The left pushes the negative rhetoric if a white policeman kills a black person: totally ignoring the fact that black policemen more commonly kill black criminals than white police do. The left eulogizes the football player who does not respect our flag in protest of perceived police aggression, ignoring the fact that because of all the protests the police have backed away from aggressive policing, which has led to far more blacks being killed. Black Americans are far more often killed by other blacks than by the police (black or white). Sally Q Yates former United States Deputy Attorney General is praised by the left for defying a legal order by the President. *THE LEFT IS THE PARTY THAT NEVER LOOKS AT THE END PRODUCT OF THEIR POLICIES AND NEVER ACCEPTS ACCOUNTABILITY OR RESPONSIBILITY FOR THE ACTUAL OUTCOME.* WHAT IS THE ADVANTAGE TO THE LEFT OF SIDING WITH MS-13 AND OTHER LAW BREAKERS? More recent the left police departments are allowing antifa to blackmail them into not protecting conservative speakers. Wow!

- HOW IS IT HELPFUL TO THE PEOPLE OF THE U.S. TO EQUATE ICE, WHICH IS REMOVING SOME OF THE WORSE CRIMINALS IMAGINABLE FROM OUR COUNTRY, WITH THE NAZI DEATH CAMPS? The left elite wants to make a comparison of ICE to the rounding up of Japanese Americans and slavery. The irony and hypocrisy here is that Japanese Americans were interned under democratic leadership. There are a few other notable differences: ICE is not rounding up people to exterminate them, it is rounding them up to get them out of our country where they do not belong. They are not rounding up people to purify the race (even if that is another argument of this left-oriented group of critics), they are not being rounded up to be put in slave work camps, and they are not being experimented on medically. Another difference is that Nazi Germany was killing people who were trying to leave the country. ICE and other law enforcement agencies are merely helping them find a way back home. Another inconvenient truth is that ICE is doing what the law requests. *THE ELITE LEFT IS THE PARTY OF HYPERBOLEY. One of the screaming points from the left was that children were being separated from parents when they illegally attempted to enter the U.S. The left knew as well as the right that the reason for this was that children were being brought to the U.S. by people who were not parents, because our broken immigration laws gave them priority for admission to the U.S. if they were accompanied by children. The proper approach would be to change the laws so that children would not be extorted in this way.* THE LEFT IS THE PARTY THAT WOULD RATHER YELL AND SCREAM AT TRUMP FOR SOMETHING THAT IS CREATED BY THE TOTALLY INADEQUATE LAWS REGARDING IMMIGRATION TO THE U.S. Who created these laws? Not the President: Congress did. Who needs to correct them: not a President; Congress does! The lefts claim that ICE is equivalent to Nazi death camps is like declaring the Jan 6th political protest is equivalent to the attack on Pearl Harbor. Shame on them.

- THE ELITE LEFT IS THE PARTY OF DELIBERATE DISTORTION. Trump makes a comment in a small closed meeting (granted not a great statement) and the LMP picks up on it and repeats it hundreds of times on the air. What do they blame Trump of doing? Saying the comment to hundreds of innocent children who will hear the comment on the air, because they are putting it on the air a hundred times. I think most third graders could see through that, but I guess they feel their listeners will not. Why is there not the same outrage and coverage when a senator on the left calls the President a "M….r F….r or an A..H..e?" LMP!

- THE ELITE LEFT IS THE PARTY UNABLE TO SEE BIASES. Mueller stacks his team of investigators with one of H. Clinton's previous lawyers, large donors to the democratic party, outspoken anti-Trump advocates, attorneys sanctioned for wrong doings in the past and this is all seen by the left as appropriate. H. Clinton has connections to Russia through the creation of the infamous Trump dossier but is never investigated by Mueller while Trump is put under the scrutiny of the FBI, because he said in a campaign speech that he would like better relations with Russia. Members of Mueller's investigative team talk between themselves about stopping Trump from being president, but no bias is seen. Not seeing bias here is like a 'white out' in a snow blizzard."

- THE ELITE LEFT IS THE PARTY OF SELFISHNESS AND UNFAIRNESS. Do you recall how H. Clinton made such a big deal about getting Trump to agree to accept the outcome of the election if she won? Yet for the past three years of Trump's presidency, she and the left have continued to try and negate his winning. *IN THE NEED TO MAINTAIN POWER, THE LEFT SHOWS NO SPORTSMANSHIP, NO SENSE OF FAIRNESS (WOULD THEY SUPPORT TRUMP DOING TO HILLARY WHAT THEY ARE DOING TO TRUMP IF SHE HAD WON?), NO RESPECT FOR THE OFFICE OF THE PRESIDENCY, NO RESPECT FOR THE PEOPLE WORKING IN THE WHITE HOUSE, NO RESPECT FOR CABINET MEMBERS ("YELL AT THEM, SHOW THEM THEY ARE NOT WANTED"), NO RESPECT FOR THE HALF OF THE COUNTRY THAT ELECTED THE PRESIDENT--Deplorables, NO RESPECT FOR THE ELECTORAL PROCESS THAT HAS BEEN IN EFFECT SINCE THE FOUNDING OF THE COUNTRY, NO RESPECT FOR THE PEOPLE WHO PUT THEMSELVES ON THE LINE FOR OUR PROTECTION (THE LAW AND THE ENFORCERS OF THE LAW WHICH INCLUDES THE PRESIDENT), NO RESPECT FOR THE PROCESSES OF THEIR OWN RULES (KAVANAUGH'S FATE IN THE HEARING WAS DETERMINED BY THE LEFT BEFORE HIS NAME WAS EVEN SUBMITTED, THE MAN WAS NEVER GIVEN A FAIR HEARING FROM THE LEFT—NONE OF TRUMP'S NOMINEES HAVE), ENTIRE GROUPS ARE DISMISSED AS 'DEPLORABLES' "SMELLY" "RACIST" "WHITE NATIONALISTS" "NAZI" "MISOGYNIST" "LIAR" "TOOTHLESS" "MASCULINE TOXICITY" "OLD WHITE MEN" AND RACISTS. THE DOUBLE STANDARD GOES ON TO INFINITY.* [I need to stop before I run out of ink on this point.] From a psychiatric perspective unfairness is not a feeling it is a condition where one party wants to play by a set of rules, but they are not willing to grant the other side the same rules. I.e., I get to investigate you, but you do not get to investigate me. (The left can scream in full voice that the president can be investigated--"no one is above the law"--for no identified crime, but if the focus is turned to investigate Joe Biden's self-incriminating statements, the President asking for an investigation is subjected to an impeachment attempt.) I get to yell in your face, but you do not get to yell in mine. I get to knock on your door with 17 SWAT members with guns drawn in the middle of the night, but you get a pass. I get to hold secret hearings in the basement of the House or Representees, but you can't call witnesses you want without my approval. The FBI can lose important emails and H. Clinton can destroy her computers and hard drives when under investigation, but people Trump is associated with get arrested in the middle of the night by the SWAT team for **possibly** lying to congress. [Something at least 3 of the FBI and CIA directors have been identified as doing.] There is also the inappropriate use of inductive reasoning to go after Trump and his associates. Now, Biden is asserting that Trump as president didn't have the right to declassify documents, but he on the other hand has the right to invade Trumps home to fish for, or confiscate, documents the past president has that might prove the democrats have done bad things. Not much justice there!

- THE ELITE LEFT IS THE PARTY OF PASSION IN PLACE OF REASON. Numerous people on the left have suggested that passion is more important than fact (Biden and Alexandria Ocasio-Cortez among them). The left seems to prefer not doing studies in the first place, but frequently distorts the outcome when they have been done. One of the most blatant areas is around gun violence and climate. In psychiatric language this is seen as emotional reasoning. "Guns kill people." To anyone with the ability to think, this is not accurate. The gun controversy is based on a desire to control and uses emotion rather than fact to promote a point of view. For each use of a gun for mischievous or criminal acts, it is used thousands of times for protection and to secure safety. In every state where open carry, or concealed carry, has been initiated, major criminal acts have gone down. In countries, or in our states, where things like gun registration were initiated there have been zero associations with decreasing crimes from guns, or in finding perpetrators of crimes; only the cost of ownership has gone up for those enjoying the sport of legal shooting. The emotional left simply doesn't get it. Why do you think people (a lot were ladies) went out and bought guns during the Obama years? Sales have markedly gone down since he left office, but they are up again with a Biden presidency. People recognize and are coming closer to the realization that we are the first responders: not the police or some Good Samaritan who happens to be standing around. Each of us needs to be able to protect ourselves and our families. "No guns allowed" has never stopped a bad guy. As a psychiatrist I openly admit to a prejudice that all girls should be enrolled in Martial Arts programs. Sexual violence has been reported to occur every 98 seconds in America. [RAINN 25] The ages 12-34 are the biggest target for predators. The left appears to be mainly concerned that the predators are not injured. Fact: Guns are equalizers: they give targeted victims a chance. In countries like England where guns have been taken from the public, it has not stopped bad guys from using guns. I have had individuals in my practice from England who reported to me one of the most rewarding things they can say about coming to America was that they feel they have a means of protecting family and themselves. **IF GUNS KILL PEOPLE, THEN PENCILS MISSPELL WORDS, CARS MAKE PEOPLE DRIVE DRUNK, AND SPOONS MAKE PEOPLE FAT**

(JODIE CANTOR) Climate is their next greatest emotional issue. Their claim to have all the facts is simply another lie. They constantly distort the science by dishonestly providing numbers that are inaccurate or made up to fit their narrative. The second thing they do is treat computer generated outcomes as fact when **in fact** their computer projections are not confirmed by what can be directly measured and compared. Republicans do not **deny climate** is a factor in life or that it should not be a concern. Republicans actually look at the climate facts and do not find a legitimate reason to destroy the country for something that a computer is predicting. Something there is no reason to believe it is capable of predicting at this point in time. Climate has been changing since the birth of the world and there is no reason to suppose it is going to stop changing. Republicans just don't agree that the science (remember it is inductive reasoning) of climate is a done deal. Read Jane M. Orient, MD **The Physician and 'Climate Change'** in the appendix.

- THE ELITE LEFT IS THE PARTY OF LIARS. Adam Schiff said he had proof Trump collaborated with the Russians. Where is your proof after 6 years Adam? Former CIA Director John O. Brennan lied before congress several times and called the President a traitor. Where is your proof after 6 years John? Since his testimony under oath has come out it shows he was lying to people about things he knew were inaccurate. The LMP declared some new impeachable conduct by Trump every other week and now declares he is braking other laws nearly daily. How often have these hysterical proclamations been shot down when evidence and **facts** were revealed? This is inductive reasoning at play again. Comey is a liar and an informant (fact), but he is a hero on the left. Peter Strzok was fired from the FBI for lying, but the left set up a 'fund me account' to help him with his retirement funding lost because of the disgraceful way he conducted himself in the FBI (but not disgraceful apparently to the left or the LMP). The congressional left and the LMP jumps all over Trump for dealing with Stormy Daniels' accusations (with a financial agreement) while ignoring the fact that congress has had a fund they used for years, at taxpayers' expense, to do the same thing. The left has called the President a liar for things he has not done; they surely must be looking at his world through a mirror. Sounds like they are talking about themselves.

- THE ELITE LEFT IS THE PARTY OF BULLIES. Have you seen the glee on the side of the LMP when Manafort or Roger Stone are arrested in the middle of the night and dragged off in handcuffs and barefooted? Common decency would identify that as a Gestapo technique and unbefitting behavior toward citizens of the U.S. accused of l y I n g. REALLY! Almost makes me want to see the same behavior directed to Brennan and Comey. ALMOST! Not really, I personally do not want to be a bully even when dealing with liars. Have you heard of the left getting behind an investigation as to why 20 percent of our Uranium was transferred to our arch rival Russia (players in that decision included Clinton, Brennan, Comey, Rosenstein), the amazing money (Estimated $145,000,000.00) contributions to the Clinton foundation when Hillary was Sec. of State but seemed to dry up immediately after she lost the election surely didn't have anything to do with it. (?) What is the comparison of Trump saying he wants a better relationship with Russia and Clinton's role in the uranium deal? Or the reset button? Where is the follow-up to Douglas Campbell's (FBI informant) accusations that millions of dollars were paid by Russia to Clinton charities and lobbyists to influence Hillary's decisions? Where did Douglas go? Alexis de Tocqueville said, "Laws are always unstable unless they are founded on the manners of a nation; and manners are the only durable and resisting power in a people." [Wikiquote] By these criteria the country currently is completely a failure.

- THE LEFT ELITE IS THE PARTY OF EQUALITY OVER LIBERTY AND OF EQUALITY ONLY FOR THOSE WHO THINK AS THEY DO. There is nothing wrong with equality in certain areas: the law for example (The left does not appear to support that idea). There are some arguable issues with equality in education: some people really should not be going to college and would do far better in alternative educational venues like Trade Schools. The need for skilled people in the US is equally as important as a college education. I think it was Newt Gingrich who coined the term 'Intelligent but idiots." The world needs hands-on people, not just intellects. My father used to say if the people who designed farm equipment had to come to the farm and repair the equipment, they would put it together differently. Benjamin Franklin said, "Those who would give up essential liberty, to purchase a little temporary safety, deserve neither liberty nor safety." Liberty is the freedom of individuals to speak, think and act as he or she wants ("Men should shut up and step up" is not a good example; Antifa's attempt along with educational leaders of our higher academic facilities to stifle speech of independents and conservatives is not a good example). Equality is treating everyone in the same manner, according to the same standards and the same rules. I do not have a problem with some people believing that equality is more important than liberty but the people pressing in that direction should be aware that equality across the board puts a damper on creativity, and ambition; liberty "has a tendency to prevent full equality." [internet] Which is the more important of the two for me is clearly liberty. Without liberty the fabric of our society falls apart and we become homoclites. It is my perception that every day we lose liberty in the U.S. When one person in our society who does not like something can cause it to be lost by all who enjoy it, we have a major issue in liberty. If one person does not like "under God" in the Pledge of Allegiance, it should be taken out? Everyone should have access to all the portable bathrooms, or you can't build (New York). Everyone should be able to get to the top floor of your building, or you can't have a home for the homeless (Mother Theresa). When will every car have to be handicapped usable or no cars can be built? When will every house have to be built to accommodate little people, or they can't be built? When does every statue have to be approved by everyone or they will have to be torn down? When does everyone have to think liberal, or they shouldn't speak? Melton Friedman reportedly said, "Those who put equality before liberty are not likely to have either."

- **THE ELITE LEFT IS THE PARTY *CLAIMING* A HIGH MORALITY.** It is professed with vehemence that walls are immoral. Abortion is moral. Letting millions be affected by drugs and criminals coming over the border is moral, but stopping murders, drug traffickers, and rapists from coming into our country is immoral. Taking care of illegal immigrants is moral but giving legal citizens the same consideration is immoral. Abortion is moral even if it is done just prior to the baby being born but encouraging adoptions as an option to abortion is immoral. Limitations placed on what women can do regarding disposal of a baby are immoral but having abortion parties is the newest best thing that can happen, and it is moral! Liberal points of view are moral, conservative points of view are immoral. Lying to congress is moral if you are a democrat, being a republican is immoral. Being a democrat is moral, being a white person or a male is immoral. Establishing new biological classifications for humans every day is moral but calling someone by the wrong pronoun is immoral and unlawful. Not wanting to spend defense dollars for sex changes is immoral but spending defense dollars for sex change surgery is moral. Calling the President any name you want is moral; being civil to the office of the Presidency (if his name is Trump) is immoral. Spending tax money to get abortions is moral but spending tax money to protect life is immoral. Protecting myself and family from criminal behavior is immoral, deliberately removing the way I can protect myself is moral. Refusing to confirm you have a legal right to vote is immoral; allowing non-citizens to vote in federal and state elections is moral. Doing what the laws request regarding criminal immigrants is immoral, letting criminal immigrants back into society against the law is moral. Speaking out at work with conservative principles is immoral, limiting and firing people who speak out conservatively is moral. Limiting the influence media like face book is moral when it supports the left ideas and immoral when it supports the conservative point of view. Telling Russian diplomats "I will have more flexibility after I am elected" [Obama] is morally ok but saying, "I would like a better relationship with Russia" when campaigning is tantamount to treason. Having judges create legal precedence is moral but limiting legislation to the elected bodies of the country is immoral. The President enforcing the laws of congress is immoral, but the President breaking the law (DOCA) is moral. Supplying guns to be shipped to cartels on the Mexican side of the border is moral but reporting the real benefits of equalizers in the hands of non-criminal Americans is immoral. Using children to get better immigration status when illegally crossing our borders is moral, using the tragedy of childhood killings in schools to push the scenario of gun control is moral, but attempting to change the laws so children are not exploited is immoral. The second amendment is immoral for the left and constitutional for the right. The left feels socialism is morally right, and conservatives support capitalism (which helped all those on the left aspiring to be president to make the millions of dollars it takes to get where they are). The left feels that more government and more laws are morally good (equality) and that limiting the rights of government and decreasing the number of rules and regulations is morally wrong. The left wants more equality and less liberty; the right wants liberty with equality, especially legal equality. [I really might run out of ink on this track.]

Did you know that guns are a lot harder to get now than they were in the past: Sears and Roebuck catalogue in the 1900s had 35 pages of guns you could buy right out of the catalog?

- <u>THE RELIGIOUS MIND; Why good people are divided by Politics and Religion</u> by Jonathan Haidt indicates that the two sides have somewhat similar talking points but define them differently. Both sides would likely say caring is important: The left seems to care only about power, so they frame caring around immigrants who might become left voters. The right cares about the condition of the people in the United States. Caring on the right is directed more clearly to what might be the U.S. family. The left cares more about immigrants then citizens. Liberals at the grass root level seem to have strong opinions about fairness in a class action sort of way (all poor people should be allowed into the U.S. if they will vote democratic.) Conservatives want fairness, but it starts at the basic root of the family, county, state, and country before embracing the rest of the world. The liberals are strong on fairness when it comes to everyone should be able to vote, even if you are here illegally. The right has a concern that people who are citizens of the country should have a priority in running the country. They also have a loyalty to their group, but a higher sentiment is placed on sanctity and liberty. Haidt seems to frame it this way:

Liberal concerns: 3 foundations of morality: Care/harm---Fairness--- Equality

Conservative concerns: 7 foundations of morality: Liberty-----Loyalty -----Concern about their group-----Sanctity-----Authority-----Fairness foundation--- Hate tyranny

Dennis Prager (radio) says that equality is such a central theme of the left that they want children to be equal to parents and students to be equal to teachers. That explains a lot of what I see in my office from day to day. It may also explain the change in the judicial system occurring around 1980s when courts began to give children power over their parents. Kids started carrying around the telephone number for CPS, and parents were bullied into letting them do what they wanted. Guess this may also explain the movement to socialism.

I have not done this book justice, so read it yourself. I thought it was clarifying.

- THE ELITE LEFT IS THE PARTY OF HIGHER TAXES. Conversation on the left is that the tax relief begun by the right is "crumbs" for the people (Nancy P) and that the government does not get enough of the people's money. Newly elected members of congress on the left are talking 70-80 percent taxes. I expect most people would accept that a 100 percent tax might be called slavery. Is a 90 or 95 percent tax in the slavery area? Since 1619 the left has endorsed slavery. As they push the tax higher and higher, it appears that perhaps they still wish that condition for all but the elite. I am likely pushing history too quickly. Before slavery there was indentured service. Like most ideas of greed, it took some time to become full blown slavery. (Somewhere around the 1640s). The right is the party of lower taxes and less spending toward non-citizens of the U.S. Trump wished for other countries to pay a fair share for their defense (a radical idea on the left I guess—since it is so often criticized by the left), he wanted to stop other countries from taking advantage of Americans in trade (another radical idea on the left I guess—since it is so often criticized), he wanted countries to stop stealing our intellectual property (another radical idea I guess—since it is so often criticized), he wanted corporations to have the money necessary to reinvest in the productivity of the U.S. (another radical idea I guess), he wanted the people of the U.S. to have and keep more of their earnings/salary to spend the way they want (a radical idea I guess), Trump appeared to want government money to be spent on protecting American citizens and not on abortions (another radical idea on the left), Trump appeared to want to make decisions based on the best understanding available and not on some political claim of superior insight based on nothing but a desire to keep people on the defensive. Science is inductive reasoning (climate change arguments are based on inductive reasoning). Remember how science said we should not eat butter and then later that butter was ok? That is the way of science—what we think we understand today may be totally different tomorrow. If the 'left's' science is correct we should all quit our jobs and have a ball for the next 10 years because that is when they have predicted the world is going to end. The party of the left (Harris, Booker, Warren, Sanders, etc.) want 'free' health care, and 'free' college at a projected 'cost' of up to 44,000,000,000.00 dollars over 10 years. PLEASE HELP ME UNDERSTAND HOW SOMETHING THAT COSTS THAT MUCH CAN BE CONSIDERED FREE? [Did you catch my propaganda style?] Of interest also is how the pre-midterm election propaganda was that conservatives were **too radical.**

- THE ELITE LEFT IS THE PARTY OF BLAME, ANGER AND HATE. Anger is blaming. No blaming; no anger! Trump makes a joking comment at a rally about sometimes just feeling like you wanted to punch someone (protesters interrupting him) and off the cuff offered to pay the defense if someone did, was understood as a joke by the thousands of people at the rally (no one stepped up and did it), but not by the angry blaming left that used (They didn't need excuses, because they were already doing it.) his comments as a battle cry to physically attack people supporting him. The battle cry of Maxine Waters is just another example of the hatred pushed by the left. The left-oriented talk shows openly display their level of hatred for the Trump as does/did the LPM daily. H. Clinton says "if we win back the congress, we (democrats) can start being civil again." Eric Holder says, "When they are down kick them." Maxine Waters says, Get in their face and tell them (the Trump cabinet) they are not wanted." The elite left is not very nice.

- THE ELITE LEFT IS THE PARTY THAT WEAPONIZES SPEECH. Guns that are used to protect thousands of times more often than they are used to assault are referred to as "assault" weapons by the left. I would label them "equalizers" as Colt did. The LPM uses Nonsense speech on a continuous basis. Rarely does the left answer a question addressed to them, but they continue propagandizing, using emotional speech, logical fallacies, irrelevance, diversion, ambiguity and incorrect inference, confusion of cause and effect, oversimplification, erroneous comparison and contrast, evasion and selective reporting. They conspire to prevent anyone who might speak directly to the issues to be shut out even before they can speak. Individuals at Grand Canyon University in Phoenix AZ protested until a speech by a conservative was canceled, because "his appearance on the Phoenix campus would be too divisive and run counter to the school's mission." Does that mean the mission of the school is to bane conservative thought and speech? Is the school's mission to ban free speech. I do give the left credit for understanding what I fear the right has yet to learn: If you control the speech, you control the person: one of the main reasons they likely hate Trump—They can't keep him from saying what he believes.

THE ELITE LEFT IS THE PARTY ENCOUIRAGING INFANTILISM. Women who do not want someone to ask them out to dinner or tell them they look nice need to learn to "woman up and tell them," not run to HR and make a complaint (at least until the person is given a chance to back off). Students in college who do not like Trump don't need a 'crying room' or 'safe room' they need to be given some accurate information about our government and the way it works, and not nursed and patted on the head for their self- imposed self-created pain. If they don't want to hear a conservative speaker stay home. Do not be a fascist and try to prevent everyone else from hearing the talk. Individuals who have had some difficulty being accepted into the American society (Irish) didn't do it by playing victim. "Coming out" is a step in saying, "I am a person like everyone else, treat me like everyone else." Individuals need protection from hate crimes, but not from other's opinions. [Not claiming my situation is equal, but as a child I raised and rode Arabian Horses (in a community of Quarter horse breeders). He was good enough that we usually won the contests we entered. I was not liked, and my horse was not liked. I still have Arabian horses.] Women who feel infantilized when a man offers to hold a door open for them have a problem. Tell him you don't appreciate it, and he will stop. Scold, cuss or insult him for being thoughtful and he will properly think you are nuts. Psychiatrically, people need to be given the chance to comply before someone "steps on their neck". Every few months in my practice, I see someone who has been accused of doing something someone doesn't like, and their job is threatened. My last was a very talented well-educated female (white) who appeared to be ganged up on by several co-workers because she was being picked out to head projects. She was leaning toward isolation; I suggested she take the situation on frontally. If her boss as worth his salt, he would support her. Ronald Reagan said that we lose rights every time the legislative body passes a law. The FAA has a lot of regulations on flying. Several years ago, a very popular site for small airplane pilots to congregate in Wisconsin had a tower failure. Hundreds of

Pilots continued to safely land for hours without the tower. They simply "co-operated" with each other. In Virginia 1000s of gun advocates brought guns to a rally. The press must have been disappointed when none of the violence they predicted happened. Too bad left you were wrong again. People who like guns are no different from those who like swimming, boating, archery or darts. Another inconvenient truth.

- THE ELITE LEFT IS THE PARTY OF THE 'ELITE'. Movie stars for whatever reason congregate to the left. It seems to have gotten to the point where if you admit you are conservative you may not be able to work in movies. DIDN'T THE LEFT USED TO BE AGAINST SEGREGATION? Are they trying out for roles in McCarthyism? If you are a conservative teacher, or movie star, you may be at risk of losing your tenure, or working role, if you say something that is not sanctioned by the left. DIDN'T THE LEFT USED TO BE AGAINST SUPPRESSION OF SPEECH? I guess it makes sense that if you want to be elite you should join the Democratic Party. Personally, until the restriction related to Covid 19, I had stopped going to a movie weekly or even more often and was going once every two to three months instead . The role of movie stars in politics gets them an F in my grading system. Even looking at the elite movie star is no longer a pleasure. It has become hard for me to separate faces from politics. Who wants to go to a movie and watch someone who has demonized your President and you because you supported him? It seems McCarthyism is being reinvented by the left elite. Trump's Vice President Pence was confronted as he watched the play Hamilton. There is a time and place for everything, I don't agree with the M Waters approach to politics.

- THE ELITE LEFT IS THE PARTY OF POLITICAL CORRECTNESS. You certainly would not see that if you listened to the comments on the View or other LPM broadcasts as they use all kinds of cussing and derogatory words directed to people on the right; but to wish someone Merry Christmas you had better look out, because the speech police might show up on your door. I recently wished one of my patients "Merry Christmas" and she responded "thank you, but I don't celebrate Christmas." I said, "Thank you for telling me, I wish you happiness for anything you do wish to celebrate." Her response was "I know that and thank you for the thought." We concurred together that the inaccuracy of speech was not the issue; it was making speech an issue that was the problem.

- THE CURRENT POLICY OF THE ELITE LEFT SEEMS (Now established as is ...) TO FOSTER OPEN BORDERS. Until president Trump campaigned on border security the left (Pelosi, Schumer, Obama) seemed to be in favor of border security and were verbally willing to build barriers to illegal immigrant passage. We have all seen them expressing a need for borders. They appeared to hate allowing Trump to secure the nation more than they want safety and security for the American citizen. Denying the importance of border security openly supported by multiple democrat leaders is failed 'slight of hand.' I can't help but wonder if the change has something to do with the fact that a lot of lower income, left, voters are moving to the right. Perhaps they like "crumbs." Those crumbs have turned into thousands of dollars, which have now been taken back because of Biden economic policy.

- THE PARTY OF THE LEFT ELITE SEEMS TO SUPPORT VOTER FRAUD. Identifying one's self is not a very difficult thing to do in the U.S. if you are a citizen. Identification is required if you fly on planes, drive cars, take out a loan, deposit cash into a bank, receive medical treatment in a hospital or doctor's office and buy items from stores of all kinds. Obtaining false credentials to do those things is breaking the law. It is generally considered unlawful to vote illegally in a state and federal elections. [This is being challenged by states on the left.] Wanting identification to identify people who are eligible to vote is certainly as reasonable as asking for it when participating in the other activities I mentioned. When we are told by the left that it is suppressive to require identification to vote (arguably the most important single thing a person who is a member of a free society can do) there is no other way to legitimately look at it, except that the purpose is to support election fraud. Another option on the left, of course, would be to help individuals, who can legally vote, secure the identifications needed. That of course is clearly not the direction taken by the left. Voter fraud seems to be essential to maintaining power by the left. As Judicial Watch has discovered the Supreme Court seems to back the idea that asking for identification when voting does not foster "voter suppression." A community in Mexico established voter identification rules and actually more people turned out to vote. Apparently, they believed their vote meant more if it was protected.

- THE ELITE LEFT IS THE PARTY OF REGULATIONS. In 1960 there was an estimated 20,000 pages of regulations for the U.S. Current estimation is closer to 185,000 pages. Not all created by democrats of course. Cutting unnecessary regulations has allowed the business world to blossom under Trump who insists when creating new regulations others must be taken away. The simplicity of this is remarkable. The left of course continued to scream that the President is not capable of governing the country for his entire term. Look at the results! It raises the question of whether the left can understand the concept of governing?

- THE ELITE LEFT SEEMS TO DEFINE THINGS THE WAY THEY WANT. I heard this statement on one of the LPM stations: "America elected an authoritarian, anti-immigrant, racist, strongman to the nation's highest office." Authoritarian? Google dictionary defines an authoritarian person as [synonyms] "autocrat, despot, dictator, tyrant, absolutist, disciplinarian, martinet" The chief job of the executive branch is the safety of the country. So, if Trump was all the things described above, would his desire to shut down the government to unvetted individuals from terrorist countries have had to go through the Supreme Court? Courts also knocked down Trump's order restricting federal funds to sanctuary cities. (Too bad in my world) It would appear from an outsider position that the 9th circuit court is more authoritarian than Trump. They seemed to overrule the president Trump on policies the left did not like. If you look carefully at the Biden position on topics like free speech it is easy to see he is far closer to what Trump was accused of than Trump.

The next allegation was "anti immigrant:" This, of course, is a complete lie, fabrication and continuation of propaganda that had been repeated over and over by the LPM. On occasion, President Trump advocated strongly and supported openly for LEGAL immigration.

The next noun used was "racist." Racist is a popular noun or adjective used by the left continually. It means "prejudiced against all people who belong to other races". [Google dictionary] I have listened to a lot of things the president has said, and I have never heard a racist comment from him. I do hear racist comments against whites and men coming from the left nearly daily. One commentator on MSNBC said, "Trump is the worst type of racist; he does not know he is a racist." This seems to be another of those situations where the speaker has an open channel to read Trump's mind, or to get special insights from some higher power they subscribe to. I think he was simply looking into a mirror.

The next attribute he gave Trump was "strongman." I think he may have complemented the president here: "a person who is very powerful and able to cause change, especially of a political type." [Google dictionary] The President of the US is often said to be the most powerful person in the world. One might wish that were true. I am certain the speaker was counting on the word having a mafia boss connotation.

- Where is the information on the Clinton Cartel and its relationship with Health Care?

- THE ELITE LEFT APPEARS TO BE THE PARTY OF IDENTITY POLITICS. Identity politics (IP) are hate policies and are based on a variety of forms having to do with things people have no choice over: calling people racists is racist; calling them "old WHITE men & WHITE supremacists' is racist; distorting the meaning of what someone says to create hate and anger [nationalism] is Identity Politics; Labeling someone a Nazi is racists and IP; "religion [Degrading people by calling them a Jew, a Christian, a Muslim, etc. in a negative context] is IP; social class [smell the Walmart shoppers] is IP; culture ["ten toothed"] is IP; ethnicity complaints are IP; gender identity ["Toxic masculinity"] is IP; generation [OLD white men] is IP, political party affiliation ["I could smell the Trump Support."] is IP, sexual orientation, urban and rural habitations, and veteran status [Wikipedia] are all Identity politics. Identity politics are causes of hate perpetrated by the people who use the term: the left seem to keep looking at the world through a mirror.

- THE ELITE LEFT SEEM TO GET STUCK IN PROCLAMATIONS. I turned on the Van Jones Show to hear a guest make the following comment about the President's State of The Union Address: It was a "psychotically incoherent speech with cookies and dog poop." I hope I got it right, I had to listen several times because it was so profound and clear without *emotional language, irrelevance, diversion, amphiboly, juxtaposition, incorrect inference, or erroneous comparison and contrast*. Given that at least 74 percent of polled republicans thought it was a good speech, is this person possibly someone looking through a mirror again?

- THE ELITE LEFT IS A PARTY FULL OF HYPOCRACY. Probably the things about the elite left that stands out most prominent is the continuous disregard for what they claim to stand for: Justice for me but not for you. Protection for me, but not for you. You need to believe women even if we don't. We like long investigations for you, but none for us. When you leak information, it is a crime but if we leak it is fantastic. We can collude with the Russians and it is fine but you will be investigated. We can stack an investigative team with Clinton lawyers and supporters and it is just fine but if you want some indication of fairness, it is to be ignored. Clinton can give 20 % of our uranium to Russian and it is fine but if Trump says he would like a better relation with Russia he is investigated for treason. Russians contribute $100,000,000.00 to Clinton's foundation and no one looks but when Russia is accused of spending $120,000.00 on adds the left feel support Trump it is grounds for 2 years of harassment of the President for collusion (a non crime). Democrats call the president a supporter of KKK, yet democrats have all the historical connections with that group. Democrats keep claiming the President is guilty of something, but when asked for proof none is provided. Democrats claim the President is responsible for things he has no choice about and you recognize it, but you continue to claim it anyway. Democrats belittle the office of the Presidency, because you didn't like it that the Trump outsmarted and out-campaigned your idol. Democrats used to be for free speech, but you fire, fight, slander, discharge, disown, block everyone promoting a conservative point of view. The left controls the majority of the educational programs and your teachers seem to want only to engage in left propaganda. The left claims moderation politically, only to turn to the extreme left after an election—apparently willing to lie and tell people what they want to hear to get elected. The left says Trump lies, yet they seem to lie about everything! (Another case of looking at Trump through a mirror.) The left bemoans for weeks the death of a soldier doing his duty (attempting to make it Trump's fault), but calls it a 'non-issue' when 300 Americans are killed every week from heroin--80% of which comes from south of the border—because they do not want to stop illegals from crossing the border. You can also add rapes and assaults democrats are apparently not interested in.

- The LEFT SEEMS TO BE A PARTY OF 'if I think I am right, you are amoral if you don't think the same way.' I like different opinions. I like looking at things in numerous ways. When I was in the Child Psychiatry program at UCLA I would occasionally get dressed down, because I was reading during a lecture. I have found over the years that juxtaposing different sets of data can lead to novel outcomes. My artistic patients have said the same things. Blythe Pepino appeared on Carson Tucker the other night describing how her strong negative belief in the future of our climate has led her to the solution of not wanting children. Tucker and his friends on the show seemed to focus on how sad it was that a person would allow their beliefs about climate to interrupt the great experience of being a parent. I experienced it a little differently. I thought it was great that she was willing to stand behind her belief and principles and to unite others with the same beliefs to do what they thought was right in the circumstance. This raises the entire issue of *freedom of choice*. Freedom Of Choice (FOC) is a two headed fox. The left promotes FOC in ways that usually impacts directly on someone's life: choice to own slaves, choice of abortion, and choice of becoming a socialist society. I am for freedom of choice that allows individuals to do what they feel is important if it does not force others to do the same thing. I would be happy if all the individuals concerned with climate control stopped eating beef, stopped driving fossil powered equipment, and lived the life they believe will save the planet. Groups have been doing this in the U.S. since its inception. (Amish) If it looked like these efforts were productive others might well join in. Only a totalitarian system tries to make everyone do the same thing. As with the socialist movement, I am fine if believers in socialism want to live in an environment where they give all their money to the government. I expect they would be able to get a card that says, "You get free education and health care, maybe even enough food to sustain you." I do not think it is wise, or healthy, for everyone to have to follow someone else's choice (I don't want a gun so you can't have a gun, I do not want to drive a gas driven car so you can't have a car either, I don't want to say 'under God' so you have to stop saying it, I don't like certain historical statues so they have to be removed, I want Sharia law so you need to change.) This opens, of course, the issue of what is ok to choose and what is not. This is where the constitution comes in. Progressives do not seem to like the constitution very much. They don't seem to like the law in general very much. When Trump tried to do something, the left claimed he was breaking a law. When Obama broke the law, the left thought it was fine. Save the world; live the life you think will save the world. You can start now. You don't have to wait on some legislation to be passed like the new Green Deal. Do it now! Save the world! There isn't anything you want to do you can not get started on except bullying everyone else into doing what you want. Example: Bill de Blasio has taken meat out of the diet of school children on Mondays. Maybe if the results are liked it will spread as an idea. Parents can still feed children meat for the evening meal if they want. Test it out. See if it makes children smarter or healthier. I have my doubts, but Americans should be able to deal with problems differently. Better policy would be to give parents and students a choice about eating meat on Monday. That would be democracy at work. American democracy.

A new psychiatric syndrome is being considered (Lise Van Susteren MD and David Pollack MD Psychiatric News Nov. 1,2019) "Pre-traumatic Stress DO and Ecological Grief DO." I didn't check and see what part of the states they practice in, but I have not had Arizonans present with these concerns in my office. The scientists I have listened to say we are likely to have a 1 degree increase in temperature by 2060. The condition of concern might better be called an iatrogenic or political gimmick DO. I guess that will win me the 'denier award' from the left. But I have been planting more trees on my property— What have you been doing?

- The left is the party of "fine the people doing nothing wrong and let the bad guys go free" (If the bad guys are democrats). What am I referring to? Schools are trying to collect money from organizers of conservative talks at schools because they must spend so much money to protect the speakers from the left mobs. Just how much more distorted can one get, and this from higher education facilities? I went to a college that had a policy that if you were caught driving on campus you were likely to be expelled. They were obviously interested in academic standing. I was admitted to three medical schools I applied to—after only three years of college. If schools wanted to solve the issue (Charlie Reese) they would establish rule a.) Anyone obstructing the expression of free speech on the campus will be expelled: This is to include physically blocking speakers or people coming to listen to a speech, it includes heckling the speaker giving the speech, it includes disruptions causing others to reasonably fear for their safety. B.) Anybody found on campus with identity compromising outfits (Halloween excepted) will be arrested for trespassing. C.) Everyone found guilty after being arrested for trespassing or harming another person while on campus will be expelled if a student and referred to the state law enforcement if not! I bet the problem would be resolved immediately. Democrats do not like to solve some problems!

- On occasion, when my blood pressure is less than my normal low, I will tune into one of the LPMs. Last evening, I tuned to CNN and came across an Anderson Cooper special on "Lies of the President." I thought I was watching a comedy program, all that would have been needed to complete the picture was 'black face.' The first lie they started with was Trump's statement "Looks like Alabama may be hit (referring to bad weather)." From the briefing notes it looked like the President was taking information from sheets provided for him by the weather bureau. From there the direction of the program went to the horrible damage the President did to the nation by making that prediction. It appeared that perhaps the President was given bad information. From the clip they played there was no evidence the President was predicting the weather. (If I were the President, I probably wouldn't take information from that briefer again.) After listening to a few more identified "lies," it was clear a lie was identified as anytime the President had the boldness to disagree with the left's policies. Of interest was the declaration that each time the President made a statement about the same thing it was counted as a separate lie. So, for those like Kessler who was doing the counting, each time Trump said the left was on a 'witch hunt' it would be counted as a separate lie. Each time the President disagreed that the climate was not the most pressing condition in the world his comment would be considered a lie. I have already stated that perspective is not popular among the left, but consider applying the same counting method to the number of times, over the past 3 years, the media has said there is proof the president has done something wrong only to discover it was a fake report. To be fair you must count the comments from all the LPMs and each time they were said and insisted on by friends and family of the left. Remember also, that if Trump did not stick up for himself during his first year as President, there would have been little to no reporting of his side of an issue. Whether it is Russian collusion, obstruction of justice, Stormy Daniels, impeachment, etc. the left never seems capable of counting their own blunders, they simply declare all the misinformation they have provided is an example of excellent reporting and give themselves awards. P.S. Any defense of course is labeled *misinformation!* Are they accurate that the people of the U.S. are really that stupid? I hope the people will assert their sense of fairness and objectivity and elect Trump again in 2024!

AN INTRODUCTION TO THE IDEA OF SPEAKING ACCURATELY

I would not like to read a mystery novel that gives me the conclusion at the start of the story, but in this case, it is exactly the thing I am going to do. The reason is because it is the unraveling of how the conclusion came about that makes it understandable, not the answer itself. The conclusion is that many of our problems (academic, political and psychiatric) are the product of NOT LEARNING TO SPEAK ACCURATELY. Every time I say this, I cringe at the hours I spent learning to do therapy and to write prescriptions.

After learning to speak correctly, which most students do, it is also important to learn to speak accurately which most people do not do. Like the earth's gravity, it is difficult for us to break through the mantel of inaccurate speech, because it is all around us: in our music, in our books, in our movies, on our television shows, and, at the time this is being written, the LPM shows this error on a nearly continuous stream.

There are authors who have contributed to the understanding of the role language plays in the forming of concepts: a couple of my favorites are Harry L. Weinberg <u>LEVELS OF KNOWING AND EXISTENCE</u> and Sl. Hayakawa and Alan R. Hayakawa <u>LANGUAGE THOUGHT AND ACTION</u>. Their thoughts are too important to summarize here, read the books if you want to learn what they said.

The basic error in our speech starts in childhood, should be removed in childhood, but is generally not removed at all, because it is not recognized for what it is: THE BEGINNING OF BIG PROBLEMS.

And just what is that speech error: *BLAMING*. The mind comes by this principle of thinking as normally as it learns to deal with size and volume. To understand how the concept goes wrong, it is necessary to quickly look at the age-old issue of mind and body: Rene Descartes. Not really! Another Joke! What is necessary to understand is that the mind must deal with two separate perceptions: Our *physical world* (That which we can touch in some form, or fashion) and the *psychological world* of thoughts and concepts which are real for us but cannot be physically touched. I will spell out some of the attributes of each world and why they are important.

Children experience the world around them initially through physical registers or senses: smell, touch, pressure, taste, hearing, etc. The language that is developed in childhood reflects the experiences they have with the physical world. They fall (Ouch! That hurt me!) Not the falling, but the sudden stopping caused by hitting the ground, they run into something (Ouch! That hurt me!) The pain is seen as something the event created. In their mind IT had to have caused the pain, because the child does not perceive that they had something to do with the experience of being hurt.

I recall when he was about 6-year-old my very bright son was riding his bike; he turned into our driveway and ran smack into the gate that had been pulled across the entrance. The bike of course stopped rather suddenly against the gate causing him to take a spill. He got up and kicked the bike. I was a witness to the event, and I asked him, "Why did you kick the bike?" His response was, "It made me fall down." I asked him, "How did the bike make you fall down." His response was, "Dad, don't give me any of that psychiatric bull, it just did."

Children, in conjunction with their physical world experience, form a speech pattern of blame. "It made me. It caused me. It hurt me. It...." This formative interpretation becomes a screen through which everything is processed. It is actually a delusion. Another inconvenient truth.

The blame configuration is not entirely inaccurate. In the physical world items do hurt us. This is the basis of the traditional cause and effect model. When one steps on a nail, the nail tears tissues in the body that sends pain sensations to the brain in abundance. It is not bad speech, or framing, to indicate that the nail is the source of the damage that led to the pain experience. The same could be said for a knife cut, stepping on a rough stone barefoot, being hit by a falling object or the ostentatious swing of a bat striking the body.

The problem begins with the overgeneralization* of the physical world's <u>form of speech</u> when dealing with psychological issues or conditions. E.g.: The child wants to go to a movie and the parent tells them, "No." The child blames the parent for the feeling of disappointment in not being able to do what he wants, which leads to feelings of helplessness and then comes anger. The anger is directed at the parent whom the child mistakenly sees as causing their hurt feelings. In logical cognitive progression this is akin to 2+2=5. It is an inaccurate frame of speech and thinking. It is a mistaken perception. It is delusional thinking. [Merriam-Webster's New Collegiate Dictionary defines delusion as "A false belief regarding the self or persons or objects outside the self that persists despite the facts."]

* One of the fifteen styles of distorted thinking.

Stop where you are! Do you comprehend what I am suggesting? From the very earliest days of childhood children are creating (More accurately, they are being taught to create "delusional" concepts about the world) an inaccurate belief system about their world.

How is this delusional system being taught; by repetition and by familiarity? This error is repeated over and over in our music, in our books, in our movies, in our television programs and on the LPM almost non-stop in the same way they badgered President Trump. Because it is so seldom understood by parents or teachers, they simply repeat the perception the way they were taught (which was inaccurately) and the process is perpetuated from one generation to another. The educational system, which does a great job of teaching people how to speak correctly, does not pay as much attention to the accuracy of speech. Those teachers and parents who try to convey accuracy in speaking are facing a Tsunami wave. If states like California and New York wanted to help people they would not make laws to punish people for using the wrong pronoun or the words 'illegal alien,' they would encourage their teachers to teach children and adults how to speak accurately.

The most important thing to take away from this is that much of a child's emotional experience is a product of "delusional" thinking. It is not accurate and is generally not reality based. It is seen through the filter of BLAMING. Blame language will become the thread that runs through most of our interactions with other people and all our interactions with the physical world long before we start making psychiatric diagnoses for the products of this form of speech. To see the end products of this form of thinking look no farther than the current political scene.

Anger is an exploited problem. Courts send individuals to Anger Management classes which run from 3-9 months and which I see as an oxymoron. Why would people want to learn to manage anger—when it takes about ten seconds to learn what you need to get rid of it forever. Unfortunately, that seems to be the current American way.

The number of conditions that seem to disappear when people stop blaming is mind blowing yet this error in speech that sets up a lot of psychiatric illnesses is not even identified in the psychiatric literature.

Blaming in the psychological world is a speech disorder. Perhaps the reason it is not in the psychiatric literature is because it is actually an educational problem. At issue here, however, is that this educational problem creates a lot of psychiatric diagnoses. I might add, in the bizarre state of our political conflicts that it is at the base of unresolved issues in that venue also. Arabs and Jews have been blaming each other for thousands of years without resolution. One might think that would be an eye opener, but it seems not to have caught on yet except for the work of Jared Kushner. Maybe in another 2000 years: or maybe now! Does it really surprise anyone that if we cannot speak accurately we cannot resolve conflicts?

Understanding the language (and paradigms) of the physical and psychological worlds helps us comprehend the world better. Not understanding the language of each lead to mixed metaphors that can be confusing at all levels.

The power words for the physical world are change and control. These words only confuse when applied to the psychological world.

Blame language which recognizes cause and effect in the physical world is an accurate frame of speech. In the psychological world blaming/cause-and-effect-language is generally confused with sequential ordering of events. In the psychological world events only precede our feelings and actions, they do not cause them. Again, this is an educational issue from the beginning, but it creates psychological problems and political disasters.

Physical World: To make a chest-of-drawers one starts with raw wood and creates fine boards. There is a need for tools, and hopefully the skill and special understanding about how to use those tools to create a product which is stable. This **process cannot be reversed**. There is a definite change that has occurred. This paradigm is not very useful in the psychological world. In fact, it prevents things from happening quickly. Control is applicable as a concept in the physical world (keeping your car between the lines when driving), but not very useful in psychological context.

In the psychological world the **power words** are choice, selection and movement. It is also helpful in framing accurately to understand we live in a predominately <u>creation world</u> rather than a change world at the psychological level. What I tell myself about the events (my thoughts) in my life determine how I feel and what I do.

It is useful to think of the **psychological world** as a huge <u>smorgasbord</u> on which are <u>all the options</u> that are available to us. It is certainly true certain choices may have place and time qualifications. Generally, we take concepts and ideas off the smorgasbord and they begin to create a product for us, or we put them back on and they stop creating the original product. Think of choosing to drink (alcohol) or choosing not to drink. Drinking/Not drinking is always an available choice but the outcome is different depending on which choice is made. AA reflects awareness of this in speaking only of 'recovering alcoholics' not recovered alcoholics. (The wording is reflective of fact that there is <u>no change</u> only <u>choice</u>.)

Once that concept becomes understood, it is easier to understand the power of choice, selection and movement. All three of these may take place <u>immediately</u>. When John McCain was running for president, I wrote him a letter saying he needed to stop talking about changing things, because everyone knows people who talk about changing things never get anything done. He obviously didn't listen to me. [smile!]

When I ask groups how long they have been trying to change something the answer is generally, "Six months to a lifetime." Nurses at St. Luke's Hospital used to complain to me that my patients got well too quick. One of the first things I would do when seeing a new patient was to get them to stop framing issues in *physical world paradigm* and to re-frame them in *psychological paradigm*. Whether you believe it, or not, it makes a difference in the time necessary to resolve an issue.

Back to blaming!

As mentioned, when we blame, we metaphorically <u>give away our power</u>. Being without power is a <u>very unpleasant experience</u>. The progression from powerlessness> hopelessness> helplessness > resentment > anger > desire to hurt something > (here there is a division) 1) hurt others > marital abuse > child abuse > murder; 2) hurt self > burning > cutting> escape behaviors like > drugs and alcohol > Suicidal ideation>Suicidal attempts > Suicide. How many different psychiatric diagnoses did you count on the path I just laid out? How much political rhetoric is based on the same error? This is the source of the Left's pain and misery!

The slippery slope here is initiated by giving away our power: an act called BLAMNG. Where do we start the repair: in our homes and in our schools. By the time it reaches the psychiatrist's office we are about ten years too late to stop the ascension into a psychiatric disorder.

There are **common errors** contributing to conflicts between people.

- Arguments are almost always *errors in framing*. When we frame issues without blame, they are much more likely to be understood and there is a much greater likelihood of solution.

- The second reason for arguing is the attempt to *steal power*. If we have the power (parent) we should never get into an argument with a child because at best, we can only come out with what we had going into the argument. It pays children to argue with parents who are not aware, because parents will sometime give away power to the child. The left's childish blaming is not likely to prevail when dealing with a President who is focused on problem solving (Trump). Problem solving is the way we keep our power, blaming gives power away.

    There are a lot of inconsistencies in the human interaction. The origin of these issues is frequently not properly and sympathetically appreciated. There is an important interaction between our THOUGHTS, FEELINGS and ACTIONS.

Each influences the other. If I say I want to go to Chicago, but I buy a ticket for Houston there is an inconsistency present between thought and action. If I tell a first date, I really enjoyed the date, but I don't call again there is an inconsistency between feeling and action. I call these conditions internal *inconsistency*--sometimes referred to as spinning one's wheels. If I say I want to go to Chicago, I buy a ticket for Chicago and I am looking happily forward to the trip there is *internal consistency*. Psychopaths present one of the worst forms of internal inconsistency, but they can be spotted quicker if we apply this observation technique.

- *Superficial Communication/Superficial Intimacy*: Individuals are not able to communicate with each other honestly when they feel responsible for the other's feelings. If Jon feels responsible for June's feeling, he will not speak to her in the same way he might if he did not feel that way. This is likewise the danger of politically correct speech. (The Left's excuse for making laws that penalize certain speech is that it hurts people's feelings. This is so unhealthy! It fosters system 1 problems and teaches people to use blame to hurt others. This shows healthy people their leaders do not have a clue.) Both are examples of attempting to control others. If I can tell you how to speak, I can control your life. This can also be understood as a basis for starting an affair: two strangers meet, start talking and because they do not feel responsible for each other they can convey the way they really feel about life and perhaps about each other. They may share more intimate thoughts in an hour than they have shared with spouses in the past year. It feels good, "Let's do this again."

- *Self-Esteem*: We greatly hurt self-esteem when we try to exist in a blame world. Blaming is the act of giving our power away to others. Doing that and expecting something to turn out well is inaccurate about 90% of the time (my estimate). That dismal outcome leads people to feel poorly about themselves and others. Both lead individuals to withdraw from others emotionally and often physically.

- *Dependency*: In relationships, people who blame often experience being too dependent on others. When that occurs, the tendency is for people to attempt to become more independent. This creates two more problems; one is that becoming more independent leads to more emotional isolation and secondly, independence is not the best opposite of dependency--*healthy dependency* is a better choice. The word dependency is used negatively so much it isn't generally recognized that there is a healthy dependency. This is manifested for example in individuals seeking help for mental illnesses or psychological conditions. They are not hopefully coming to have someone do for them what they can and should do for themselves: they are coming to get help for things they either do not recognize how to do or cannot do for themselves.

Control: A fairly large percentage of the population likes to approach issues through a mechanism of control. I see control as mainly an illusion, unless we are dealing with the physical world. Even there it is frequently inaccurately employed. I see it as much more useful to understand that Nature is in control. I tell my patients, "All things are as they should be." In simple words, if we are depressed all the conditions are as they should be to be depressed. If we are happy all the conditions are as they should be to be happy. People who try to control are the same as those trying to change things. If we can control, we can change: if we can change, we can control. People who epitomize the saying, "Insanity is continuing to do the same thing over and over hoping for a different outcome" are the ones believing they can change things. I frequently suggest to my people that if what they are doing is not working, they need to mess up something--choose a different approach. [Jared Kushner] Again, shifting to *a creation world outlook* is frequently more productive than trying to change something.

The use of inaccurate speech contributes to our failure to recognize these pitfalls. We say we are going to "change the oil in our car." What we mean is that I am going to take the old oil out and replace it with new oil. If I were able to change the oil in the car, I would never have to replace it. The alcoholic who comes home and tells his wife, "I am a new man, I no longer drink" needs to understand her husband has not changed, he has merely made a choice not to drink for the moment, and that choice can be reversed in the future.

A huge problem exhibited on the left is a complete misunderstanding of cause and effect and sequential ordering of events. A does not cause B. 1 does not cause 2. These are sequential events. When Trump says something and the left gets mad, upset, overcome, or frightened these are all sequential events and have no cause-and-effect attribute. The left leadership seems to be on a course of misinforming people to the point that it creates criminals and psychiatric illness.

One of the pleasant events in my office since Trump became President is that people can unapologetically say, "Merry Christmas doctor Campbell." Too bad we need a President brave enough to say it to show us the way back to sanity.

WHO TOOK MY MONEY???? [From the internet]

Democrat President Kennedy and Sergeant Shriver were the first ones to misuse the Social Security account. They used Social Security funds to start the Peace Corps. Not the first or last time our money has been taken from American citizens and given to foreign nations.

Things every US citizen should know and remember about Social Security and changes made.

A History Lesson on Your Social Security Card Just in case some of you young whippersnappers (& some older ones) didn't know this. It's easy to check out if you do not believe it.

Be sure and show it to your family and friends. They need a little history lesson on what's what and it doesn't matter whether you are Democrat or Republican.

Facts are Facts.....

Social Security Cards up until the 1980s expressly stated the number and card were not to be used for identification purposes. Since nearly everyone in the United States now has a number, it became convenient to use it anyway and the message, **NOT FOR IDENTIFICATION**, was removed.

Franklin Roosevelt, a Democrat, introduced the Social Security (FICA) Program. **He promised**;

1) That participation in the Program would be completely voluntary. **No longer Voluntary**

2) That the participants would only have to pay 1% of the first $1,400 of their annual Incomes into the Program.
   Now 7.65% on the first $90,000.

3) That the money the participants elected to put into the Program would be deductible from their income for tax purposes each year. **No longer deductible**

4) That the money the participants put into the independent 'Trust Fund' rather than into the general operating fund, and therefore, would only be used to fund the Social Security Retirement Program, and no other Government program.
Under Democrat President Johnson the money was moved to the General Fund and Spent.

5) That the annuity payments to the retirees would never be taxed as income. **Under Democrats Clinton & Gore, up to 85% of your Social Security can be Taxed**

Since many of us have paid into FICA for years and are now receiving a Social Security check every month and then finding that we are getting taxed on 85% of the money we paid to the Federal government to 'put away' -- you may be interested in the following:

Q: Which Political Party took Social Security from the independent 'Trust Fund' and put it into the general fund so that Congress could spend it?
A: It was Lyndon Johnson and the democratically controlled House and Senate.

Q: Which Political Party eliminated the income tax deduction for Social Security (FICA) withholding?
A: The Democrat Party.

Q: Which Political Party started taxing Social Security annuities?
A: The Democratic Party, with Al Gore casting the 'tie-breaking' deciding vote as President of the Senate, while he was Vice President of the U.S.

Q: Which Political Party decided to start giving annuity payments to immigrants?

A: **That's right! Jimmy Carter and the Democratic Party. Immigrants moved into this country, and at age 65, began to receive Social Security payments! The Democratic Party gave these payments to them, even though they never paid a dime into it!**

Then, after violating the original contract (FICA), the Democrats turn around and tell you that the Republicans want to take your Social Security away!

And the worst part about it is uninformed citizens believe it!

If enough people receive this, maybe a seed of awareness will be planted and maybe changes will evolve.

Actions speak louder than bumper stickers.

I have left a lot of blanks Fill them in with the following references:

Book 1
The Russia Hoax: The illicit scheme to clear Hillary Clinton and frame Donald Trump Greg Jarrett

Book 2
The Deep State: How an Army of Bureaucrats Protected Barack Obama and is Working to Destroy the Trump Agenda.
Jason Chaffetz

Book 3
Death of a Nation: Plantation Politics and the Making of the Democratic Party Dinesh O'Souza

Book 4
Idiot America: How Stupidity became a Virtue in the Land of the Free.
Charles P pierce

Book 5
Ship of Fools: How a Selfish Ruling Class is Bringing America to the Brink of Revolution. Tucker Carlson.

Book 6
Hands off my Gun: Defeating the Plot to Disarm America. Dana Loesch

Book 7
The Subtle Art of not Giving a f*ck; A Counterintuitive Approach to Living a Good Life. Mark Manson

Book 8
Liars Leakers and Liberals: The Case against the Anti-Trump Conspiracy Jeanine Pirro

Book 9
The Big Lie: Exposing the Nazi Roots of the American left. Dinesh O'Souza

Book 10
The Religious Mind: Why good people are divided by Politics and Religion Jonathan Haidt

Book 11
The Conservative Sensibility
George F Will

Book 12
Unfreedom of the Press
Mark R. Levin

Book 13
Bullies
Ben Shapiro

Book 14
Witch Hunt: The story of the greatest mass delusion in American Political History
Gregg Jarrett

Book 15
The Parasitic Mind: How infectious ideas are killing common sense
Gad Saad

Book 16
Breaking History: A Whitehouse Memoir Jared Kushner

Book 17
A Republic Under Assault   Tim Fitton, Judicial Watch

Book 18
The Dying Citizen: How progressive elites, Tribalism and Globalization are Destroying the idea of America
Victor Davis Hanson

Book 19
The Real Anthony Fauci: Bill Gates, Big Pharma, and the Global War on Democracy and Public Health
Robert F. Kennedy Jr.

Book 20
Thinking Fast and Slow
Daniel Kahneman

Book 21
Predictably Irrational
Dan Ariely

Book 22
THE RELIGIOUS MIND; Why good people are divided by Politics and Religion Jonathan Haidt

Book 23
THE SUBTLE ART OF NOT GIVING A F*CK
Mark Manson

Book 24
THE RIVER of CONSCIOUSNESS
Oliver Sacks

Book 25
LEVELS OF KNOWING AND EXISTENCE
Harry L. Weinberg

Book 26
LANGUAGE THOUGHT AND ACTION.
Sl. Hayakawa and Alan R. Hayakawa

What recent events should teach us about a left oriented governing body:

The left will continue to weaponize the English language against the right and people in general even more than they have already. E.g., democracy, secure borders, inflation)

The left will continue Obama's attitude of hate for the U.S, its people, it's Pledge of Allegiance, it's National Anthem, it's standing in the world and will attempt to finish what he started: make the U.S. mediocre.

The left will do whatever it takes to get back power and keep it. (Lie, lie, lie and lie)

The left will continue to shift positions quicker than a sand dune in a windstorm and more often as they have no established policy except to do what will destroy the USA.

The left will continue the policy of accusing the right of using every dirty trick they employ.

They will expand "Trump Derangement Syndrome" as they have no insight into how they are creating it. It seems easier for them to continue to destroy rather then rebuild.

The current left elites relish becoming the most dangerous grouping of people in the U.S. Their actions show an intent to destroy freedom of speech and the Constitution of the U.S.

The Left's idea of democracy is complete totalitarianism

By way of the 'deep state' they want to destroy the opposing political party and the will of the people who vote.

The Left's idea of honest elections is that anyone that wants to vote should be allowed to vote as many times as they want as long as they vote democratic.

They will continue to encourage and support some of the most cherished institutes in the U.S. (FBI, CIA, AG, etc.) to become political activists against rivals.

No amount of "lack of evidence" will be enough for them to stop their oppression.

They will continue to show no respect for the law or the people who enforce the law while at the same time supporting fascist groups like antifa and media propaganda organizations. (LPM) that support their destruction of the American way.

They will continue to support news organizations reporting only the stories they feel that meet their agenda and labeling everything else *disinformation.*

They will continue to praise their failure in governing as if it were success.

They will continue to destroy healthy cities across the U.S. by encouraging sanctuary status for illegal aliens. (San Francisco, New York, Seattle, and Chicago are already injured.)

They will ignore the disease prone tent cities they support until the spread of diseases start to affect their own. (San Francisco and Seattle are already suffering.)

They will continue to be supported by the LPM that makes up news against political opponents.

They will enjoy parties of celebration where they can insult members of the opposing party. (I.e., Sara Sanders, Trump)

They will continue to pat themselves on the back for the great reporting they made up over the year. (CNN, MSNBC, etc.)

They will continue to show no insight and will not learn from failure as they believe that only they have the right answers for everything and that they do not error.

They will continue to support the universally flawed system of government: socialism.

They will continue their practice of interference with other countries elections (I.e., Brazil, England)

They will continue to support the idea of 'homoclites' as ideal citizens.

They will continue to oppose discussion and favor propaganda, oppose teaching and favor propagandizing, oppose law and order for mob rule.

They will continue to claim they are supporting democracy while they stymie free speech and support totalitarianism.

They will continue the practice of rewarding and protecting non-citizens and punishing and debasing citizens.

They will continue their effort to destroy the protection of the check and balance system in our government.

They will more aggressively determine which laws are ok to ignore and which to enforce.

The elected left will continue going outside of chambers to the streets to lash out against those who oppose them and the bills they have produced.

The left will continue to talk about being compassionate, but will direct all actions away from citizens of the U.S.

The left will seek, but at the same time degrade, any office, or holder of an office, held by someone not of their party.

The LPM will spend a lot more (if that is possible) time on things like "taking off shoes."

They will likely give out "Eric Holder awards" to the person or group best at "kicking them when they are down."

New York will have a huge display in Time Square showing when the left has gotten back enough power that they no longer need to be angry and violent. (H.R. Clinton will be the score keeper.)

They will establish new writing awards for who can destroy the most people with one journal article.

The LPM will establish a world series for the most outlandish story told that people believed.

There will be new awards for "Height of Hypocrisy."

They will require Textbooks to eliminate the words they do not like: him, her, she, illegal alien, man, manhole, riot, electoral college, rural America, mobs Trump. Etc.

They will continue to distort the understanding of the First Amendment to mean they, the LPM, can make up and say whatever they want, but to be criticized for distortions will be made unconstitutional and will create a "constitutional crisis."

They will continue to test peoples' credulity by keeping some absurd story in front of people for the purpose of dividing the country and selling print.

They will continue to believe that night-n-day shifts in what they report will not be noticed by the public, because all the LPMs shift rhetoric at the same time making it appear they have always had that point of view.

The left will remain unable to recognize prejudice and conflict of interest.

Whenever the left controlled congress has a conflict with the President of a different party, they will 'judge' that they are in the right and the President is in the wrong, so he/she must be impeached for "obstructing congress."

Given that the left is perfectly happy with judges appointed by Obama blocking actions a conservative President wants at almost every turn, they will attempt to run the executive branch of the government themselves through liberal judge appointments. Challenges to their rule will be "obstruction."

The left will continue the policy of ignoring fairness. [I.e., They spent nearly three years supporting a special counsel investigation of Trump where he released thousands of documents and allowed his staff to participate without restraint and be questioned for hours by the special counsel. He did not assert executive privilege once through the entire investigation. After millions of dollars (Estimated from 25 to 42 million--nineteen left supporting lawyers plus 40 FBI agents) and hundreds of hours of cooperation with the special counsel the congress wanted to start another investigation because the special counsel did not find a crime that would warrant impeachment.]

They will continue the operational belief and contingency that "If you haven't done wrong," you should agree to and want more investigations, except when it applies to a democrat.

They will continue the cloaked hypocrisy that "no one is above the law" – unless your name is Biden, Clinton, Obama, or Holder.

To protect its own, a left controlled Congress will attempt to block investigations related to the sons of Biden (president) and Nancy Pelosi's (speaker of the house) working for companies in China or the Ukraine.

They will continue to block a conservative exploring corruption on the part of the left by insisting any investigation is a violation and is being done for personal benefit, but at the same time they completely disavow any personal benefit when they do the same thing.

They will continue to plead "not guilty' while they try to prevent a look at the use of a foreign government to support a democratic contender for president. (Christopher Steel dossier.)

If you are unpopular with the left, or your views are unpopular, expect the left to turn its back on you and shun or attack you as it has the Trump administration and family, and his supporters.

If you dare to stick up for yourself, you will be accused of obstruction of justice.

If your policies are not liked, expect that you will be accused of treason and bribery based on someone else's *presumptions*.

People who may support you or your perspective can look forward to being ruined financially, and personally by the attacks against them.

The law will only support one perspective and if it is not yours you can expect midnight raids on your home with guns drawn, helicopters flying overhead, boats at your back door and TV cameras running all because you have been accused of lying. An alternative is to be accosted in the airport, put in shackles and paraded through the crowd to have a point made.

You can expect that your comments will be reworked, and then spread over the news outlets over and over as if they were yours.

After the news repeats over and over their ill-conceived comments they will attack you again for saying those things in front of the children watching their program at the times they choose.

You can expect that if your policies are not liked the fascist acting mobs will be ready to attack you without protection from the police who will have been told it is ok not to protect your rights.

Expect that your guns will be taken away, so you may not protect yourself. In the name of safety and to protect the environment you will eventually have to give up your swimming pools, boats, bikes and roller blades. Possibly hard toed shoes (they all kill more people than the rifles the left now wants to confiscate).

You will be encouraged to blame others for your misfortunes by the educational institutes.

The government, not your doctor, having full management over your medical treatment will decide what medicines you will be entitled to receive, and which programs you must purchase whether you deem them necessary or not.

The democrat government will establish a Chinese style grading system to judge how well you are complying with their demands

Men will be told they have no say in government or anything else when opposed by a woman.

Our money will be confiscated and we will be forced to use credit cards for any purchase so big government can follow every detail of your life.

Men and women will enjoy the company of a new species of humans every few months

Religion will be considered a nuisance and outlawed because it gives people comfort.

If you are on the wrong side of an argument expect to be subjected to no privacy and opinions substituted as facts at your trial.

You will no longer be assumed innocent until proven guilty, but you will be held to the new standard of having to prove your innocence if you are not a democrat.

If you are a Republican President, each time the democratic power-to-be does not like what you do, you can look forward to being impeachment.

If you are not on the democrat's side of power, you may not investigate corruption.

Property will slowly be taken from you over time and you will receive only what the power-to-be says you may have. (Looks like this will start with your salary and extend to your other possessions.)

There will, over time, become more and more words you may not say without being fined. The government will begin to impose penalties on certain thoughts. They have already demonstrated that they, without a doubt, know what people are thinking and what their intentions are, so that will be a logical next step: creation of the Thought Police.

When the left congress is unable to get cooperation for its political agenda from a non-democrat President, it will simply impeach him. If they have their way there will never again be a republican president to impeach.

When the left is unable to find a reason (like breaking the law) to impeach a President not doing their bidding they will make up new standards of impeachment like "standing up to congress" and "resisting the political agenda of the majority members of congress."

Whenever the democratic majority in congress does not like the policies of a non-democrat President, they will declare a "state of emergency and a national security breach" and will launch years of investigation (in the name of oversight) along with their media friends to destroy the President.

Then as Hilary Clinton indicated when they get power back, they will be "less violent."

Whenever the democratic party believes they cannot win the general election with the current constitutional rules they will attempt to abolish the electoral college, will try to expand the Supreme Court by adding more democrats to the court (tried by F.D.R.) or they will open the gates and encourage illegal immigrants to vote. Oh, actually they are already doing all that. Sorry.

They will fight to bring into the U.S. as many low wage immigrants as possible to keep Americans from getting higher wages and a better lifestyle, all the time pretending they are supporting Americans by making them dependent on the government for a livelihood (putting and keeping more people on welfare).

They will continue to support the protectionist elements of labor unions to the detriment of non-union workers, because it gives them more political clout.

The new democratic policies will be for every union to obey the government as the Teacher's Union has done (at the expense of our kid's education).

The Left Academic Establishment (LAE) seems to support the promotion of the left propaganda machine's (LPM) practice of making the news rather than reporting it. The LPM makes up the news and then gives themselves awards for excellent fabrications. Common sense might suggest their reasoning needs some work; but, remember Obama was awarded the Nobel Peace Prize apparently for getting elected. (Maybe his contributing billions of American dollars to the world's largest terrorist regime was not a part of their consideration.)

The LAE shares the idea with the left that there should be no debate about issues but only acceptance of the liberal points of view. Debate will continue to be discouraged on liberal college campuses.

Grades in school will continue to be lowered because students will not follow the left party line. (New York families have reportedly been leaving the city because they feel teachers are propagandizing rather than teaching children. This point of view might be supported by the global ranking of basic educational skills of U.S. students. Not good!)

The LAE will continue wanting to hold speakers at college functions (if on the right) responsible for the expenses incurred for protecting them from the violence that is a product of what they are taught by the teachers at the institution.

The LAE will continue to promote the concept that it is someone other than themselves who are responsible for the animosity students feel for conservative points of view.

There will be increased disregard for the concept of self-accountability on the left.

The LAE disingenuously promotes the protection of the poor students who are too traumatized to deal with a republican being elected President, but at the same time encourage indirectly and deliberately students to riot against conservative speakers.

The LAE will continue to promote free speech only when the speech promotes liberal points of view.

The LAE will continue to strongly promote the concept of the judicial branch of government making laws through their rulings.

The LAE will build power by promoting the concept that left appointed judges should be able to overrule elected officials of the government whenever they do not like the conservative policy of the elected individual.

The LAE will continue to work at getting rid of the constitution of the U.S. because it does not allow the rapid changes proposed by the left. (The mechanism for governing laid out by our founders was intentionally stacked against rapid changes in government. It was engineered to encourage incremental changes.)

The left once entrenched in power will make a 2-day work week in Congress because more time might allow more dissention and besides the deep state runs everything anyway.

The LAE is continually cultivating the people of the U.S. to risk destruction so they can experiment with socialism, a form of governance that has failed repeatedly across the globe.

The LAE is supportive of the practice by the left of choosing which laws should be followed and which may simply be ignored.

The LAE will continue supporting the idea that governments should be able to dictate what health insurance you must buy, what words you must not use, what clothes you are not allowed to wear, who you should allow into your country, who should or should not be charged with a crime, who should be labeled as a male or female in sports activities, and that it is perfectly fine for local governments to support theft (by not charging someone if the stolen property is less than 750 dollars).

The LAE continue its smugness with the rich buying the election of members to congress and senate as well as to buying admittance to the educational institutions of their choice.

The LAE supports charging students more for less education.

The government will support working men and women paying tuition to college for students who will come out of college making much more money than they do.

The LAE supports the government giving schools large amounts of money while they establish billion-dollar endowments.

The LAE seems to be comfortable with charging huge tuitions but not sharing the risk of students not getting employed after the completion of their education. (Carson Tucker) This, in turn, encourages students to support free education promises by the left, with the apparent lack of understanding that free means they will pay in a different manner.

The LAE seems unworried about encouraging students to blame others to manage issues.

The LAE supports the totally unsupportable position that there are no differences between the sexes. They want to rewrite the concept of what it is to be a male or female. At the same time, they adhere to terms like "toxic masculinity" and other demeaning ways to define the male.

The LAE to get the vote of the transgendered community will remain incapable of understanding the unfairness of genetic males competing with genetic females in sports after the male has defined himself as preferring the female identity.

The LAE will continue to ignore the history regarding capitalism over socialism.

The LAE will continue to ignore the difference between sequential ordering of events and cause and effect events because this way of thinking supports in part the belief in mind reading capabilities.

The LAE will continue to distort cause and effect; misunderstanding simple associations like people kill people (themselves and others).

The LAE will continue supporting the concept that if the left calls it a crime it must be a crime, or if the left declares it is unconstitutional it must be so.

Removing the instruments used by different people to kill self or others will mean getting rid of cars, pools, knives, hammers, shoes, all types of poison materials, tall buildings, bridges, and hands.

The LAE will continue to join the left in a desire to provide for foreign illegal aliens' needs over those of U.S. citizens.

The neglect of U.S. citizens will continue to be made worse by not following federal laws, developing more sanctuary cities, encouraging tent-city developments in the heart of cities, encouraging more drugs to enter the country, and giving more support and help in the abuse of drugs.

The LAE sides with the left's desire to debase the legal system and those who are tasked with enforcing the laws and they provide one-sided bias in favor of criminals and not citizens.

The LAE will continue to endorse the 'black lives matter' idea and condemn those who believe that all lives matter as racists.

The LAE will continue to support ideas like open borders where anyone who wants can come into the country and use up our resources and compete with lower income Americans to keep wages down.

Criminality will be further encouraged by laws declaring not only that people can steal up to 750 dollars from merchants without worry of being arrested, but the hungry can merely go in and get what they want off shelves as long as they stay below the 750-dollar amount. The amount they can freely steal will likely increase over time.

The left will begin to discourage the sale of locks and security cameras.

The LAE will likely contribute to the number of books declared as disinformation or racist a will encourage their burning.

The educational institutes on the left will continue to support homeless people being able to pitch a tent in town, to urinate on the streets when no facility is available, to spread diseases without check, and break drug laws without consequences when and wherever they wish.

The LAE will continue compassion for alien drug dealers, murderers, sex traffickers, drug cartels, antifa, and MS-13 over Americans.

The LAE believes children and children's opinions should be used to champion social goals when they agree with the left's talking points, and that they can be attacked openly when they have opinions different from the left (Nick Sandmann).

The LAE will offer classes supporting attacks on employees of conservative presidents.

The LAE will stand with law non-enforcement when conservatives are being attacked.

The LAE will more actively support getting rid of the flag, the pledge, and the national anthem. They still want the government to keep funding them, however.

The LAE seems to support the idea of **accusation** first and apology later.

The LAE is complicit but will become more assertive about teaching that victims of crimes are not first responders, that people should not take self-accountability for actions, should not learn the difference between sequential ordering and cause and effect events, and should perfect the ability to be mind-readers.

The LAE will encourage propagandizing over open debate and over actually teaching.

The LAE will aggressively support accumulation of large salaries for teachers without accountability for getting graduates good jobs.

The LAE will spend its time rewriting and recreating history rather than reporting it.

The left academic establishment will continue to be an obstacle to the development of knowledge and learning how to evaluate perspectives and come to conclusions, since only one point of view will be presented.

Psychiatrists will likely support the left because in their mind they cannot separate the issues of needy and mentally ill.

Psychiatry will ignore the lessons from Galen of Pergamum, Eli Metchnikoff, or Linus Pauling and put one persons (Fauci) point of view before equally or better qualified individuals.

Psychiatry will continue looking for the cause of anger in each diagnosis

Psychiatrists will ignore the obvious vulnerability to the field of medicine of having an autocratic system where one person (Fauci) determines the placement of millions of dollars of research funding --a really short-sighted arrangement in a democracy.

Psychiatry will lose track of individuals as it tries to solve all the social inequities in life.

There will be new specialties of psychiatry created to look at the dynamics of why there is resistance by some psychiatrists to lean to the left.

Psychiatry will become increasingly divided along political affiliations lines.

In the attempt to be fair, psychiatrists will continue to overly identify with the plight of patients.

There will be increasing resistance to holding patients responsible for their own conditions in life and the decisions they make.

Psychiatrists will give up the concept that keeping parents healthy is better for the children, because doing so will have a negative political connotation.

Psychiatrists will avoid debate on what political policies support behaviors that weaken the family (not following laws if you don't like them, learning how to have an abortion without telling your parent, cheating to get into the college of your choice, and how it is ok to steal if it only amounts to 750 dollars.) but will never come to a conclusion because the answer would be politically incorrect.

Psychiatry will continue to see guns as the cause of homicides and suicide instead of looking at the contribution of blaming, disrespect and inaccurate speech.

Psychiatrists will likely agree college should be free as it helps make everyone more equal.

Psychoanalysts will become even more hostile to psychiatrists using therapies that help people quicker and definitely will desire to disbar any psychiatrist teaching a patient how to live better. Psychoanalysts will petition insurances not to pay for therapies if patients are being taught something during sessions.

Being responsible for other's feelings and making others responsible for your feeling will become a point of separation in residency programs.

Psychiatrists will continue to struggle with the cause of violence because the answer will not be politically correct.

Psychiatrists will continue to avoid looking at actual psychiatric issues in the political world that should be addressed such as unfairness and prejudice. [These concepts have nothing to do with politics they have to do with reasoning.]

Psychiatrists will continue to confuse politics and mental health.

Psychiatrists will be informed by organization like the APA, that if they do not go along with the democratic agenda on things like Covid 19 immunizations they will be charged with ethical violations for not following the government's faulty reasoning. Excuse me, did I say that wrong? Perhaps not.

Psychiatry will put its resources into making everyone wok instead of looking at :1. How the family is being destroyed by encouraging children to report their parents to authorities if they are too involved in their schooling or ask too many questions. 2. How the government is attempting to sabotage parents' rights to sustain family values. 3. How the government is supportive of abortion that kills far more black babies than white babies (which is what the founder of planned parenthood wanted) while, at the same time claiming and at the same time trying, to make it look like they are pro black families. 4. How there is complete disregard for equality in the law along political lines. 5. How the rule of *do no harm* is dominated by the rule of *do what the government tells you to do* regardless of outcome. 6. How it is extremely harmful to people, (parents, children, everyone) when topics are not allowed to be debated (climate change, rigged elections, unfair administration of the law, loss of jobs because of political differences, etc.). 7. How shutting down medical opinions about the treatment of Covid 19 (as disinformation) may have caused hundreds, possibly thousands of lives, over the past 2 years. 8. How setting laws that allow people to steal up to $750.00 without considering it a crime is a major rule violation in boundary issues and is bad for family and country. It does not help raising of children either. No boundaries. 9. How providing "safe places in colleges for students to go if the wrong president is elected" is not only among the more stupid ideas around but is an indicator that our college students are not being taught basic coping skills. 10. How one of the most liberal organizations, and in my opinion, least prejudicial (non-racist) organizations I have ever belong to buys into Marxist concepts like "black lives matter." 11. How biological males are not females and women should not be forced to compete with them in sports regardless of what they call themselves. 12. How much damage there is to children over the ambiguity of gender? 13. How has the gender of a person all of a sudden become the priority of the educational system? Is this not a family/medical issue? Teachers have always been good role models for children. Is this current trend of 'sexually oriented teacher guides' helping or harming children? Personally, I think teachers should teach, doctors should practice their branch of medicine and parents should raise their children. 14. How is it that psychiatry does not see a social issue when every legal outcome is tied/predictable according to the political party who appointed the judge-a very clear indication people see the judicial system as political in its determination. 15. How is it that psychiatry is not more outspoken about the direct attempt by the left to diminish or destroy the family unit? 16. How is it that psychiatry does not have anything to say about the obvious disparity in the way the law is used against republicans and democrats? 16. How is it that psychiatry is not outspoken about the 10 million illegal aliens invading the U.S and the effect it is having on our educational and social systems.? 17. How is it that psychiatry is not expressing an opinion about the negative effect of homeless people lining the way to our children's schools? 18. How is psychiatry not addressing the psychological impact of laws allowing people to steal, up to a certain amount, before they can be arrested for stealing? 18. How is it that psychiatry is not concerned about 500,000 possible deaths from Covid 19 related to the deliberate withholding of cheap treatments (shown to be effective in treating virus diseases) for hugely expensive immunizations that were known to have no treatment benefit and potential lethal effects. Of course, there is also the fact that the person insisting on not giving the treatments was also making a lot of money from the immunization process. 20 -200. Etc.

The biggest issue in academia, and psychiatry is the total and complete lack of respect the left has for members of the American family on the right.

I love America and the American People on either the Left or the Right. Please **help** *establish a conversation free of NONSENSE!*

PS: I asked my friend and liberal in California to tell me where he thought the left was headed. His response was essentially that I was being too negative about the leaders on the left. When I started writing this book, I asked for his involvement again; I offered to include comments he wanted to make about what I had said if it was simply not a propaganda statement. His answer was that he did not want to debate me. For a second time my request for information or dialogue was ignored, not because of what I had requested, but obviously for some other reason. I certainly was not asking for a debate. I have not heard back from a second friend and liberal I sent a copy of what I had written to for comments. (His wife was kind enough to tell me he was not interested in participating.)

As someone who has always been very proud of the United States I am deeply saddened by the total lack of civility from the left toward the office of the President and to President Trump himself and to the people who do not agree with them. This lack of civility is manifested by the democratic congress, by the LPM, and by the citizens who are willing to do Maxine Waters dictum to "Get in their faces and tell them they are not wanted." I am appalled by schools of higher education attempting to block free speech (speech not agreeing with their point of view). I am disgusted by the division and fear the left has created by the unrelenting attacks on the average person. I am disappointed by the left's disregard for the citizens of the United States **in favor of** illegal immigrants. I am disheartened by the constant lying and the way the left tries to frame me: I am not deplorable, I am not anti legal immigration, I am not a racist, I am not a misogynist, I am not a hypocrite, I am not a white supremacist, I do not want a border on the South of the United States to keep people of color out of the country—I want it for security from drugs and to keep thousands of people from thinking they can come into the country without an invitation, I did not like Obama, but I did not attack the Presidency of the U.S. I do have concerns that the running of the country not be turned over to people who are not in this country legally (illegal voting). I have concerns that the needy citizens of this country have not, and are not, being cared for appropriately. I find it sickening when the LPM moderators seem so gleeful that Trump might have done something wrong, and so unwilling to report what he is doing to help the country. I sincerely hope there are others like me who want the United States to stay strong and not to be put up for sale to the highest bidders. (It is believed by many that the Biden family has received millions of dollars from China for only they know what). The movie stars (supremacist) on the left project the worst example society have to offer. President Trump demonstrated courage and steadfastness in the face of unearned criticism on the left. He was a model for those being bullied. He pushed through the left's hopes for his failure and did the best job he could given the relentless attack on him, his family and his political supporters. The left spent a lot of energy and money attacking President Trump and bullying his supporters. Bullies are basically cowards at heart, and they are not comfortable with open discussions. They want power (often from basement enquiries) and they don't care who they must destroy to get it.

When I started writing this section, I thought I was going a little overboard but since the Biden Regime these projections seem to be coming true.

Actions for the right to consider

1. Immediately stop financially supporting schools that restricts free speech and certainly any with endowments greater than a billion dollars.
2. Stop supporting the overthrow of conservative governments in other countries.
3. Stop sending money and support to countries who profess a desire to destroy our country or acts in a way that does harm to our country.

4. Educators and psychiatrists should point out NONSENE in speech. There is no way to have a discussion or solve problems with people who talk nonsense.
5. Educators and psychiatrists should realize good people on the left may not understand the ramifications of what the left is suggesting. The right needs to find better communication systems. Since the left controls the news outlets in paper and a majority of those in TV they must find other ways to communicate their visions.
6. Educators and psychiatrists need to find some way to push back on constant propaganda from the left. If the LPM stopped talking NONSENSE, they would be on the air about four hours a day.
7. Educators and psychiatrists need to accept If people are told something over and over, they will begin to believe it even when it is not true.
8. A country that can build a computer to predict weather changes and stock movements surely can develop a lie detector that works. Do it! Why has it not been done already? Or has it? Is everyone afraid of the truth? Just because there has been improvement in the weather predictions a few weeks ahead does not mean there is technology to accurately predict weather for the next 10 years or 100 years.
9. Educators and psychiatrists need to recognize anger is synonymous blaming!
10. Educators and psychiatrists should recognize that blaming has probably been at the root of more deaths than diseases.
11. Educators and psychiatrists need to confront nonsense speech.
12. Everyone needs to return to a state of respect for free speech and open discussion.
13. Everyone should recognize and deal with deaths from guns in the same manner deaths are dealt with from auto accidents, drownings, overdoses, etc. If they did that there would no longer be an attack on the NRA which provides education and gun safety classes all over the U.S.

14. Blaming the NRA for gun problems is like blaming AAA for auto accidents.
15. The NRA should include a statement about decreasing or attempting to eliminate accidents in their policy statement.
16. Murder needs to be understood as either an act of disrespect or anger. Both can be addressed, but not eradicated, by teaching people to stay out of blaming. Some people kill because they are mean!
17. Suicide needs to be understood as the culmination of the helplessness generated by a life of blaming. Blaming leads to a state of powerlessness. A sense of powerlessness is an awful experience: hopelessness, helplessness, frustration and anger are additional products.
18. It would be nice if the Left gave up identity politics and went back to addressing problems with some level of common sense.
19. Recognizing anger is inseparable from blaming and constitutes nonsense speech and thinking could help the world immensely.
20. Recognize it is necessary to frame life's experiences accurately to be free of blame/anger.
21. Anger frequently leads to harm of self or other (suicide and homicide)
22. Blaming is giving away our power to an event. It makes me …
23. The left should be careful about using moralistic arguments as it suggests something important existed before government: a conservative point of view.
24. Teachers do a good job of teaching children how to speak correctly, but they need to pick up their game and teach children how to speak accurately as well.
25. It would be helpful if the left understood the difference between sequential ordering of events and cause and effect events.
26. It would be helpful if the left were able to recognize the difference between wishes ("truth") and facts.

27. It would help if the left recognized they do not have the power of mind reading. They continuously assert motivation on others that is not supported.
28. The new attack (new because it was never intended by the constitution that elected judges should be co-executives with the President) by appointed judges on the executive branch of our government needs the ability for an immediate fix [Perhaps a priority referral to the Supreme court]. This might also stop the need for the opposing branch of government to try and settle policy differences through an impeachment.
29. Perhaps schools should not be charging more for tuition than an average student can pay back on the salary generated by the education that is provided within 5 years.
30. Biological women should refuse to compete in sports with biological transgendered men. The game is stacked against them. Taking a stand is the only method likely to be heard by the religion of wok.
31. Removing the instruments used by different people to kill self or others would mean getting rid of cars, pools, knives, hammers, shoes, all types of poison materials, tall buildings, bridges, and hands.
32. A more practical solution to homicide and suicide might be to help people learn to respect others and stay out of blame (nearly the same thing).
33. Perhaps the LAE should pay more attention to one of their graduates (Dula) and promote eliminating nonsense in speech. The silence that would ensue would be music to our ears.
34. Teaching people how to recognize what they have responsibility for and what they can do something about removes conflicts people create that turn into psychiatric diagnosis.
35. If there is an honest desire to get rid of drug abuse in the U.S. there must be a step in the so far avoided area of charging the users a fine. Sanity would say that there would be less drug

deaths if the use of drugs illegally had some cost for the users, besides dying.

36. Most states do not yet support assisted suicide. It is still illegal in others. Why are sellers of drugs that cause deaths not prosecuted for assisting in cases of death? Medical doctors are not even allowed to pass out drugs without special licenses. They would surely go to jail if they acted in the same manner as drug dealers.

37. Cities wanting to clean up drug deaths should establish geographical areas within the city, identify individuals selling drugs in those areas, and on the death of a person within that area it should trigger the prosecution of every drug dealer in that area. If the law does not yet allow that, change the law.

38. The right should consider using billboards to assert the basic beliefs and principles of conservativism. They might reach more people.

39. More education needs to be done to help the black communities understand that aggressive policing helps save their lives. If I were black living in a metropolitan city with huge death tolls, I would support "stop and frisk." It worked!

40. It does seem to be time to look at how to make governing more representative for the people. It should not be the lobbyist who determine the laws of the U.S. nor should the rich be able to buy elections. Personally I support getting rid of lobbyists completely or capping their salaries to the average income of a person in the U.S.

41. My psychiatric mentor at UCLA and at least a one-time friend would not allow me to park in front of his house because I had a bumper sticker supporting a republican on my car. How can a teaching psychiatrist in a leading psychiatric program not realize how unhealthy that act was? How could a group of psychiatrists and psychologists write a book declaring half the population of the United States was wrong to elect a president the group concluded (violating their own society's rules) without doing a personal evaluation, was a narcissist with grandiosity

who would destroy the U.S. They would appear to need to get rid of the mirror they look at the world through. More interaction, more conversations seem to be necessary.

42. It is reasonable for psychiatrists not to want patients to be harmed by anything (guns included). What I do not find reasonable is for them to go outside the field for solutions. I think the study that should be supported is not one on guns but on blame/anger as causes for the behavior of killing self and others. This would be in the preview of psychiatry. It might add something of importance to the field. The solution and cure would have to be handed over primarily to the teachers. That might keep it from happening for years.

43. Some German psychiatrists were complicit with Hitler's abuse of Jews. Psychiatry in the United States should be cautious not to contribute to the division of people in the United States, but we should use the skills we learned to help people reason with sanity.

44. I was taught at Michael Reese by Dr. Reid that to fight segregation (like that in our congress) people had to interact with each other at a personal level. We understand as well as any group that when good people do not stand up to bad ideas the end is disastrous. Jewish psychiatrists might appropriately understand this even more clearly than others. The Senate and House of Representatives needs to integrate.

45. Personally, I would have been fine never being involved with politics, but when politics create such an obvious frontal attack by use of things like prejudice, unfairness, destruction of the integrity of families, destruction of the concept of self-defense, failure of equality under the law, judgments without facts, "truth" over facts, opinion over facts, women over men, black and brown over everything (identity politics over sound judgment) it seems like a time to speak out in favor of sanity.

46. Psychiatrists should be able to see when policies are destroying the fabric of reason. We should take to heart the multiple

examples of the derangement in thinking that surrounds us (The Death of Common Sense by Philip K. Howard is a great starting place.).

47. **School organizations serous about stopping violent behavior on campus would simply have a rule that if you interfere with free speech on campus, you will be expelled. [Out of control behavior over.]**
48. Billionaires like Soros, Bill Gates, Jeff Bezos and Mark Zukerberg should not be able to buy elections through their various schemes of contributions. Our government should stop funding Soros associated organizations which in turn attempt to destroy **our** democracy.
49. Term limits seem like a long overdue consideration for our legislative branch of governance. Perhaps there should also be term limits for the people making up the deep state since, is seems clear, they are the one's actually structuring our laws after something has been passed by the elected members of house and senate.
50. It seems like there should be an automatic investigation done on any member of congress that leaves that a gust branch more than four times richer than they were when they were elected.

Definition of words as used by the left:

Abortion:
- considered an appropriate means of birth control
- to be at the unfettered choice of the mother as to when it is appropriate
- a behavior that should not be restricted by court, spouse, or God
- a form of birth control that everyone should want to pay for others to have
- freedom to kill a fetus whenever the fetus is inconvenient up to the time of birth.

- a form of birth control more frequently used by non-white ladies (I am not certain if any men have had abortions yet. I guess under democratic belief that men can get pregnant it is only a matter of time.)
- promoted by the left as a women's health issue
- Pregnancy is not seen as a normal condition supporting the continuation of the race

Administrative state [Ballotpedia]:
- "refers to federal executive branch agencies collectively and routinely wielding powers that exceed statutory authority and elude accountability, including the exercise of judicial and legislative functions in violation of the U.S. Constitution's principles of separation of powers."
- the group designated by the congress to fill in all the blanks in created legislation, so congress does not have to work more than three days a week (Tuesday through Thursday) --apparently supported by the left governance.

Antifa:
- gangs dressed in black hoods and clothing supported by democrats and CNN claiming to be antifascist that attack cars, and schools with bats and fire-bombs.
- a group attacking conservatives, news reporters on the right and conservative sites using fascist tactics
- a fascist like mob supported and protected by democrats

Anti-Trump:
- heroes of the left
- academics
- MSNBC, CBS, New York Times, Newsweek, HuffPost, Washington Post, ABC, NBC, CNN etc.

CNN:
- left propaganda machine currently raising money for the fascist group known as Antifa

Conservative:
- someone who believes the 'outdated' Constitution of the U.S. is a useful instrument of government
- someone who believes all rights are not the sole gift of the government
- someone with the audacity to see themselves as responsible for their own well being
- people supporting 'those old' traditional values: free speech, love of country, community, and family.
- people who do not like abrupt major changes in government policies
- people thinking that telling the truth is a positive characteristic
- people believing that truth has something to do with facts and not just feelings
- people believing that bigger government is not always better
- people described as 'deplorables' by last presidential contender (Clinton) on the left and neo fascists by the current president (Biden).
- smelly Walmart people according to some high-ranking FBI leaders
- anti-constitution according to the left
- anti-democracy according to the left

Deep State:
- also known as administrative state
- the people behind the scenes of our government who have immense power over how legislation is actually framed and executed

Elite democrats:
- high minded and superior beings with special powers of foresight and mind reading ability.
- unfalteringly assert exactly what opponents are thinking (mind-readers)
- developers of new math: 'everything is free'
- unlimited ability to find projects that will cost billions/trillions of dollars
- have unlimited capability to deny a roll in what they create
- have uncanny ability to blame others for crises of their making
- believe in violent verbal and physical attacks on political opponents
- believe destroying others is ok when marching to power
- support creating a socialist government

Fact Checker:
- another left supporting group helping to weaponized the language and promote arguments, frequently with no facts involved at all. "Immoral wall"

Fake news:
- according to the LPM and the left it is accurate news not accepted by the right
- as used by the right it is news that is inaccurate or deliberately fake to foster a political agenda

Free **medical care for all:**
- 'all' here means illegal immigrants
- 'free' here means an estimated "tens of trillions (25-30 T) of dollars over a decade' [New York Times] Bernie Sanders says his bill "would save 5.1 T" ??
- Free college is estimated to cost 70 Billion dollars a year. Estimated cost of the program is 67% of the 70 billion. Taxpayers (working people) would be paying the bill so those

with higher educations who will eventually be making more money in general will not be bothered by the payback.

Government:
- the left wants larger government
- the entity capable of telling people what should make them happy
- the entity given the ok to make laws if the President is a democrat and not if they are republican.
- the entity we should want to give all our money to

Hate terms (terms used by the left not to identify or reveal hate but to assign hate and create division in the country; "weaponized words"): racist, misogynist, xenophobe, toxic masculinity, male, fascist, homophobe, anti-immigration, nationalist, border supporters, etc.

Impeachment:
- fall back plan for losing the election
- The absence of a crime is not important
- the President resisting being lynched is seen as obstruction

Inconvenient truth
- the counter label for the democrats *disinformation* claims.
- An apparent lapse on the left is the understanding that if the country is forced to expend all its resources to care for the needy there comes a point when there are no resources and there is no country.

Language:
- mechanism to control people: if you can tell people what to say you can control them
- 'politically correct' speech is speech designed to force people to see things a certain way
- the left has successfully 'weaponized' speech against the right. Examples; rifles become "assault weapons" even though they

are used as weapons less often than knives, hammers and boots; "racist" becomes a word to beat up on people disagreeing with the left's agenda having nothing to do with race; "bullies" we are told is a term that cannot be used to describe the men in black who go around beating up reporters and conservatives; use the right pronoun or get fined in Calif.; recognize 'toxic masculinity' by getting rid of the 'man' in *man*hole, wo*man*, *Man*chester, *Man*hattan, etc.; not wanting illegal aliens becomes 'hates Mexicans' and "is a racist"; wanting NATO members to pay a fair share becomes 'hates our friends around the world;" believing people who hate the U.S and Israel should not be in the U.S. Congress becomes "racist;" believing a working relationship with countries like Russia and North Korea is good for the U.S. becomes "Putin's buddy" and a "lover of dictators;" being in favor of border security becomes one is a "racist, immoral, hates Mexicans, is caging kids, is taking kids from families (statistics show 30 percent of kids coming across the border did not come with family members-never reported on by the left-these kids are being exploited by the left-and when they are not immediately united with a family member (no family came with them) the left screams about how they are being separated from family-just another lie)

Laws:
- a rule of behavior seen as binding except by the left
- guidance created by the legislative branch of the government felt to be optional by the left
- inconvenient to the left unless they created it
- optional to the left if they do not like it
- enforceable only when desired by the left
- selective enforcement seen as appropriate by the left
- frequently ignored by the left
- distorted to mean whatever the left wants it to mean.

Leak free investigation:
- Mueller's claim about his investigation: There were only 25 leaks (good news) but they all put the President in a bad light (interesting!).

Left Propaganda Machines (LPM):
- CNN, MSNBC, ABC, NBC, CBS, etc.
- Anti-Trump in 95+ percent of their reporting

Liar:
- anyone who does not agree with the left's propaganda
- white republican men regardless of what they say
- term designed as a media attack on republicans (especially white republican men) whenever they oppose the LPM
- one of the over used weaponized words that is supposed to get people to support the left (same category as racist, misogynist, conservative, xenophobe, white nationalist, assault weapon supporter, family separator, immoral border seeker, Trump supporters, anti-sanctuary city deplorables, Walmart Shoppers, etc.) Typically, mobilized every election year but in this administration used daily. [meaningless as used by the left]
- among the hate terms used by the left to divide the country.
- Make America Great Again (MAGA) is seen as a lie "America was never great" according to the left.
- according to the left MAGA is racist, MAGA is neo fascist, greatest threat to our constitution, more of a tragedy then WWII, more of a disaster then Pearl Harbor, [Obviously, they do not want America to be America or to be great.]
- according to the left making America great again is going back in time 30 years [Another look in the mirror perhaps]
- is to inappropriately recognize the power of our history, the progress we have made toward issues and to reclaim the apologetic position on the stage of the world created by the last Obama administration

Misogynist:
- a person who criticizes a democratic woman
- supersedes justification for the statement or comment
- defines men in general
- a person who believes the female sex is a biological phenomenon and not a choice

MS13:
- an invasive criminal group from South America encouraged by open borders and favored over citizens by Nancy Pelosi
- defended by Nancy Pelosi as humans who should not be criticized by Trump
- Individuals and groups preferring to kill others with knifes or machetes who Nancy Pelosi sticks up for when criticized by conservatives.

Open Borders:
- goal of the left, no restriction to entry to the U.S.,
- source of disease, drugs, and death for Americans
- invitation to break the laws of immigration in the U.S
- the left's only hope for replacement voters lost because of their socialist agenda
- supported by businesses wanting cheap labor and low wages & to continue democratic power

Politically correct:
- lefts attempt to control speech
- a Yale study shows liberals "dumb down speech" when talking to minorities; the right does not
- a mechanism of control

Racist:
- a person disagreeing with an elite democrat
- especially directed toward all white republican males
- useful accusation to generate emotions and division in the country
- considered truthful even if the target has no history of or personal racial feelings
- "the worse racist is someone who does not even know they are a racist"
- is at home in the democratic party

Sanctuary Cities:
- havens for homeless squatters
- havens for law breakers
- havens for illegal immigrants
- havens for disease
- havens for drug use and abuse
- a place to ignore criminal behaviors if you are homeless or illegal
- a place where it is ok to steal from businesses up to $750 with minimal charges
- protection for illegals from U.S. immigration laws
- zone where the left feel taxpayers of the nation should put more money
- zones free from the laws that others are required to respect
- zones where officials do not have to follow oaths of office
- areas where illegal immigrants are "better and more deserving than citizens."

School choice:
- disliked by democrats and favored for all students by Trump's team
- supported only for the children of the elite on the left

Smelly Walmart Shoppers:
- Trump supporters

Socialism:
- form of political system preferred by the left
- a system typically advocating for an end to private property and free speech
- a Marxist form of government marked by distribution of pay according to work done
- a form of government associated with collectivism, communism, Marxism, Leninism and Maoism.

Ten Million:
- number of illegal aliens the left claims have a right to be in the U.S. (studies show the number may be over 20 million)

Totalitarianism:
- a centralized government system in which a single party without opposition rules
- Democratic dream state
- a system free from discussion with other political parties
- a system in which government determines what people are to consider pleasurable

Trump Derangement Syndrome:
- New York Times declares Trump causes hurricane off East coast
- democrats claim Trump caused their use of mobs to beat up on conservatives
- left claims Trump caused the border problem because he is enforcing laws passed by legislature
- left claims Trump failed to get legislation passed to get rid of Affordable Care Act (more accurately a product of the democrats and John McCain deciding to support Democrats instead of republicans over the issue.)

- belief that Trump created the cages immigrants were shown on TV to be housed in. (Actually created under Obama)
- belief that $100,000.00 dollars in internet purchases from Russia was responsible for getting Trump elected President
- belief that under Trump the stock market would collapse
- belief that Trump would start a war with China, North Korea, Russia, Iran, etc.
- belief that not letting friendly nations take advantage of US is disrespectful
- belief that asking countries to step up and protect themselves is disrespectful
- belief that protecting yourself from dishonest persecution is obstruction of justice
- belief that "Make America Great Again" is a Nazi tactic
- belief that a member of the Trump Campaign could in 6 months orchestrate a deal with Russia to get a person elected President with 100,000.00 dollars spent on adds
- belief that any member of the Trump election team that talked with a Russian was plotting against the American free election policies
- belief that "I would like better relations with Russia" was grounds to initiate a counter espionage investigation of the Trump camp
- belief that Trump is responsible for all the hate the democrats have toward him
- belief that having borders is un-American and immoral
- belief that the US can support the poor from everywhere in the world
- belief that enforcing the laws of the U.S. is somehow being a bad President and/or a bad person
- belief that Trump is dividing the country
- belief that Trump is mean to enforce laws passed by the people complaining about him
- belief Trump is a White Nationalist

- belief that Trump makes me feel bad, think bad, and act bad
- belief that Trump did not beat HRC at the poles
- belief that God does not approve of Fences
- belief that it is the right (Trump) that manufactures crisis
- belief that if you are proud of your heritage you are a xenophobe
- if you believe in laws and the people who enforce the laws you are a right-wing-extremist
- if you believe in hard work, fair play and fair compensation you are an anti-socialist
- if you believe in self-defense and the military you are a right wing-militant
- Trump is making everyone unhappy
- TRUMP IS THE REASON FOR THE TRUMP DERANGEMENT SYNDROME

Truth:
- this is whatever the left feels it should be.
- "more important than facts"
- a conclusion arrived at not by fact or reality but by prevalent feelings.
- Joe Biden and Alexandria Ocasio-Cortez say "Truth is more important than fact."

Twenty-one million:
- estimated number of illegal aliens living in the U.S. currently according to actual studies by Yale University

White men:
- racists
- misogynist
- xenophobes
- individuals with 'toxic masculinity'

Women:
- individuals who are to be believed even if they are lying
- the part of the population not affected by masculine toxicity
- the half of humankind who should be allowed to determine when they abort babies

545 People

545 PEOPLE By Charlie Reese (545 vs. 300,000,000; Republicans & Democrats Alike - No One Is Blameless.) Charley Reese has been a journalist for 49 years. Received by e-mail July 27, 2009.

Politicians are the only people in the world who create problems and then campaign against them.

Have you ever wondered, if both the Democrats and the Republicans are against deficits, WHY do we have deficits?

Have you ever wondered, if all the politicians are against inflation and high taxes, WHY do we have inflation and high taxes?

You and I don't propose a federal budget. The President does.

You and I don't have the Constitutional authority to vote on appropriations. The House of Representatives does.

You and I don't write the tax code, Congress does.

You and I don't set fiscal policy, Congress does.

You and I don't control monetary policy, the Federal Reserve Bank does.

One hundred Senators, 435 Congressmen, one President, and nine Supreme Court justices -- 545 human beings out of the 300 million are directly, legally, morally, and individually responsible for the domestic problems that plague this country.

I excluded the members of the Federal Reserve Board because the Congress created that problem. In 1913, Congress delegated its Constitutional duty to provide a sound currency to a federally chartered, but private, central bank.

I excluded all the special interests and lobbyists for a sound reason. They have no legal authority. They have no ability to coerce a senator, a congressman, or a President to do one cotton-picking thing. I don't care if they offer a politician $1 million dollars in cash. The politician has the power to accept or reject it. No matter what the lobbyist promises, it is the legislator's responsibility to determine how he votes.

Those 545 human beings spend much of their energy convincing you that what they did is not their fault. They cooperate in this common con regardless of party. What separates a politician from a normal human being is an excessive amount of gall. No normal human being would have the gall of a Speaker, who stood up and criticized the President for creating deficits. The president can only propose a budget. He cannot force the Congress to accept it.

The Constitution, which is the supreme law of the land, gives sole responsibility to the House of Representatives for originating and approving appropriations and taxes.

Who is the speaker of the House? Nancy Pelosi. She is the leader of the majority party. She and fellow House members, not the President, can approve any budget they want. If the President vetoes it, they can pass it over his veto if they agree to.

It seems inconceivable to me that a nation of 300 million cannot replace 545 people who stand convicted -- by present facts -- of incompetence and irresponsibility. I can't think of a single domestic problem that is not traceable directly to those 545 people. When you fully grasp the plain truth that 545 people exercise the power of the federal government, then it must follow that what exists is what they want to exist.

If the tax code is unfair, it's because they want it unfair.

If the budget is in the red, it's because they want it in the red.

If the Army & Marines are in IRAQ, it's because they want them in IRAQ .

If they do not receive Social Security but are on an elite retirement plan not available to the people, it's because they want it that way.

There are no insoluble government problems.

Do not let these 545 people shift the blame to bureaucrats, whom they hire and whose jobs they can abolish; to lobbyists, whose gifts and advice they can reject; to regulators, to whom they give the power to regulate and from whom they can take this power.

Above all, do not let them con you into the belief that there exists disembodied mystical forces like "the economy," "inflation," or "politics" that prevent them from doing what they take an oath to do.

Those 545 people, and they alone, are responsible.

They, and they alone, have the power.

The people, who are their bosses, should hold them, and only them, accountable and responsible for the current state of affairs.

Provided the voters have the gumption to manage their own employees.

We should vote all of them out of office and clean up their mess!

Charlie Reese is a former columnist of the Orlando Sentinel Newspaper.

224

Internet humor:

RIGHT ON MAXINE!!!

This is the best analogy yet! Leave it to Maxine to come up with a solution for the mess that America/Canada/ UK/Germany/ Australia/NZ are?

I bought a bird feeder. I hung it on my back porch and filled it with seed. What a beauty of a bird feeder it was, as I filled it lovingly with seed. Within a week we had hundreds of birds taking advantage of the continuous flow of free and easily accessible food. But then the birds started building nests in the boards of the patio, above the table, and next to the barbecue. Then came the shit. It was everywhere: on the patio tile, the chairs, the table ... everywhere! Then some of the birds turned mean. They would dive bomb me and try to peck me even though I had fed them out of my own pocket. And other birds were boisterous and loud. They sat on the feeder and squawked and screamed at all hours of the day and night and demanded that I fill it when it got low on food. After a while, I couldn't even sit on my own back porch anymore. So, I took down the bird feeder and in three days the birds were gone. I cleaned up their mess and took down the many nests they had built all over the patio. Soon, the back yard was like it used to be .... quiet, serene.... and no one demanding their rights to a free meal. Now let's see...... Our government gives out free food, subsidized housing, free medical care and free education, and allows anyone born here to be an automatic citizen. Then the illegals came by the tens of thousands. Suddenly our taxes went up to pay for free services; small apartments are housing 5 families; you must wait 6 hours to be seen by an emergency room doctor; Your child's second grade class is behind other schools because over half the class doesn't speak English. Corn Flakes now come in a bilingual box; I have to 'press one ' to hear my bank talk to me in English, and people waving flags other than "ours" are squawking and screaming in the streets, demanding more rights and free liberties.

Just my opinion, but maybe it's time for the government to take down the bird feeder.

Respect Can Help Us Heal:
Why do we make things so complicated?

"You cannot do a kindness too soon,
for you never know how soon it will be too late."

Ralph Waldo Emerson

ABOUT GUNS

There is a continuous witch hunt that has gone on for years that did not start with Trump. To put it succinctly, it is the hunt for a way to stop gun related murders. This is another one of those events that is approached from the insane right/wrong perspective the people of the United States seem to like as much as watching soap operas or tennis matches. I tell my patients that life is like mathematics, you cannot get a good outcome unless you frame the problem accurately.

The left frames the murder problem as a need to have more laws regarding possession and use of firearms. They do not use the laws already on the books, because then they might not have a reason to try and get even more laws. The cities with the most and the strictest gun laws are of course the cities with the most crimes. I guess in some ways that makes sense, but it raises the chicken and the egg type argument. The left wants to crack down on lawful gun owners making it easier for criminals to perpetrate crimes—which they do.

The right sees what the left is doing as in infringement on constitutional rights to keep weapons, to thwart crime, and for the security and the enjoyment they experience through the sport. Neither side understands the problem properly. The left really wants to make the issues one of disarming the American people. They ignore the fact that as the number of guns has increased in the U.S. the number of gun deaths has, contrary to what the left wants you to think, decreased

According to Everytown there were 12,830 homicides by guns in the year they studied. Guns did not do this. People did this. There is some agreement between right and left regarding this, but then the telescope is focused in on the wrong place: mental illness. (Remember I am a psychiatrist.) It is certainly true that on occasionally there has been a suspicion of a mental illness when a school shooting has occurred and the perpetrator is a fringe or disengaged student, but what about the other 12,800 shootings. Mental illness is rare as a cause of murder. There is something that is present, however, in nearly every murder, and it isn't even mentioned by either side: Lack of Respect (Sara Sanders excepted).

There is another subtle concept owned by a lot of people (mainly men) when it comes to children and marriage. It is the ownership implied by "my wife, my children." I have often wondered if this is not at the root of why couples who have lived together for years, after deciding to get married, have the marriage fall apart in a few months under the new umbrella of marriage.

Where do people learn respect? How about from the LPM that spends all day and night putting down the President of the United States? How about the candidates who are running for President who claim the President is a liar, and a ____ (fill in the blank)? How about from observing the way the senate runs a confirmation hearing? Remember how there was a united decision on the left not to support anyone appointed by the President, and the reasons for not supporting were determined before the hearings even started. Only the name was needed. How about witnessing a congress member telling people to "hunt them down and yell at them and tell them they are not wanted." (Target: the people who are trying to help run the country). How about encouraging people to go to the homes of our senators and yell obscenities at them. How about TV shows where the participants sit around a table and call our President obscene names? How about movies that are made showing the left elite hunting down deplorables (conservative neighbors) and killing them. How about a contender for presidency calling a quarter of the population of the U.S. deplorables? Or a President calling 70 million

Americans neo-fascists. Please note the disrespect is not just toward a President, it is toward nearly half of the population of the country.

Five thousand priests, and 8000 Boy Scouts being implicated in sex crimes and there are only a few dozen convictions would seem to represent real disregard. The left is publishing in magazines directed to youth information on how to get an abortion without telling their parents. When did common sense completely stop?

There is another source of disrespect. It is in the blame system that I have discussed with you. When we blame another person for the way we feel, for what we do, or for how we think, we are being disrespectful and completely inaccurate. *Anger and blaming* are one in the same thing. I will bet you that the majority of the 12,800 people who were murdered by shooting were blamed for "making me mad, hurting my feelings, causing me to feel bad, etc."

This would also be a good place to bring in the 22,000 people who suicide yearly. When people blame, they give away power. When they give away power, they feel helpless, hopeless, resentful, angry and then they frequently aim the gun at either themselves, or others. Along the way they may try drugs, alcohol or physical abuse of others. The more times they blame and the quicker they blame the faster they draw the gun.

The concern about being hurt, or hurting others, is shared by those who feel words have power (to hurt) and by those who want to use the fact some people believe words have that power to create chaos. (Words are not clubs, guns, pitchforks, etc.) The proverb says, "Sticks and stones may break my bones, but words will never hurt me." The left seems to have missed the point of this saying. People who understand words have only the power we give them are free from this burden. Recognizing the destructive role of blame language is essential to the accurate framing of a sentence or a mission statement. *It is necessary to frame life's experiences accurately to be free of blame/anger.*

Some people see it as <u>morally</u> right to care about how others feel. There is an intrinsic dilemma here that most people apparently do not recognize. The first component of the quandary is that we are not responsible (responsible--meaning to have an actual ability to cause, or choose, other's emotional state or reasoning) for how others feel. Part of the confusion is that when dealing with physical activities the opposite is accurate (we can inflict physical pain on others). The proper way to frame an interaction with other people is to understand/accept that we each create our own psychological experience. Our feelings are generated by mental intermediation. This makes the emotional interaction with, or about another person, a sequential ordering (1234 or ABCE) of events and not a cause-and-effect event (which is a characteristic of the physical world interaction). Misunderstanding this causes people to frame psychological/ emotional products in cause-and-effect nomenclature: that is an inaccurate framing. It is the Adam Schiff and Jerry Nadler approach to issues. It is what children do. When people hold others responsible for their feeling, they are simply trying to control others. Being seen as hurting is one of natures greatest manipulations.

The second component of the quandary is that we often do care about how others feel, or how they feel about us, so we want/hope/wish/try to influence them to think the way we would want them to think about us. We may also have a genuine concern for the other person's experience. As normal/common/and reasonable as this state of the mind is, it does not alter the reality that we are each the creator of our own emotions. This is both fact and truth. This reality was recognized as far as 1000 years ago in Rome.

The problem boils down to an error in our education. Society and social media through inaccurate framing of speech teach us to frame life inaccurately. We are taught through the messages in our books, our music, our TV programs, our movies and our news programs to blame and hold others responsible for the way we feel. Unfortunately, this is an unrecognized, and under attended error in our education. We are taught by our schools to speak correctly, but little attention is paid to the accuracy of our speech. This is an error of omission. There are two worlds we must learn to navigate in life: physical and emotional. They work on different principles. If you apply wording that is accurate in the physical world to the psychological world you are framing life inaccurately.

<u>Moralistic</u> arguments are frequently employed by the religious, or the elected, as the authority for their actions. Because it is a <u>moralistic</u> argument, however, does not make it "right" except for those who subscribe to that moral point of view. For example, we are appalled at Hitler's extermination of millions of Jews, yet in the Christian Old Testament there are multiple reports of God telling the Israelites to exterminate a population of people. In all my early years in Sunday school, I never heard criticism registered about those stories. It seems disrespectful to accept this behavior in one instance and condone (if just through not addressing it) it in another. When people claim a moral high ground, they should be aware that Germany's Head of the Department of Jewish Affairs Adolf Eichmann felt it was his *<u>moral duty</u>* to exterminate as many Jews as possible. In his mind, he was only following the laws of his country and the head of his state. (I will not address this issue here except to say it touches on the original sin issue in the creation of our constitution. Those who believe in Natural Law see Eichmann as nuts. Those who believe all things come from the government surely must have some identity with him.)

I think it is painful for people to accept there is nothing we can call absolute truth. People are certainly not short on opinion about what is right, true, good or bad even when the only support is their own opinion. When they have strong enough opinions, they add <u>moralistic</u> labels to the beliefs: "A wall is immoral." In a nutshell, it is highly possible things we have been told about right and wrong may be relative. Will Rogers said there are many people who know things for a fact which are not true. I think he was referring to democrats. Maybe Adam

Schiff fits in this group: he claimed for years that he had absolute proof that Trump colluded with the Russians (which would not be a crime, even if it were true), but he has never provided his proof. Seems he is trying to manufacture some, since he can't get it any other way. [Did you hear his audition on the floor of the Congress?]

Teaching children and adults to stay out of blame (be respectful) has the potential to decrease suicides and homicides by the thousands without costing a cent, possibly saving millions of dollars in outlay for mental health treatment, and it works without creating another law that can do nothing but cost law abiding citizens more money and freedoms. I have no issue with looking for the emotionally disturbed person and attempting to keep then away from a gun, and with hundred of thousands of dollars spent on that task, it might save a couple people along the way.

The left supported slavery and supports making people dependent on the government for their wellbeing and wants to make them dependent on the government for their safety. Each of these positions is one of making citizens more and more dependent on handouts or interventions by government and less on taking care of one's self. I think Rome tried something like that, and it did not work out well for them.

If the left or right want to decrease the number of deaths from guns the direction is quite clear: 1) Enforce the rules already on the books, 2) Alter the costs for doing a crime with a weapon to double what it would have been without a weapon. (I see signs along the road "Double fines if workers are present.) 3) Make families of murderers and attempted murderers potentially culpable for fines. 4) Most of all work through learning accurate speech to get rid of hate and other progressions of blame.

BLAMING KILLS

Teachers do a good job of teaching children how to speak correctly, but they need to pick up their game and teach children how to speak accurately as well! Accurately/factually/truthfully *blaming kills people*! Lack of respect is not the thing that kills people, but it is the background for blaming which does kill and destroy people!

For further discussion of the issues of anger, I refer you to my book:

Blame and Anger found online only.

Martin Luther King framed the issues of his time and ours best when he said: "Now's the time ......"

APPENDIX I

Letters

PRESIDENTS TRUMP AND LINCOLN AND THE MEDIA

Originally published at Fox News

When *The New York Times* printed a <u>wildly false headline</u> asserting that President Trump was possibly a Russian agent, I was furious. However, I was also reminded of another time in our nation's history in which the press was this hostile to the American President.

I called President Trump and told him no president since Abraham Lincoln had faced the kind of unending bias and hostility that he is living through.

Indeed, the Media Research Center reported for both 2017 and 2018 that the mainstream evening TV media had been at least <u>90 percent</u> anti-Trump in its reporting. This relentless hostility parallels what President Lincoln had to endure in the media.

As I wrote in my #1 *New York Times* best seller *Understanding Trump*, many news outlets opposed Lincoln from the beginning – much like President Trump.

Upon Lincoln's election, the *Memphis Daily Appeal* wrote on November 13, 1860:

> "Within 90 days from the time Lincoln is inaugurated, the Republican Party will be utterly ruined and destroyed. His path is environed with so many difficulties, that even if he had the ability of Jefferson and the energy of Jackson, he would fail, but he is a weak and inexperienced man, and his administration will be doomed from the commencement. If he takes that radical section of the Republican Party, the conservative wing of it will cut loose and repudiate him. If, on the other hand, he courts the conservatives and pursues a moderate conciliatory policy, the radicals will make open war upon his administration."

These criticisms of Lincoln were not confined to the South.

In his book *1864: Lincoln at the Gates of History*, author Charles Bracelen Flood noted that *The New York Herald* once wrote that "his election was a rash experiment, his administration is a deplorable failure." The northern paper's editors also said, "As President of the United States he must have enough sense to see and acknowledge he has been an egregious failure. One thing must be self-evident to him, and that is that under no circumstances can he hope to be the next President of the United States… [He should] retire from the position to which, in an evil hour, he was exalted."

Does this sound familiar?

Just as President Trump rails against "fake news," President Lincoln felt that a significant front in his war to preserve the Union was against the news media. This made Lincoln highly critical and skeptical of media.

According to Noah Brooks, a reporter who had regular access to Lincoln, President Lincoln often said, "the worst feature about newspapers was that they were so sure to be 'ahead of the hounds,' outrunning events, and exciting expectations which were sure to be disappointed." Lincoln, who was embroiled in a civil war in which the very survival of the country was at stake, was also much tougher and more aggressive with the media than one could imagine in the modern era. This included shutting down newspapers and imprisoning journalists who supported secession from the Union.

But the hostility toward Lincoln within the Washington establishment and the political elite was just as ferocious.

Edward Everett, the famous orator who spoke for hours at Gettysburg while Lincoln gave a very brief but historically and morally a much more powerful speech, wrote in his diary that Lincoln was, "evidently a person of very inferior cast of character, wholly unequal to the crisis."

According to George Templeton Strong, a prominent New York lawyer, Lincoln was "a barbarian, Scythian, yahoo, or gorilla."

Even the general who Lincoln chose to lead the Union Army, George McClellan, dismissed President Lincoln as a frontier hack, "an idiot," and "the original gorilla."

Even among his fellow Republicans, Lincoln encountered fierce attacks.

Republican William M. Dickson of Ohio wrote in 1861 that Lincoln "is universally an admitted failure, has no will, no courage, no executive capacity … and his spirit necessarily infuses itself downwards through all departments."

You decide whether attacks on President Trump's hair or attacks on Lincoln's intelligence are more demeaning.

President Lincoln was a very different man facing a radically more dangerous situation than President Trump. Yet each president represents a direct threat to a national establishment by an outsider.

The next time you hear a nasty attack on President Trump, consider what people wrote and said about President Lincoln.

There is a lot more similarity between the Lincoln crisis of the Union and the Trump crisis of the Establishment than most people will want to even consider.

Your Friend,

Newt

P.S. In my *New York Times* bestselling books, *Understanding Trump* and *Trump's America*, I discuss more on the media's unending hostility toward President Trump.

A word from Tom Fitton on voter fraud.

Dear Mr. Campbell,

We have all heard about voter fraud and attempts by liberal media organs like *The New York Times* and leftist politicians to dismiss it as a nonexistent problem. **But voter fraud is in fact real, widespread, and substantial to the point that it can and does decide elections. It also drives honest citizens out of the democratic process and breeds distrust in our government.** I, like most Americans, believe that voting is a highly valued right and serious responsibility of American citizenship. <u>And clean, accurate voter registration lists, as well as commonsense laws requiring voter ID help stop voter fraud and voting by individuals ineligible to vote</u>. That's why Judicial Watch's filed lawsuits against the states of **Indiana, Ohio and Kentucky** that resulted in those states agreeing to comply with that National Voter Registration Act (NVRA) by cleaning their voter lists.

But there's more to do. You see, there are other states that have not been cleaning their voter lists as required by law and we've issued notices to a dozen of them that they need to comply with the law – or perhaps face a lawsuit from Judicial Watch.

<u>**And that's why I hope you will help Judicial Watch now as we expand our fight for clean and fair elections.**</u>

Lawsuits are costly, especially when we're fighting the government! But this is indeed a critical battle for the rule of law, and for the future of our nation. And that's why your support of our work is so important.

Thankyou!

Sincerely,

TomFitton

President

From the Desk of
BISHOP E.W. JACKSON

U.S. Marine Corp Veteran
Reagan Conservative
2013 GOP Nominee for Virginia Lt. Governor

Dear Racist Conservative,

Got your attention?

I hope so, because this is exactly what millions of young black children are being told every day by the racial demagoguery of Louis Farrakhan, Jesse Jackson, Al Sharpton, and even former President Barack Obama.

These professional, "Blame America First" hatred-mongers are scamming millions of black children into believing the debilitating LIES that:

** America is a racist, hate-filled country, not worthy of our love and respect!

** Conservatives like you and me are all racists who don't care about Black Americans. We're their enemy.

** Morality, personal responsibility, and hard work ONLY work for white people.

** Black Americans can't thrive, they can only survive -- and the only hope of survival is through Big Government handouts.

But with your help, I'm going to set the record straight. I'll explain how in just a moment, but first let me tell you why this is so important.

As a conservative, I'm disgusted by the hopelessness intentionally peddled by so-called black "leaders" like Farrakhan, Obama, Jackson, and Sharpton in order to benefit from keeping blacks under their thumbs.

Radio America | PO Box 96848 | Washington, DC 20090-6848

Page 2

They don't want to solve the problems of poverty, violence, drugs, and gangs in the Black Community -- rather, they want to perpetuate them so they can blame America and posture themselves as champions of "social justice."

Having risen out of poverty and a broken home, I'm living proof of what is possible for any American who rejects these race-baiting lies and takes responsibility for his or her own life.

Honestly, when have you heard Jesse Jackson preach the value of personal responsibility? When have you heard Al Sharpton say that hard work and moral values are the keys to success?

You know as well as I do that they have no interest in seeing people get off welfare.

They want Black Americans to see themselves as victims, completely-dependent on them and their Big Government handouts...

If you turn on your TV or radio, you'll almost always hear the same old loony liberals pushing for more government in your lives and more of your taxpayer dollars wasted on more government welfare programs.

My friend, I've seen the so-called liberal "compassion" of government welfare. Instead of improving black people's lives, it destroys them!

And instead of providing a "safety net" for people in temporary need... it has become a death trap that promotes laziness, destroys human dignity, and wastes your hard-earned tax dollars.

Welfare dependency has discouraged marriage, discouraged the entrepreneurial spirit and discouraged personal responsibility.

Is this the liberals' idea of compassion? It would be comical if it weren't so sickening.

You won't hear any of that kind of talk from me, my friend. Unlike these hate-mongering liberals, I believe that:

"Government isn't the solution, government is the problem."

This may shock a lot of liberals out there -- they think a government handout is the answer to every problem.

But they're dead wrong, and I'm not afraid tell them or the American people so.

My name is Bishop E.W. Jackson, and I've dedicated my life to spreading the truth about conservatism and America to the black community, where it's needed most.

My mission is to teach our young men and women -- both black and white -- the value of a hard work ethic and a strong moral code... something you just don't hear from today's black "leaders."

I'm not afraid of Louis Farrakhan, Barack Obama, Jesse Jackson, Al Sharpton, or any of their comrades. In fact, I've been fighting these race-baiting liberal extremists for decades!

I'm fighting back against their hate-mongering by spreading the word that hard work, family values, moral principles, and personal responsibility are the keys to success in America...

...NOT A GOVERNMENT PROGRAM OR HANDOUT!

That's why I'm so excited about my new radio commentaries airing on Radio America.

I feel so blessed to have this amazing chance to tell America there's an alternative to the Left's race-baiting, fear-mongering LIES.

I'm on a mission to open America's eyes to the fact that black liberal "leaders" like Barack Obama, Jesse Jackson, and Al Sharpton have scammed, cheated, and exploited the black community for their own selfish gains...

...and Radio America -- as "The Voice of the Nation" -- is uniquely positioned to make this critical mission a reality.

Parenthood, the Brookings Institution, Common Cause and the Center for American Progress. Among the specific causes and the Soros-supported groups that advocate for them are:

- Anti-Israel (**Al-Haq, Amnesty International, Arab American Institute Foundation, New Israel Fund**);

- Anti-conservative judicial appointments (**Alliance for Justice**);

- Anti-educational choice (**American Federation of Teachers**);

- Pro-abortion rights (**Catholics for Choice, Center for Reproductive Rights, National Women's Law Center**);

- Radical and LGBT agenda (**Human Rights Campaign**)

Judicial Watch is proudly conservative, but we are non-partisan. Our commitment is to support government transparency and the rule of law, and to expose and prosecute public corruption in both political parties.

Consequently, George Soros' contributions to candidates and political party organizations, presuming they are within legal limits, are not of direct interest to Judicial Watch. And many of the groups and activities that George Soros and his **Open Society Foundations supports are not of direct interest to Judicial Watch, either, although we firmly believe Americans should be educated about the degree to which George Soros and his network are funding the entire American Left.**

However, commensurate with our mission to support the rule of law, **Judicial Watch** has long been a leader in fighting for enforcement of our nation's laws against illegal immigration; and enforcement of our nation's laws that protect election integrity. Our ongoing investigative and legal actions in these two closely related areas frequently bring us into direct contact with **Soros-funded** organizations.

That is because we believe that **George Soros** is committed to degrading America into a European-style socialist state and knows that the surest method of achieving that goal is to open our borders to unlimited illegal immigration and undermine existing laws that limit voting in American elections to American citizens.

I. THE FACTS ABOUT GEORGE SOROS FUNDING OF THE OPEN-BORDERS AND AMNESTY FOR ILLEGAL ALIENS MOVEMENT

Through his **Open Society Foundations**, **Soros** has founded dozens of radical groups dedicated to effectively erasing America's borders and any legal distinctions between citizens and non-citizens in our country. A key component of these groups' strategy is to enact amnesty for illegal aliens, inevitably leading to illegal aliens voting in American elections. Here is a partial list of open-border and pro-amnesty groups that the **Open Society Foundations** has funded:

- **America's Voice** (pro-comprehensive immigration reform);
- **American Bar Association Commission on Immigration Policy** ("opposes laws that require employers and persons providing education, health care or other social services to verify citizenship or immigration status");

- **American Immigration Council** (pro-amnesty);
- **American Immigration Law Foundation** (legal actions in support of amnesty);
- **Brennan Center for Justice** (legal actions, *pro bono* support to activists, media campaigns);
- **Casa de Maryland** (radical state lobbying organization for amnesty and expanded rights for illegal aliens residing in Maryland);
- **Center for Constitutional Rights** (pro-open-borders);
- **National Council of La Raza** (pro-amnesty and expanded rights for illegal aliens);
- **National Immigration Forum** (pro-amnesty for illegal aliens and more visas for individuals wishing to immigrate legally to the U.S.);
- **National Immigration Law Center** (pro-full access to government social welfare programs for illegal aliens)

Soros, and the organizations he funds are major supporters of **"sanctuary"** policies in cities, counties and states across America. Most **sanctuary** policies undermine and violate federal immigration law by forbidding local police from cooperating with federal immigration authorities. These policies, which are on the books in major cities including Los Angeles, New York, Washington, and San Francisco, as well as hundreds of counties and smaller cities, block local police from informing federal immigration authorities when during the course of their work they detain a criminal alien subject to deportation from the United States.

In a new twist on subverting the rule of immigration law, a spin-off of the Soros-funded **National Immigration Law Center** called **United We Dream** launched a smartphone application ("app") that helps illegal immigrants detect and avoid federal immigration authorities. That's not all. Eight open-borders groups that receive funds from the **Open Society Foundations** reportedly helped promote, organize and support the massive **"migrant caravan"** through **Central America** to the U.S. border that manipulated large groups of migrants for political purposes prior to last November's U.S. congressional midterm elections in an unsuccessful effort to embarrass President Trump!

Judicial Watch has distinguished itself fighting sanctuary policies since 2005 and has become the national leader in challenging sanctuary policies through the legal system and fighting to enforce federal immigration law.

II. THE FACTS ABOUT GEORGE SOROS FUNDING GROUPS THAT WANT TO WEAKEN BALLOT INTEGRITY AND OPEN VOTING IN U.S. ELECTIONS TO INELIGIBLE VOTERS

George Soros made national headlines in 2016 when it was revealed he was funding legal challenges across the country to state efforts to ensure honest elections

Specifically, a **Soros-funded** legal team headed by **Marc Elias** (who at the time was legal counsel to **Hillary Clinton's** presidential campaign) looked to augment legal challenges that the **Obama Justice Department** mounted against states attempting to protect the honesty of their elections by attempting to block states from enacting common-sense measures like voter ID and regularly cleaning voter rolls of ineligible voters (including deceased individuals, and those who moved out of the jurisdiction).

Today, the organized Left continues its efforts to weaken ballot integrity. Under the guise of "protecting minority voting rights," the Left has undertaken a massive legal effort to undermine and oppose election integrity laws. **Soros-backed** groups are deeply involved in this effort. Here is a partial list of "voting rights" groups that the **Open Society Foundations** has funded:

- **The Advancement Project** (which advertises itself as "the next generation, multi-racial civil rights organization");
- **Bend the Arc Jewish Action** (condemns voter ID laws as barriers that make it harder for minorities to vote);
- **Demos** (whose board is now chaired by the daughter of radical U.S. Senator Elizabeth Warren);
- **Project Vote** (the voter-mobilization arm of the discredited ACORN organization, which also received Soros support);
- **Southern Coalition for Social Justice** (involved in several challenges to voter ID and redistricting legal challenges in the South)

Inflammatory rhetoric from **Soros-funded** groups like these, and echoed in the mainstream media and by Democratic politicians, argues that commonsense ballot integrity measures like voter ID and cleaning voter rolls somehow create "barriers" for minority voters.

It is clear that **George Soros** and the Left see weakening ballot integrity, along with amnesty, as keys to ensuring victories for leftist allies far into the future.

Judicial Watch does not endorse or oppose candidates, but we firmly believe that our elections should be conducted honestly and free of corruption, and that only eligible voters should be allowed to cast votes.

Judicial Watch is the national leader in enforcing federal laws that require states to take reasonable steps to clean their voter rolls between elections as required by federal law, and in supporting a number of state efforts to enact ballot integrity measures like voter ID laws.

III. **THE JUDICIAL WATCH RECORD IN EXPOSING AND PROSECUTING GOVERNMENT WRONGDOING AND PUBLIC CORRUPTION**

Judicial Watch was founded in 1994 and over the past quarter-century has become the nation's most active open records litigator. It is our contention that dishonest politicians and government bureaucrats both fear and are innately hostile to transparency in government. This rule applies whether Democrats or Republicans are in power.

Consequently, **Judicial Watch** has sued every presidential administration since **Bill Clinton's** over the release of public documents that the American people have a right to see. And today, even as we expose the corrupt **Deep State conspiracy** to take down President Trump, we are now in court against agencies of the **Trump administration**, including the State Department, the Justice Department, and the FBI, that are continuing to fail to honor our open records requests on behalf of the American people. **Judicial Watch is uniquely qualified to successfully investigate and litigate this nexus of potentially unlawful taxpayer financing for left-wing activism.**

Congressman Mark Meadows

Dear Friend,

If you believe that in life you reap what you sow, then I have a very important warning for you.

Right now, the seeds are being sown by the Progressives in this country for what is one of <u>the most audacious attacks on your freedoms ever contemplated</u>.

Very importantly, it is an assault that will also directly jeopardize the health and well-being of you, your family, and your loved ones.

What's worse, some of the more reliable public opinion polls are showing that they are already having frightening success. The polls also indicate if their efforts are not countered in the next 12 months, it may very well be too late.

Let me explain what is going on and what you can do to protect your family and your freedoms.

As the Chairman of the House Freedom Caucus, let me tell you that Progressives are sowing the seeds of their most audacious assault on freedom ever!

They are now very effectively laying the groundwork for an expansion of government **that will make virtually every American dependent on government forever.**

Here's how. You would think that in the face of the failure and misery that Obamacare has created, the Progressives would abandon their assault on our nation's healthcare and freedoms, tuck their tail between their legs, and run in the other direction.

Stunningly, they are doing the exact opposite.

Have you heard about the new litmus test for all Progressives called "Medicare for All" ?

The Progressives are doubling down on a full and complete takeover of your healthcare. This time they want only the government to provide health care and <u>they are even calling for outlawing private insurance</u>.

That is so important – let me repeat that. **<u>Under their "Medicare for All" plan, government bureaucrats would determine what care you receive and when you receive it</u>**.

Cleverly, the Progressives have figured out that calling it a "government takeover" or "single payer system" is not popular, so they are repackaging their authoritarian program as "Medicare for All."

Not printed or mailed at government expense.

Strategically, they are not seeking a vote on their radical Medicare for All program today or anytime soon. In fact, they don't really want a vote anytime soon because they know it would likely fail at this moment or President Trump would veto it.

Instead, they are waging an intense grassroots campaign to build broad-based citizen support so in the not-too-distant future they can ram it into law.

Tragically, *their* efforts are bearing fruit. Recent opinion polls are showing that Progressives are very effectively sowing grassroots support for Medicare for All.

In a Gallup Poll taken at the end of 2017, a whopping 62% of Americans were undecided about Senator Bernie Sanders' Medicare for All proposal.

That may sound good, but it is actually a disaster since it shows how many can be won over to support taking away all healthcare decisions and giving them to Washington bureaucrats.

What's worse:

1. The same poll shows that of those with an opinion on Medicare for All, a **MAJORITY NOW SUPPORT Bernie Sanders' Medicare for All,** full government takeover of all medical care in this country.

2. In a separate question looking at government-run healthcare, Gallup also concluded that, "Republican's shift in attitudes accounts for most of the overall increase in support for the government system in this year's update."

In other words, most Americans have not yet made up their mind on the Progressives' radical Medicare for All single-payer government takeover of all healthcare.

But, because of their current propaganda, **when they do make up their minds, they are casting their support for a government takeover of all health care – Medicare for All.**

Under the banner of "Healthcare Justice" and promising "health care as a right that Americans should enjoy universally and equally," they are working to very wrongly convince your fellow Americans that handing over control of their healthcare will result in better care and lower cost.

Slowly and frighteningly, this propaganda is working.

If they continue uncontested to build support for "Medicare for All," it will be unstoppable when they do force a vote on it – the public demand will simply be too great.

In short, they are patiently and very successfully sowing the seeds of Medicare for All right now.

You and I must act immediately to counter this devastating propaganda.

WITH EVERY PASSING DAY MORE AND MORE OF THAT 62 PERCENT OF AMERICANS WHO ARE UNDECIDED, including many who should know better, ARE

DECLARING THEIR SUPPORT FOR THIS AUTHORITARIAN MEDICARE FOR ALL PLAN.

Put simply, the Progressives are doing it again! <u>They understand that politics is downstream from culture.</u>

If you create a broad-based "cultural demand" for something, the laws will soon follow.

But how can you and I counter this growing government healthcare juggernaut that is gaining speed and momentum every day?

To counter the propaganda that the Progressives are sowing, we must wage our own drive to sow the seeds of truth.

We must tell Americans the truth about Medicare for All.

But let me warn you, it won't be easy. Some people automatically gravitate to the seemingly simple answer of "just let the government do it."

Additionally, the Progressives' propaganda campaign is growing in strength and it will be difficult to catch up and pass them.

As the old saying goes, "a lie makes it around the block before the truth can get its shoes tied."

We need to give Americans the frightening facts about Medicare for All, including:

- **OUTLAWS PRIVATE HEALTH INSURANCE** - We need to tell them about how their private insurance or any supplemental insurance will be outlawed under Medicare for All and they will be totally dependent on government bureaucrats.

- **CLOSING HOSPITALS AND FEWER DOCTORS** - We need to tell them how Medicare already underpays hospitals and doctors and many experts expect many hospitals not to survive – Americans will have to start competing and waiting for hospital beds. The lower reimbursements of doctors will mean fewer doctors continue to practice and many bright young people will pick other professions. All of this means Americans will have long wait times and fewer choices in doctors.

- **DON'T EXPECT BREAKTHROUGH DRUGS AND TREATMENTS** - We need to tell them how even *The Washington Post* has reported how Medicare for All will likely mean less research and fewer new drugs and medicines, since they will be too expensive. All of this means that the hopeful cures for cancer, heart disease, Alzheimer's, and many other diseases will remain just that: a someday hope for other countries to solve.

- **MEDICARE ALREADY HEADED TO BANKRUPTCY AND RATIONING** - We need to tell Americans the cold-hard fact that Medicare is already going broke and expanding it will mean its financial demise is accelerated. The only option to slow bankruptcy will be to ration care – particularly for the elderly and sick whose medical costs are often higher.

- **ABSURDLY HIGH TAXES AND TAKING MONEY FROM OTHER PRIORITIES** - For decades, Americans have seen how, once a government program gets started, its costs skyrocket. The rosy cost projections of the Progressives are no more truthful than the last time we heard "if you like your insurance and your doctor, you can keep them." In fact, the center-left Urban Institute projected Medicare for All would increase federal spending by $2.5 trillion annually. Federal tax collection would need to increase by an opportunity crushing 70%. Bernie Sanders proposed to pay for his Medicare for All plan with a 7.5% payroll tax. That is an ENORMOUS tax increase. Medicare for All will mean a crushing tax increase that will hurt the financial security of every American and will still need more funding. This will result in taking money away from other government priorities. This will jeopardize the well-being and safety of all Americans.

I could go on and on about how Medicare for All will mean low quality of care especially for complex procedures, the government getting in the way of decisions that should be left between patients and doctors, and much more.

In short, we need to powerfully remind Americans what they already know – that government does very few things very well and all the government attempts at healthcare indicate that Medicare for All will create widespread suffering and needless deaths.

A good example of government run healthcare is the VA. Year after year, month after month, day after day, there has been a continual stream of horrifying stories that tell the failure of government health care – not in some foreign land – but right here in America with the Veterans Administration, the second largest department of government.

In fact, we need to share stories such as the one in *USA TODAY* that reported:

"A veteran with diabetes and poor circulation checked into the Memphis VA Medical Center for a scan and possible repair of blood vessels in his right leg last year, but he ended up with a piece of plastic packaging that VA providers had mistakenly embedded in a critical artery.

Doctors didn't discover the 10 inches of tubing — used by manufacturers to protect catheters during shipping and handling — until the veteran had to have the leg amputated three weeks later.

When they cut into his leg, they found a 3-inch segment, and after the procedure, they found another 7 inches in the amputated limb."

Or other *USA TODAY* stories such as how a surgery at a VA hospital was canceled after the patient was already under anesthesia because a retractor was unavailable — it had not been sterilized since its last use a week earlier. Or how a surgeon had to improvise when a tool used to prepare a skin graft was broken and the graft failed. Or how a surgical staff member had to run to a private-sector hospital across the street to borrow mesh to repair a hernia mid-procedure.

These stories must be told. Under Medicare for All, all the hospitals will be effectively under complete government financial control and there won't be any more running across the street for emergency supplies.

We must also remind Americans of the pervasive and persistent problems with government officials manipulating patient wait times to make themselves look good as veterans *suffered* and died.

We need to ask Americans if this is what they want for themselves, their children, and their grandchildren – with no chance of retreating to private insurance and care when things go badly, as they surely will.

But publicizing and educating Americans about the truth about Medicare for All and this Progressive assault on our freedom is a massive undertaking.

You and I are now faced with the question of what organization is large enough, tough enough, and principled enough to take on the deceptive propaganda and effectively counter the Progressives' Medicare for All.

Who is out there that can counter it so successfully that the Progressive efforts on the grassroots to sow support for Medicare for All not only fail, but there is a new, robust call for more freedom?

I can tell you I think there is only one organization in America that is equipped *to counter the* Progressive Medicare for All propaganda on the grassroots and turn the tide of public opinion against this authoritarian takeover of health care.

That organization is Americans for Prosperity. Seeded several years ago by David H. Koch, Americans for Prosperity (AFP) has quickly grown far beyond anyone person. Today, AFP is fighting for freedom and opportunity at the local, state, and federal level.

They are active in 36 states with 144 offices and 3.2 million grassroots activists. AFP's rapid growth is aimed to undo the damage the Progressives have done in their years-long effort to build support for their supposedly "compassionate and fair" big government.

I can tell you they were critical to the passage of the tax cuts proposed by President Trump. AFP's leadership role started even before President Trump released his framework for tax reform. As the first proposals were being floated by some in Congress, AFP made tax reform its Number One federal policy priority. AFP immediately started fighting harmful proposals such as the Border Adjustment Tax (BAT). In fact, AFP was the leader in killing the BAT.

AFP then worked very closely with the White House to win passage of the tax reform plan President Trump outlined. From their leadership and grassroots activists holding more than 1,000 meetings on Capitol Hill with elected officials to dozens of town hall meetings in key areas of the country to leading a coalition of organizations pushing for tax reform, AFP had a major impact inside the beltway.

But it was the mobilization of their unmatched grassroots organization that may have carried the day. *The New York Times* reported,

> **"Americans for Prosperity and its field staff and volunteers have hit more than 41,000 homes and made 1.1 million phone calls."**

By knocking on tens of thousands of doors and making more than a million calls to likely supporters of tax reform, they lit up the telephones of key Senators and Representatives. Elected officials felt the "heat" from home so they saw the "light" in Washington.

And if all of that was not enough, they also amplified their grassroots efforts with millions of dollars of paid media advocating tax reform in states of wavering Senators. AFP focused on several members of the majority such as Senators Lisa Murkowski (R-AK) and Susan Collins (R-ME) who should have been fully committed from the outset.

You may be familiar with AFP's all-out efforts to support the record number of confirmations of President Trump's judicial nominees to the federal courts. You may also be aware of how they are partnering with the Administration in eliminating the regulatory overreach of the Obama era. You may also be aware of their hard-hitting efforts to curb the overspending that is driving the deficit and threatening the future of every American.

But what you might not be as aware of are all AFP's efforts in states from coast-to-coast to win important opportunity-expanding policy battles that seek to shrink the size, power, and ability of *government to rig* our system. They range from cutting taxes and slashing wasteful spending to winning Right to Work to expanding school choice to eliminating occupational licensing requirements that do not make us safer and are simply designed to stop competition, and much more.

In short, AFP is rapidly growing and becoming the most important grassroots force for freedom and opportunity-expanding policies in America today.

But taking on the Progressives' very effective propaganda that is winning support for Medicare for All will be a herculean task and, candidly, AFP needs your help.

If they are going to undertake this massive effort, they need the support and participation of patriotic Americans like you.

They need evidence of a growing number of Americans who recognize the grave danger that Medicare for All poses to our health, financial security, and freedoms. So, I urge you to take a moment now to sign the enclosed Declaration of Opposition to Medicare for All. Your signed Declaration will help generate media attention to the dangers of Medicare for All and it will potentially aid in recruiting other Americans to oppose this authoritarian, freedom-robbing programs.

And I urge you to please combine your signed Declaration with a special donation to enable Americans for Prosperity to wage this expensive but essential campaign against Medicare for All and the Progressives' entire drive to push us toward a society characterized by big government, cronyism, poverty, and control where individuals are pitted against each other as they vie for government largess.

Please sign your Declaration of Opposition to Medicare for All and return it with your largest possible donation today. Many Progressive groups receive funding from the government. AFP does not. Their success in this and all their battles against freedom-robbing policies depend on the generous, voluntary contributions of people like you.

That is why I want to ask you to join as an Americans for Prosperity Donor Activist. Some new Donor Activists are contributing $25, $50, or $75. Others who have concluded that AFP *gives them the greatest impact for their contribution are sending $100, $250, or more.* Please join this vital effort at your earliest convenience. You will be helping to build a movement of millions to get the truth out about the extreme dangers of Medicare for All and the other Progressive threats to our freedom. Your support right now is very important.

Again, time is running out. As the Gallup polls show, the Progressives are very effectively sowing the seeds of grassroots support for Medicare for All. If we don't counter their efforts with the cold-hard facts, I can tell you that when it eventually comes to a vote, it will become the law of the land.

If that happens, your children, your grandchildren, and all Americans will suffer terribly. AFP, with their 144 offices and 3.2 million grassroots activists in 36 states <u>is the one and only organization that can counter the Progressive push for Medicare for All</u>. Please help them today with your signed Declaration and best donation possible. Thank you in advance for your help and participation in this historic campaign. Please answer today.

Sincerely,

[signature]

Mark Meadows
Member of Congress

P.S. As you decide how much you decide to invest in this historic campaign to stop Medicare for All and reverse the Progressives' efforts to turn Americans away from their faith in and love of freedom, let me share with you another AFP success.

In AFP's early days, there was a growing Progressive push for the disastrous policy of Cap and Trade – the carbon tax-like scheme that would have devastated our economy and thrown millions of Americans out of work. Very early on, AFP saw that it was going to come to a head in legislation on the Hill and they went to work. In key areas of the country, they rebranded "Cap and Trade" to "Cap and Tax." They conducted massive grassroots operations and hard-hitting media efforts against this job-killing policy. They mobilized a growing number of Americans against Cap and Tax.

To the dismay of the Progressives who a short time earlier were all but assured of victory, AFP's grassroots efforts turned the tide of public opinion against Cap and Tax and it failed in Congress. The fight against Medicare for All will be much tougher and larger. Please support this critical battle and all that AFP is doing to expand freedom with your largest possible donation and signed Declaration today. Time is short. Please respond today.

BEN SHAPIRO
Radio Host
Editor-in-Chief, *Dailywire.com*
New York Times Bestselling author
Speaker, Young America's Foundation

Dear Fellow Conservative,

It's urgent I hear back from you right away because the Left is using the threat of violence to silence conservative voices at our nation's colleges and universities.

I'm sure you've heard about leftist bias on college campuses before...

...but I don't think you have any idea how bad it's gotten.

You see, it's no longer just bias. It's all-out thuggery.

Let me share with you what recently happened to me when conservative students at the University of California, Berkeley invited me to speak on campus:

THE PEOPLE'S REPUBLIC OF BERKELEY LOST ITS MIND!

Immediately anonymous members of hard-left groups like "Antifa" and "Black Bloc" vowed to come to my speech for the purposes of starting a riot.

In fact, the fear of violence from hard-left groups was so great that:

*** Hundreds of policemen and more than $600,000 in security expenses were required to ensure that these leftist thugs didn't disrupt or try to cause violence at my speech.

*** The university shut down six buildings on campus during my speech and erected concrete barricades (yes, they built a wall!) to secure the Berkeley campus.

*** For the first time in 20 years, the city of Berkeley voted to allow the use of pepper spray against violent protesters.

*** In the end, nine leftists were arrested for trying to sneak banned weapons

11480 COMMERCE PARK DRIVE, SIXTH FLOOR, RESTON, VIRGINIA 20191

into our event — no doubt, with the intent to do harm.

You see, on college campuses it's no longer just about belittling or ignoring conservative viewpoints...

...it's about using the threat of violence to make sure no young person hears about the conservative values you and I share.

Meanwhile, schools roll out the red carpet for leftists like Angela Davis, Bill Ayers, Bill Clinton, and Bernie Sanders.

At Berkeley itself, administrators tried to derail my event from even taking place, as they have done with other conservative speakers. The leftist administrators at Berkeley said they had no lecture hall available for me, which was a lie.

Then, the administrators cut our venue in half, by not allowing students to sit in the balcony – a dirty tactic to minimize attendance.

Leftists at Berkeley tried to force students to pick up tickets to my speech days before the actual event — another shameless trick to discourage student attendance. Hundreds of students were turned away at the door!

Now the good news is that the hard-left's attempts to silence me completely backfired.

Even with the uproar over my speech, we were able to bring a civil and engaging event to 600 students and community members at Berkeley — without violence, and without bending to leftist thuggery.

And then YAF won a landmark free speech lawsuit against Berkeley forcing them to stop engaging in these discriminatory unconstitutional practices.

This incredible victory for the Conservative Movement would not have been possible without my friends at Young America's Foundation (YAF).

Young America's Foundation sponsored my appearance and fought Berkeley through a lawsuit to bring me to campus (which they won!).

Why did YAF do this? So Berkeley students could have the opportunity to hear your conservative ideas.

Heard them they did!

Thanks to Young America's Foundation promoting the event to students on social media, **an additional ten million people watched my speech online!**

THAT'S MORE VIEWERS THAN ANY OF THE MAJOR NETWORK EVENING NEWSCASTS!

YAF broke the free-speech deadlock at UC Berkeley.

Let me tell you what they did for me.

You see, Young America's Foundation filed a lawsuit against UC Berkeley, because UC Berkeley refused to allow YAF speakers a lecture hall.

That lawsuit and the pressure YAF brought to bear against Berkeley enabled me to finally speak at the school. And their subsequent victory guarantees what happened to me won't happen to other conservatives at Berkeley.

Young America's Foundation has sent me to <u>more than 50 college campuses</u> to promote your conservative ideas.

If you've heard of Young America's Foundation (YAF) before then you know they are devoted to reaching young people with your conservative values.

That's why Vice President **Mike Pence** recently said, "Since its founding in 1960, YAF has been a bulwark of American greatness."

Even the *New York Times* recognized Young America's Foundation's effectiveness in recruiting students when they stated that YAF is *"The Conservative Force Behind Speeches Roiling College Campuses."*

They are **the leading youth outreach organization in America** enlightening the largest audiences of young people with your conservative ideas. What sets Young America's Foundation apart?

Well, Young America's Foundation is #1 for a reason.

*** YAF inspires the largest audiences of high school and college students with conservativism through their campus lecture program...YAF's is the largest

- 3 -

in the nation!

Steve Forbes, Lt. Col. **Allen West, Dennis Prager,** Dr. **Walter Williams, Michelle Malkin, Steve Moore,** Attorney General **Ed Meese,** Dr. **Robert George,** Peter Schweizer, **Dinesh D'Souza,** renowned historian Dr. **Burt Folsom, yours truly, Katie Pavlich, Carly Fiorina,** Senator **Rick Santorum** and many other great conservative leaders have recently spoken to YAF's student audiences.

You see, YAF works with students to host these and many other conservative leaders at their schools. These lectures end up being the BIGGEST events on campuses of the entire year. YAF lectures drive the campus leftists CRAZY, because they are so effective at reaching new audiences.

*** YAF teaches hundreds of thousands of students across the nation your conservative ideas through breakthrough conferences, training seminars, and campus activism initiatives and activities.

In fact, they are the only Conservative Movement organization that has a full suite of conservative educational programs for high school students!

*** And Young America's Foundation preserves and protects President Ronald Reagan's ranch in Santa Barbara, California. They saved this national treasure so young people can learn about Ronald Reagan's conservative ideas.

And there's more. They operate a 22,000 square-foot Reagan Ranch Center, a "Schoolhouse for Reaganism," in downtown Santa Barbara.

Young people escaping their intolerant leftist schools come to the Ranch and Ranch Center as safe havens to learn your conservative ideas! What a valuable treasure to the Conservative Movement.

You can see, no other organization reaches conservative students with your ideas on a bigger scale than Young America's Foundation.

In fact, just recently I signed an exclusivity contract with Young America's Foundation, who will be my sole sponsor for future campus appearances this school year.

YAF is THE organization I want to work with because they are the most

<u>effective at spreading conservative ideas</u>.

Already other schools are trying to silence our conservative message. Recently one of the Ohio State University's Student Advisory Councils warned students that my lecture had the "potential to threaten the emotional and mental safety of much of the campus community."

I'm glad I have YAF fighting to protect my rights and the rights of students.

But, trust me, YAF can't do this alone.

Especially when the Left is willing to stoop to any low and use any means — even violence — <u>to make sure your conservative values aren't shared with the next generation</u>.

We may have won the day at Berkeley, but we need to make sure we keep bringing your conservative values to colleges across the nation.

We can't let the Left silence us. If we're going to win the battle for the soul of America, we must win the next generation over to conservative ideas.

Which is why I'm writing to you today.

I'm writing to see if you'll help change a young person's life forever by helping introduce them to your conservative values that are the bedrock of our nation.

It can cost more than $2,000 to fund the attendance of just one student at one of YAF's conferences or seminars (lodging, food, speakers, books, and venue space all add up!).

My friend, I hope you'll stand with my friends at Young America's Foundation by rushing back your tax-deductible gift of $25, $35, $50, $100, $250, or even $1,000 or more.

Your gift could help support a current or future lawsuit against a rogue, leftist administration which denies students a fair forum for conservative ideas.

So, please consider a kind gift to help teach young people your conservatism by sending a tax-deductible gift of $25, $35, $50, $100, $250, or even $1,000 or more.

Supporters who give $1,000 or more have their name (or the name of a loved one) engraved on Freedom Wall at the Reagan Ranch so that future generations will know that you helped save both the Reagan Ranch and our nation.

We appreciate <u>whatever</u> is in your heart to give.

Students who witnessed YAF's victory in bringing me to UC Berkeley to speak have realized that if it can be done at Berkeley, it can be done at their schools, too.

Yet, they need help and resources to bring conservative speakers to their schools so that their peers can hear your ideas.

This is our opportunity to win a generation for freedom. There is no better investment.

It was Vice President Mike Pence who stated that Young America's Foundation is "winning the hearts and minds of America, one student at a time."

I, and students eager to hear your values, look forward to hearing back from you.

With Great Thanks,

Ben Shapiro

P.S. President Ronald Reagan stated, *"There is no better way to establish hope for the future than to enlighten young minds."* That's exactly what YAF does and I hope you'll help them share your conservative values with the next generation. <u>So please rush your tax-deductible gift to Young America's Foundation today</u>.

P.P.S. If you know of a young person who would benefit from attending a Young America's Foundation event, please call 1-800-USA-1776.

FROM THE DESK OF
ROY W. SPENCER, PH.D.
PRINCIPAL RESEARCH SCIENTIST • UNIVERSITY OF ALABAMA IN HUNTSVILLE

September 28, 2022

Mr. James E. Campbell
4747 W Country Gables Dr.
Glendale, AZ 85306-3509

Dear Mr. Campbell,

Let me introduce myself. I am a scientist. I am a meteorologist to be exact, and a Principal Research Scientist at the University of Alabama in Huntsville. I have also served as Senior Scientist for Climate Studies at NASA's Marshall Space Flight Center.

So yes, I am a "climate scientist."

In fact, my research has been entirely supported by U.S. government agencies: NASA, NOAA, and DOE. And I've never been asked by any oil company to perform any kind of service.

But you should know I completely reject the Doomsday climate scenarios we constantly hear about in the so-called mainstream media. I am convinced the "climate change warriors" who are so outspoken today are much more motivated by ideology than by science.

People say to me, "But what about the 'Scientific Consensus' in climate research?" I tell them that "consensus" on climate science is worthless.

The fact is only 36% of scientists agree with the end-of-the-world scenario of global warming that fuels the UN climate agenda. That's a far cry from the false but often-quoted "97% scientific consensus" claimed by the global warming industry.

And yet we are bombarded daily with frantic warnings of climate calamity.

I see the negative impact of the climate alarmists' apocalyptic message. I see how it is used to *silence* dissenting voices in places where freedom of speech is supposed to be especially treasured. I especially see how it warps the minds of some of our most promising *young people*.

Climate alarmism is the foot in the door that ideologically driven hardliners are using to convince young people to join their side.

But, there are also *solutions* to this relentless climate alarm indoctrination.

Mr. Campbell, I am writing you today about one of those solutions: the **Committee for a Constructive Tomorrow – "CFACT"** for short.

Believe me when I tell you, CFACT is unique in the way it confronts the climate hysteria so prevalent today. My good friend Craig Rucker founded this non-profit, strictly non-partisan organization in 1985 to offer a constructive, **fact-based** voice on consumer and environmental issues.

For years, CFACT has been warning America about the Radical Green agenda. *It's a war.* **Not a war to "save the planet," but an all-out war on capitalism and freedom.**

And make no mistake about it, the Left is going all-out to use the issues of the environment and global warming to lasso young people into embracing a radical worldview.

You may have heard about the United Nations' scary climate report, its "Sixth Assessment Report" or "AR6." The Secretary General of the UN called it a "code red" for humanity.

Yet the AR6 report only focuses on the worst-case-scenario predictions for our world, and purposefully downplays the more realistic, less extreme models regarding temperature increases and weather.

Is it a coincidence that the same person who called the report a "code red" for humanity, Secretary General António Guterres, was once the leader of the Socialist Party of Spain?

I don't think it is.

Socialists have long tied their hopes for a radical new future to environmental policy because they know it pulls at the heartstrings of people – and most especially **young people.**

You might recall how teenage climate activist **Greta Thunberg** became the darling of the liberal media establishment after she gave a rant to the United Nations Climate Action Summit in New York City on September 23, 2019:

> "You have stolen my dreams and my childhood with your empty words ... People are dying. Entire ecosystems are collapsing. We are in the beginning of a mass extinction, and all you can talk about are fairytales of eternal economic growth. How dare you! ... if you choose to fail us, I say: <u>We will never forgive you</u>. *We will not let you get away with this!"*

Greta was joined by thousands of other young people for a **"Youth Climate Summit"** organized at United Nations headquarters for, according to the UN's website, "a full-day of programming that brings together young activists ... [and will be] <u>action</u> oriented."

This was a week after Greta testified to Congress, and then participated in a rally outside the White House at which fellow students staged an 11-minute "die-in" to represent how many years we supposedly have left until the world ends.

Meanwhile, two newly formed radical youth organizations – the **U.S. Youth Climate Strike** and the **Sunrise Movement** – have formed to advance climate alarmism and the very dangerous and very socialist "<u>Green New Deal</u>" that was first advanced by **Rep. Alexandria Ocasio-Cortez and embraced by the Biden Administration.**

Rep. Ocasio-Cortez is attempting to frame the debate in Washington even while capturing the imagination of the next generation with her grandiose (and entirely insane) policy initiatives.

Who can forget her remarkable – and totally fact-free – outburst upon entering Congress as a naïve 29-year-old former bartender:

"The world is going to end in 12 years if we don't address climate change ... This is our World War II!"

Yes, young people today are being manipulated. They're being indoctrinated. And they are being played as pawns in a long chess game that radical environmentalists and Green socialists are determined to win.

I am proud to support CFACT's efforts to push back against this tide. *Especially* their extremely successful effort on our college campuses to free students from the grip of climate-alarm indoctrination.

They call this program, **CFACT Collegians**.

For the past 20-plus years, CFACT has organized active chapters of this campus program at dozens of colleges and universities across the country.

Students in the CFACT Collegians program have the opportunity to hear about and advocate free-market solutions, counter junk science, and promote economic growth.

CFACT is the only group in America solely dedicated to confronting global warming hysteria and other misinformation spewed by the radical environmentalists at America's colleges and universities. And on campus after campus, CFACT Collegians has become a major obstacle to the Green Left's obsession with shutting down any debate on climate issues.

Thanks to CFACT's Collegians program, every day on campuses across America a rising group of bright, articulate, enthusiastic young students (the leaders of tomorrow!) are challenging leftist orthodoxy – and especially their climate change "religion."

They are challenging the notion that "the debate is over."

And they are living proof that the Left has not yet managed to stifle all opposition on our campuses.

With socialism now apparently winning vast numbers of converts among our young people, and with more and more pressure to smother all debate, *I believe CFACT's Collegians program has never been more important than it is right now.*

For one thing, college students across America need to hear what science really has to say about climate alarmism. Having studied this subject for decades, I know the science surrounding global warming is far from "settled."

We've been told over and over that each successive year was "the hottest year ever."

But for the climate change crowd to make even this claim, they have to cherry-pick their data and completely ignore the U.S. and U.K. satellite data, which they know full well are the best available.

The truth is that recent warmth is modest ... "record" years are only warmer by hundredths of a degree. **The world might not even be warmer than it was during the Medieval Warm Period or the Roman Warm Period, and clearly Mother Nature caused those warm events – <u>not humans</u>.**

There is also increasing evidence that rising CO_2 is causing a "<u>global greening</u>" phenomenon and might even benefit ocean life as well. Records continue to be set in grain harvests around the world, contrary to fake news reports of global warming hurting agriculture.

Despite the climate fear mongers' dire predictions, the historical record clearly shows that a warmer climate is <u>better for human beings</u> than a colder one:

- If we look at the historic record – let's say the last 3,000 years – we see that people really suffered during the cold periods. During the "Little Ice Age," from around 1400 to 1850, it was very cold in Europe. Harvests failed. Food became scarce. People starved. There was much disease. It was a <u>miserable</u> period.

- Before that, however, we had a "Medieval Warm Period" around 1100 A.D. Temperatures then were at least as hot as they are now, maybe hotter. During this time the Vikings discovered and settled Greenland (they actually grew crops there!). Life was good in Europe. Cathedrals were built. Wars and violence decreased. People prospered. There was plenty of food, even a surplus.

I wish you could see the faces of some of these kids – as I get to do – when the CFACT Collegians and I discuss these issues with them. When they first realize not everything they've been told about climate change or the environment is true.

You can literally see the transformation from indoctrinated robot to independent thinker begin to take place in front of your eyes.

It's happening on college campuses throughout America. *But it needs to happen on more of them!*

That's why the Collegians program is so important. Not just to CFACT but to the entire great debate surrounding energy and the environment, and yes, even to America's very future.

CFACT Collegians <u>defy climate censorship</u> on their campuses.

They hold lectures and debates, hand out fact sheets in student centers, and talk to fellow classmates. Through debates, discussions, literature, speakers, and events, they are asking the tough questions about the "science" behind the global warming scare campaign.

CFACT Collegians stress that most consumer and environmental problems can best be met and overcome – not through excessive government regulation and bureaucracy – but rather by unleashing the power of the free-enterprise system and the ingenuity of science and technology.

Chapters invite speakers on campus such as **John Stossel, Jonah Goldberg, Dinesh D'Souza, Marc Morano, Lord Christopher Monckton**, and ... I am pleased to say ... me!

During these visits, I've seen for myself the impact CFACT Collegians can have. And they have had some remarkable successes:

- CFACT Collegians at **West Virginia University** and **Marshall University** testified at a West Virginia State Board of Education meeting regarding whether K-12 classrooms should consider causes for global warming other than man-made factors. The presence of CFACT students made a huge impact, garnering impressive media attention both locally and nationally. Eventually the board ruled 6-2 to amend the standards to "allow students to use scientific models to form their own conclusions on the debated topic."

This was a tremendous victory!

- At its flagship chapter at the **University of Minnesota – Twin Cities**, CFACT Collegians hosted several powerful speakers over the past couple of years, including Ben Shapiro, Dinesh D'Souza, and Ron Paul, among others. They also received extensive local media attention supporting an important new pipeline project in Minnesota by conducting several protests exposing the financial backing of pipeline opponents – most notably Warren Buffett, who had a financial interest in opposing it.

- CFACT Collegians have also given key testimony at several important EPA and state regulatory hearings. At the **University of Georgia**, they polled 1,400 students and found that over 70% supported nuclear power in Georgia. They then shared these impressive results with state regulators. In Washington, D.C., CFACT Collegians from **George Washington University** weighed in at an EPA hearing on carbon dioxide rules that sought to shutdown coal-fired power plants. Student representatives from **George Mason University** in Virginia and **Vanderbilt University** in Tennessee submitted a letter of opposition to Biden's moratorium on oil and gas leases on federal lands and waters to the Department of the Interior.

Unfortunately, on most U.S. campuses you will hear no argument against the Green socialists and their so-called "facts" and global warming hysteria – **unless CFACT Collegians has an active chapter.**

And that is why I am writing to you today.

Right now, CFACT Collegians are active on dozens of campuses. That's out of more than 4,000 active colleges and universities in the United States. CFACT would like to establish many more chapters – at least 20 more this year.

Funding is the only thing holding CFACT back. It takes an average of $10,000 to get one CFACT Collegians chapter up and running on a college campus. This amount is used to nurture these groups from startup to the point where they can organize their own events and function as a mature, largely independent organization.

Once established, CFACT Collegians chapters become catalysts for a <u>real discussion</u> on global warming and other environmental issues. All based on CFACT's core beliefs in sound science and free enterprise.

Of course, CFACT's ultimate goal is to build a nucleus of young Americans who believe that freedom – individual and economic – is the way to solve problems.

<u>Not massive government. And definitely not socialist economic policy.</u>

I am writing to you today because CFACT has launched an urgent campaign to found up to <u>20 new chapters</u> in four regions of the country this year. That's a total of $200,000 they must raise in the next several weeks.

I ask you to please join me in support of CFACT by rushing a tax-deductible gift of $25, $35, $50, $100 – or even $250, $500, $1,000, or more.

Can CFACT and I count on your help today?

For years, radical leftists and Green socialists have used college campuses as their primary source for recruiting. No part of this leftist agenda has been more central to this effort than climate alarmism. And now they are ramping up this effort to unprecedented levels.

Our future is being cast right now in the beliefs and perceptions instilled in this generation of college students. If you and I fail to make a stand for truth on our campuses, we cannot expect that the future will be a bright one for freedom or sound public policy on the environment.

The climate-alarm industry – and its radical political agenda – will have won.

And they *will* win unless organizations like CFACT can do more to spread the truth and expose the fallacies of the global-warming hysterics. <u>We must act quickly</u> if we are to deter this growing threat to our future as a free nation. CFACT can't do that without the generous financial support of friends like you.

Thank you for your consideration and prompt response to this most urgent appeal.

Respectfully,

Roy W. Spencer

Dr. Roy Spencer

P.S. **If you can send CFACT a tax-deductible gift of <u>at least $100</u> today, it will be my pleasure to send you my book,** *Global Warming Skepticism for Busy People.*

Warning: This book is <u>outright heresy</u> to Bernie Sanders, Al Gore, and the climate-alarm industry!

Please, don't put this urgent letter aside. I urge you to respond as quickly as possible.

APPENDIX II

Breviary on Segregation:

Fact: Segregation is generally accepted as being harmful to the community. (Webster's New Collegiate Dictionary definition: The separation or isolation of a race, class, or ethnic group by enforced or voluntary residence in a restricted area by barriers to social intercourse, by separate educational facilities, or by other discriminatory means.)

Fact: Segregation is still practiced by significant entities within the United States Congress: this practice is harmful to society.

The legislative branches of the United States government are highly segregated bodies.

Goal: Consideration of an approach by this entity that might eliminate segregation, so that it could become a symbol of unity in the governance of the people. The segregation practiced by our congress is partially to blame for the division in our country. Once a person is elected to an office in the U.S., they should be interested in benefiting the entire population of the country not some political position.

Mechanism: The House of Representatives and Senate could integrate by

- Getting rid of the concept of a republican building and a democrat building.
- Integrating each office building with approximately the same percentage from each party.

- Avoiding grouping of members under a republican or democrat name
- Extinguishing the title of republican and democrat once the individual is sworn in.
- An expressed acceptance that once elected to this exclusive branch of government they are there to serve the entire populace and not just a contingency of the populace.
- Each chamber of the House and Senate should be seated in a manner that no more than two members of the same party (while the parties are segregated) can sit next to each other during deliberation of bills or during presentations to the body.
- If party affiliation is kept primary, and the approach to legislating is only obstructionist in nature a simple plurality should suffice to pass legislation, where sincere collaboration is apparent legislation should be expected to have at least 25 % of the minority contingent to pass.

Expected Outcome:

Integrated groups are more likely to have stereotypes broken down. Segregation of deliberative bodies does not encourage the best people to step forward.

Establishing the principal that everyone in the legislative body is there to do what is best for the country as a whole, might break up the continuous deadlock between the two components of the legislative bodies and allow them to work together to solve the country's problem, rather than waste both time and money fighting each other.

If the majority understood they must have a minimum of 25 % of the minority party's consent to pass legislation, it might lead to people learning to compromise for the good of the whole. Collaboration might come to replace stagnation.

Obstructionism would be seen for what it is: hurtful to society as a whole and a waste of money.

Progressing from one day a month the speaker could request a political party occupy only every other seat when in chambers.

It might also be reasonable for all members of congress to be reminded that our political structure is only able to function if each side accepts the other side as a legitimate entity. What is being done today is petty and harmful to democracy. It is a breakdown of the **covenant** every America should support.

APPENDIX III

Breviary on Medical practices:

HIPAA (Health Insurance Portability and Accountability)

HIPAA was established to further legalize what physicians have been doing since Hippocrates. It appears to those of us in practice that this was done to make medical records more easily available to the Government, not to protect the patient's medical information (which doctors have always done). More paper; fewer trees! Disclosures without patient permission may occur under HIPAA in the following situations: when required by federal, state, or local law; if requested by law enforcement agencies; if requested by national security agencies; if requested by public health agencies; for mandatory government audits or investigations; etc. See what I mean.

Pre-certifications:

Currently, in my office, we have to pre-cert approximately 50 percent of our orders for Class 2 drug use and sometimes other categories. Once we get the medication approval, we must do it again about 30 percent of the time if we simply change the dosage. We have had to wait up to 2 weeks (not common) for the answer from the insurance program. I have seen cost figures in the area of 40 billion dollars a year from doctor's offices in expenses for this request from insurances. I have never understood why doctors should have to pay for serving their patient's needs. Even a charge of $10.00 per pre-certification to the insurance program could help keep this problem more manageable.

If that happened, perhaps health care CEOs might not be among the highest reimbursed individuals in the business arena. [United Health CEO David Witchman was paid 18 plus million in 2018 according to Biz Journals News.] Guess which medical groups require the most precertification's in my office? Medicaid and Access. It is mournful that doctors do not have an organization that might help protect them from such abuses.

Malpractice:

Malpractice is a device whereby lawyers can help themselves to income from doctors by making doctors appear incompetent. Malpractice is an archaic system of redistribution of wealth to patients and lawyers. Payouts have little to do with actual medical care but are more related to the skill of the attorney. Attorneys choose which patients to represent pretty much based on what is likely to be awarded financially if they win the case, not on the merit of the case. What is the option? It would be far more equitable for everyone if insurance was for "bad outcomes." Bad outcomes can occur with the best treatments. Malpractice should be the prerogative of the Medical Boards. People should be able to get help for bad outcomes. If that were the case patient and doctor could maintain a viable working relationship and patients with a bad outcome could be compensated accordingly. In the proposed system doctors would continue to be advocates for patient care, as we naturally do anyway and not be turned into adversaries as the current system does. Another case of refusing to work together for the benefit of all.

APPENDIX IV

Guest Editorial
The Physician and 'Climate Change'
Jane M. Orient, M.D.

A "climate emergency" has been declared, echoed by Democratic Presidential aspirants and by thousands of street protesters worldwide. Pressure groups demand radical change in all areas of life, including medical ethics, with no time for reflection or evidence-gathering.

According to the first of the AAPS Principles of Medical Ethics, "The physician's first professional obligation is to his patient, then to his profession. His ethical obligation to his community is the same as that of any other citizen." The AAPS motto "*omnia pro aegroto*" means "everything for the patient."

In recent decades, organized medicine, notably the American Medical Association and the American College of Physicians, has introduced a fundamental transformation. Individual patient welfare is subordinate to a perceived collective benefit. The AMA states that there are multiple stakeholders, whose interests must be balanced.[1] Various groups seek to divert physicians' energy and capitalize on their trusted status to promote a political agenda.

In the current widely promoted extreme view, "our ailing planet" is supposed to be our first priority. In an article in the *New England Journal of Medicine*, Dunk et al. write:

> We believe that the current imperative for climate action requires physicians to mobilize politically as they have before, again becoming fierce advocates for major social and economic change. A truly ethical relationship with the planet that we inhabit so precariously, and with the generations who will follow, demands nothing less.[2]

In 1990, Physicians for Social Responsibility members Michael McCally, M.D., Ph.D., and Christine Cassell, M.D., wrote in the *Annals of Internal Medicine* that "global environmental change," including, "potentially, global warming," which is "produced by the growing numbers and activities of human beings," threatens the "habitability of the planet and the health of its inhabitants." Thus it is socially responsible for physicians to use their expertise about the environment to try to prevent such change.[3] Christine Cassell was formerly president and CEO of the American Board of Internal Medicine and the ABIM Foundation, and then president and CEO of the National Quality Forum, which is in charge of setting quality standards for every hospital in the United States.

The Medical Society Consortium on Climate and Health offered an educational program on the "Health Impact of Climate Change—Preparing your Communities and Practices" at the AMA's 2019 interim meeting. The American Public Health Association joined with the Lancet Countdown in November 2019 to celebrate the release of a list of policy recommendations that "aim to protect human health from the climate crisis."[4]

The medical sector accounts for nearly one-tenth of U.S. greenhouse gas emissions and reportedly would rank seventh in the quantity of such emissions internationally if it were its own country.[5] Thus, physicians need to "do something." Recommended actions include fostering climate action in medical schools, incorporating advocacy skills in the medical-school curriculum, and supporting divestment from the "fossil-fuel" industry.[5]

Internationally acclaimed Gundersen Health System in La Crosse, Wisconsin, claims to produce more energy than it consumes.[6] To achieve this, Gundersen has spent $40 million on such projects as two wind installations, energy-conservation measures, and a dairy digester. It trucks $800,000 worth of wood chips a year to one hospital, where they are dumped into a concrete pit holding 75 tons of wood to feed the wood-burning boiler.[6] Methane from the manure of 2,000 cows generates electricity.[7] In Manhattan or Dallas, the logistics would be far more difficult.

Doctors are urged to be aware of the environmental consequences of their actions. Should they plan anesthesia management based partly on the greenhouse potential of the anesthetic agent?[7] "Green" their office and educate their patients on how they can reduce their impact on the environment? The American College of Physicians offers a 'Climate Change Toolkit.'[8] AMA delegates are told that they, as members of a trusted profession, have a "moral imperative" to inform their patients about climate change—with easily accessible materials in their waiting rooms if there is not enough time during individual visits. Doctors "need to think of their organizations not just as healers, but also as contributors to a looming catastrophe that only massive amounts of concerted action taken now can mitigate."[9]

Beyond "Evidence-Based" Policy

Evidence alone is not enough in this "emergency," write Dunk et al., to "compel action in a nonrational policy sphere." Physicians need to "engage, on behalf of public health, with the ugly realities of ward politics, to take off their white coats and wade into the fray in which actions are taken and decisions made."[2] These authors observe that it was "an act of well-informed imagination—and evocative writing—that galvanized physician action against nuclear weapons." Physicians need "a preparedness to base policy advice upon predictions and best guesses (as opposed to empirical data) and an ability to collaborate with unfamiliar disciplines (e.g., climatology and ecology)" [parenthetical statements in original]. Epidemiologists must "anticipate the future."[1]

Despite the exhortations for physicians to make changes in their lifestyle or medical practices, the UN International Panel on Climate Change (IPCC) admits that such actions will have no measurable impact on climate. A "radical overhaul of global economy and society"[13] and "massive public investment in decarbonizing all economic sectors, not just energy," and a "swift end to fossil fuels"[13] are demanded. The cost of transition to "renewable" energy alone is estimated to cost the US. $2.3 trillion per year.[10] The ultimate goal appears to be a global socialist, technocratic regime to control industry, agriculture, energy generation and use, diet, and virtually every aspect of daily life. An early draft for a Global Green New Deal was released by the United Nations Environment Programme (UNEP) in 2009.[14]

What is the evidence for the efficacy and safety of such a regime? If (and only if) atmospheric CO_2 could be cut to pre-industrial levels, by curtailing emissions and removing and sequestering CO_2, computer models predict that global mean temperature could possibly be held to less than the dreaded increase of 1.5 °C above the "pre-industrial level." These models, however, have so far proved to be very poor at predicting temperature.[15]

It is impossible to replace the 80% of the world's energy now generated by coal, oil, and natural gas with wind or solar, given the requirements for land, minerals, concrete, and energy-intensive manufacture.[16] Could nuclear energy be developed rapidly enough? If not, the only way to achieve the "carbon-neutral" goal would be by drastic reduction in energy use—through poverty and/or drastic reduction in the human population. Physicians for Social Responsibility and most environmental groups have strongly opposed nuclear energy.

The evidence concerning the actual performance of renewables is not favorable. In Germany, after $500 billion in subsidies for renewables, 53.5% of electricity was still generated with fossil fuels. Nuclear contributed 11.8%; onshore wind, 14.3%; offshore wind, 3.0%; hydro, 2.6%; biomass, 7.0%; solar, 7.2%; and waste, 1%.[17] The wind industry is collapsing as subsidies expire and opposition mounts from wildlife and forest conservationists.[18] Electricity bills have soared, and about 300,000 German households a year have been disconnected from the grid because of unpaid bills.[19]

There is a strong positive correlation between energy consumption and life expectancy at birth, according to figures from the World Bank.[20] Energy poverty would have a strongly negative effect on human health, life-span, and well-being.

Carbon Dioxide as Climate Driver

Discovered by Antoine Lavoisier (1743-1794), the carbon cycle describes the movement of carbon through the various reservoirs on earth.

It is estimated that the earth's crust or lithosphere contains 66-100 million gigatons of carbon (1 gigaton = 1 million metric tons), of which only about 4,000 Gt C is in "fossil fuels"—coal, oil, and natural gas.[21] The name implies that these are derived from primordial forests through a process that seems to be no longer operative for some reason, making them nonrenewable. That idea has been challenged, especially for "abiogenic oil."[22] The combustion of such fuels is the only way for carbon sequestered in the lithosphere to enter the carbon cycle.[21]

The atmosphere contains about 780 Gt C; the surface ocean, about 1,000 Gt C; vegetation, soils, and detritus, about 2,000 Gt C; and the intermediate and deep ocean, about 38,000 Gt C as CO_2 or CO_2 hydration products. Each year, the atmosphere and the surface ocean exchange about 90 Gt C.[23] Human activity adds about 6.1 Gt C to the atmosphere each year. The ocean absorbs about 2.5 Gt C more than it gives off to the atmosphere. That extra amount of carbon is utilized by marine biota and eventually gets incorporated into deep sea deposits and sediments.[21]

Over geologic time, atmospheric concentrations of CO_2 have reportedly varied widely, with some estimates 20-fold higher than the present level of around 400 ppm, and a low of 200 ppm.[23] According to one estimate, one hundred million billion tons of carbon have been taken up by coccolithophores (phytoplankton), shellfish, corals and foraminifera (zooplankton) and incorporated into calcium carbonate plates, scales, or shells. Over eons, the level of atmospheric CO_2 has fallen from about 2,500 ppm to the current level. As plants die at around 150 ppm, it can be argued that human use of carbon-based fuels is saving the biosphere from CO_2 starvation.[24] But is this use dooming the planet to a climate catastrophe?

There are numerous natural factors that affect climate, which has always been changing: the sun, ocean cycles (the Pacific Decadal Oscillation or PDO and the Atlantic Multi-decadal Oscillation or AMO), and stochastic events such as volcanic eruptions.[25] The IPCC models, however, consider only atmospheric CO_2—which happens to be the only factor over which humans have some control.

Joe Bastardi asks, how can the increase of only one molecule of CO_2 in 10,000 molecules of air over 100 years have an effect that outweighs the "Grand Slam of Climate" (the very design of the system)?[25] Note that CO_2 is a minor greenhouse gas; water vapor is by far the most important one.

If the earth is "ailing" owing to a "climate emergency," and CO_2 is the cause, what is the pathogenetic mechanism?

Like other "greenhouse gases," including water vapor, methane, and refrigerants such as freon, CO_2 absorbs energy in a narrow band in the infrared region. Al Gore and other advocates portray these gases to be acting like a blanket enveloping the earth that will allow energy in but then trap it. In the most dramatic scene in his 2006 movie An Inconvenient Truth, Al Gore displays a graph of how global temperature closely tracks atmospheric CO_2 concentration. At the end, as humans are allegedly adding "unprecedented" levels of CO_2 to the atmosphere at a rate not previously seen, the temperature will soar—as Al Gore rides up on something like a forklift, the "elevator version" of the global-warming "hockey stick."

I found it difficult to see, looking at his graphs, which came first: the change in the CO_2 level or in the temperature. But from the underlying data, obtained from the study of ice cores, it is clear that the CO_2 level increase lags the temperature increase, and therefore could not have caused it. Recall that CO_2 solubility in sea water decreases as the temperature rises. In 1957, Revelle and Seuss estimated that temperature-caused out-gassing of ocean CO_2 would increase atmospheric CO_2 by about 7% per °C temperature rise. The reported change during the seven interglacials of the 650,000-year ice core record is about 5% per °C, which agrees with the out-gassing calculation. Between 1900 and 2006, atmospheric CO_2 increased 30% because of the addition of human-caused emissions. If CO_2 had been responsible for temperature rise, the ice-core record predicts an increase of about 6 °C per 30% rise in CO_2. In fact, the temperature rose only 0.1 °C–0.5 °C between 1900 and 2006.[23]

The physical mechanism for the greenhouse effect is radiative energy input exceeding radiative output. Svante Arrhenius, who has been celebrated as the "father of climate change,"[28] found a quantitative link between changes in atmospheric CO_2 and changes in climate.[27] In 1896, he argued that changes in CO_2 could have caused the ice ages, by altering the rate at which the earth cooled to space. Knut Ångström disagreed, arguing that his experiments showed that CO_2 was not a major driver of air temperatures.

CO_2 is indeed an infrared-active gas, as are water and other "greenhouse gases." However, Connolly and Connolly point out that IPCC models ignore Einstein's 1919 observation that if a gas is in thermodynamic equilibrium, the rate of infrared absorption is equal to the rate of emission—the gas does not store the energy. The Connollys' data show that the gases are in thermodynamic equilibrium. Their weather balloons "have shown quite categorically that there is no greenhouse effect."[28,29,30,31]

Radiation accounts for only 0.29 watts/m² (0.01%) of the energy transfer within the atmosphere.[28] Climate catastrophe predictions must assume a large positive feedback from a temperature increase of any cause. Paleoclimate data showing higher CO_2 levels or higher temperatures definitively refute the runaway greenhouse concept. The Roman Warm Period and the Medieval Warm Period seen on early IPCC graphs are thus quite inconvenient.

These periods were made to disappear, as was the Little Ice Age, by data manipulations exposed in the "Climategate" emails obtained from the University of East Anglia. The "hockey stick" pattern of unprecedented recent warming is an artifact that can be generated from cherry-picked data from Siberian pine YAD061, the "most influential tree in history," or by feeding random data into the computer model used by Michael E. Mann, a climate scientist at Pennsylvania State University and a prominent figure in the scandal.[30]

It is now the 10th anniversary of Climategate. James Delingpole writes that the retrieved documents showed scientists "contriving to destroy inconvenient data in order to evade FOI (Freedom of Information) inquiries; attempting to shut down scientific journals which published studies unhelpful to their cause; viciously bullying dissenters; even trying to rewrite history." Yet, "by some bizarre inversion of logic, the less and less credible the evidence for the great global warming scare, the bigger and noisier and more powerful the Climate Industrial Complex has grown."[30]

Judith Curry, whose academic career was derailed in the wake of Climategate because she expressed views uncongenial to the climate establishment, reflects on the continuing repercussions. These include putting "a halo around Michael Mann's head over his 'victim' status;" turning "politically correct and 'woke' universities" into "hostile places for climate scientists that are not sufficiently 'politically correct'"; and damage to the integrity of professional societies that have published policy statements advocating emissions reductions and that marginalize research that is not consistent with the party line.[31]

The Fake Consensus

Science, of course, is not consensus based. But the assertion that "97% of climate scientists" agree with the apocalyptic climate scenarios is highly effective in convincing the public and politicians. This conclusion by Cook et al.[32] was based on reviewing abstracts of 11,944 papers on climate change and concluding that 97.1% of those expressing an opinion supported the consensus view—after they excluded the 67% that expressed no opinion. According to Christopher Monckton, that paper actually shows only 0.3% agreement with the hypothesis that human activity is very likely causing most of the current global warming. None were shown to agree with the idea of catastrophic human-caused warming.[33]

Great press fanfare, including in the *Washington Post*,[34] greeted the announcement that 11,000 scientists from 153 countries signed by Internet to an article in *BioScience* entitled "World Scientists Warning of a Climate Emergency."[35]

The article provided no evidence for a human-caused climate emergency, but rather accepted it as a given. The "suite of graphical vital signs of climate change" shows that per-capita meat consumption has increased by 11% in 10 years, world GDP by 80% in 10 years, and passenger air travel by 64% in 10 years—all signs of increasing prosperity.

"To secure a sustainable future, we must change how we live, in ways that improve the vital signs summarized by our graphs," the article concludes. "Economic and population growth are among the most important drivers of increases in CO_2 emissions from fossil fuel combustion." It noted that "still increasing by roughly 80 million people per year, or more than 200,000 per day,... the world population must be stabilized—and, ideally, gradually reduced...."[35] "Improvement," as defined by these authors, means fewer human beings and less prosperity.

Ezra Levant reviewed the Canadian signatories[36]—which are hardly a group of accomplished scientists. This can no longer be done at the time of this writing because the list is unavailable[37] while "invalid" signatures, likely including "Mouse, Mickey," are removed.

The longest list of scientist signatories to a petition related to climate change is the Oregon Petition (www.PetitionProject. org), which reads:

We urge the United States government to reject the global warming agreement that was written in Kyoto, Japan in December, 1997, and any similar proposals. The proposed limits on greenhouse gases would harm the environment, hinder the advance of science and technology, and damage the health and welfare of mankind.

There is no convincing scientific evidence that human release of carbon dioxide, methane, or other greenhouse gases is causing or will, in the foreseeable future, cause catastrophic heating of the Earth's atmosphere and disruption of the Earth's climate. Moreover, there is substantial scientific evidence that increases in atmospheric carbon dioxide produce many beneficial effects upon the natural plant and animal environments of the Earth.

This petition was not posted on the Internet to be signed by clicking on a link. It was sent, together with an extensively referenced review article, by postal mail to known scientists from lists such as *American Men and Women of Science*. It was signed by 31,487 American scientists, including 9,029 with a Ph.D. degree. These included two prominent scientists who had raised the issue of possible climatic effects of increased atmospheric CO_2, investigated it, and concluded that it was not a serious problem warranting drastic intervention: the late Edward Teller and the late William Nierenberg.

Since even one dissenter is a problem for climate alarmists, immediate action was taken to discredit the petition. An activist group, probably Ozone Action, planted a fraudulent signature, then "discovered" it—that of a popular singer Geri Halliwell known by her stage name Ginger Spice. The mistake of accepting a signature sent by FAX was not repeated, and security measures were undertaken to assure validity of all signatures and remove duplicates. But media smears continue to circulate.

The "cancel culture," social media de-platforming, censorship of dissidents ("climate deniers") from the mainstream press and prestigious journals, and serious threats to the livelihoods of any who are not on the "correct" side of this issue keep many Americans from learning that there is even a debate.

Instead of rational discussion, the issue is dominated by a mass youth movement, at the moment starring the Swedish activist, 16-year-old Greta Thunberg, saying, "I want you to panic" and "How dare you!" Thanks to incessant indoctrination in government schools, she and her contemporaries apparently believe that their future has been stolen from them by the older generation and the capitalist system that has enabled them to live comfortably and in freedom.

The power of youth movements has been harnessed by totalitarian campaigns before. Concerning Communist infiltration in the U.S. during the 1930s, Eugene Lyons writes:

> Because of immaturity and youthful eagerness, [youth] "follow the leader" more blindly than any other age group, and are perfect raw stuff for demagogic molding. Not one of them in ten thousand would be trusted to make policies for his community. Yet the ten thousand together, as Youth with a capital Y, influence policies, and command attention beyond their numbers and without reference to their inexperience and peculiar psychological influences....
>
> I watched both Italian Fascism and German Nazism at close range in their formative stages. It is not generally appreciated to what a large extent they were both Youth movements.[10]

Members of Physicians for Social Responsibility are marching with youth Climate Strike protesters. These physicians write that they are "pleased to witness the important testimony of 16-year-old climate activist Greta Thunberg before Congress" as she "told lawmakers to listen to scientists and urged immediate action to respond to the climate crisis," and are disseminating photographs of her on social media.[20]

The Real Objective

If lowering atmospheric CO_2 would not "stabilize" the climate, even if it could be achieved, because CO_2 is not the climate driver, what is the point of the multi-trillion-dollar investments?

Climate scientist Richard Lindzen of the Massachusetts Institute of Technology states: "Controlling carbon is a bureaucrat's dream. If you control carbon, you control life."[30]

As Walter Williams points out, proponents of controlling greenhouse gases have revealed their true agenda. They themselves do not believe the narrative through which they are causing mass anxiety, depression, and even despair.[41] Ottmar Edenhofer, lead author of the IPCC's fourth summary report released in 2007, speaking in 2010 advised: "One has to free oneself from the illusion that international climate policy is environmental policy. Instead, climate change policy is about how we redistribute de facto the world's wealth." UN climate chief Christiana Figueres said that the true aim of the UN's 2014 Paris climate conference was "to change the (capitalist) economic development model that has been reigning for at least 150 years, since the Industrial Revolution." Christine Stewart, Canada's former Minister of the Environment said: "No matter if the science is all phony, there are collateral environmental benefits.... Climate change (provides) the greatest chance to bring about justice and equality in the world." Tim Wirth, former U.S. Undersecretary of State for Global Affairs and the person most responsible for setting up the Kyoto Protocol said: "We've got to ride the global warming issue. Even if the theory of global warming is wrong, we will be doing the right thing in terms of economic policy and environmental policy."[42]

Lindzen wrote in 2003 that "the scientific community is clearly becoming less ambiguous in separating views on warming from totally unreasonable fears for both the planet and mankind." But he observed that "environmental advocates are responding by making increasingly extreme claims," and his hope that "some path will emerge that will end the present irrational obsession with climate"[43] has not yet been realized.

Scientific as well as medical ethics is challenged. Lindzen stated that he didn't think any field could survive the degree of corruption that climate science has experienced without at least losing its self-respect. He believes progress may have been set back a few generations because instead of trying to figure out how the earth behaves the field was coopted into a situation where it was supposed to support a paradigm that the government or the environmental movement wanted.[44]

Conclusions

There is an existential threat related to climate, as Climate Strike activists claim, but it comes from the radical political agenda being promoted under cover of "saving the planet."

The evidence refutes the claim that human emissions of carbon dioxide can catastrophically disrupt the earth's climate. Continuing to spend trillions of dollars to "fight climate change" will have no effect on the climate and cannot meet human energy needs with "renewables."

The existential threat is to our freedom, our prosperity, our capacity to provide medical care, and the integrity of our science and our profession. Physicians need to evaluate evidence independently and shun groupthink. They must not sacrifice their patients' welfare to serve an agenda.

Jane M. Orient, M.D., practices internal medicine in Tucson, Ariz., and serves as executive director of AAPS and managing editor of the Journal of American Physicians and Surgeons. Contact: jane@aapsonline.org.

REFERENCES

1. AMA Code of Medical Ethics. Available at: https://www.ama-assn.org/delivering-care/ethics/code-medical-ethics-overview. Accessed Nov 17, 2019.
2. Dunk JH, Jones DS, Capon A, Anderson WH. Human health on an ailing planet—historical perspectives on our future. *N Engl J Med* 2019;381:778-782. Available at: https://www.nejm.org/doi/full/10.1056/NEJMms1907453. Accessed Nov 17, 2019.
3. McCally M, Cassel CK. Medical responsibility and global environmental change. *Ann Intern Med* 1990;113:467-473.
4. Watts N, Amann M, Arnell N, et al. The 2019 report of the Lancet Countdown on health and climate change: ensuring that the health of a child born today is not defined by a changing climate. *Lancet* 2019;394:1836-1878. Available at: https://www.thelancet.com/journals/lancet/article/PIIS0140-6736(19)32595-6/fulltext. Accessed Nov 18, 2019.
5. Solomon CG, LaRocque RC. Climate change—a health emergency. *N Engl J Med* 2019;380:209-211. Available at: https://www.nejm.org/doi/full/10.1056/NEJMp1817067. Accessed Nov 17, 2019.
6. Baier E. Wisconsin's hospitals energy push brings the green. *MPRNews*, Jun 1, 2015. Available at: https://www.mprnews.org/story/2015/06/01/gundersen-renewable-energy-hospital. Accessed Nov 17, 2019.
7. Anon. Wisconsin plant turns cow manure into electricity. *La Crosse Tribune*, Oct 6, 2014. Available at: https://www.postcrescent.com/story/money/2014/10/06/wisconsin-plant-turns-cow-manure-electricity/16804325/. Accessed Nov 17, 2019.
8. Gadani H, Vyas A. Anesthetic gases and global warming potentials, prevention and future of anesthesia. *Anesth Essays Res* 2011;5(1): 5-10. doi: 10.4103/0259-1162.84171.
9. ACR Climate Change Toolkit. Available at: https://www.acpoline.org/advocacy/advocacy-in-action/climate-change-toolkit. Accessed Nov 18, 2019.

10. Clark C. Climate change: is addressing it part of the doctor's job? Medpage Today, Nov 18, 2019. Available at: https://www.medpagetoday.com/meetingcoverage/ama/83423?xid=nl_mpt_DHE_2019-11-19&eun=g403576d0r&utm_source=Sailthru&utm_medium=email&utm_campaign=Daily%20Headlines%20Top%20Cat%20MeC%20%202019-11-19&utm_term=NL_Daily_DHE_dual-gmail-definition. Accessed Nov 19, 2019.
11. McMichael AJ. Global warming, ecological disruption and human health: the penny drops. Med J Aust 1991;154(8):499-501.
12. Gilding P. Why I welcome a climate emergency. Nature 2019;573:311.
13. Editorial. Act now to avert climate crisis. Nature 2019;573:309.
14. Barbier EB. Rethinking the Economic Recovery: A Global Green New Deal. UNEP; April 2009. Available at: https://www.cbd.int/development/doc/UNEP-global-green-new-deal.pdf. Accessed Nov 18, 2019.
15. Michaels P, Knappenberger C. Climate models versus climate reality. Climate Etc.; Dec 17, 2015. Available at: https://judithcurry.com/2015/12/17/climate-models-versus-climate-reality/. Accessed Nov 18, 2019.
16. Hiserodt E. An open letter to Alexandria Ocasio Cortez. New American, Feb 27, 2019. Available at: https://www.thenewamerican.com/print-magazine/item/31579-an-open-letter-to-alexandria-ocasio-cortez. Accessed Nov 18, 2019.
17. Appunn K, Haas Y, Wettengel J. Germany's energy consumption and power mix in charts. Clean Energy Wire; Oct 30, 2019. Available at: https://www.cleanenergywire.org/factsheets/germanys-energy-consumption-and-power-mix-charts. Accessed Nov 19, 2019.
18. Hinderaker J. Wind energy collapsing in Germany. Powerline; Aug 4, 2019. Available at: https://www.powerlineblog.com/archives/2019/08/wind-energy-collapsing-in-germany.php. Accessed Nov 19, 2019.
19. Darwell B. Behind the Green New Deal: an elite war on the working class. NY Post, Mar 26, 2019. Available at: https://nypost.com/2019/03/26/behind-the-green-new-deal-an-elite-war-on-the-working-class/. Accessed Nov 21, 2019.
20. Pielke R Jr. Graph of the day: life expectancy v. energy use. Available at: https://rogerpielkejr.blogspot.com/search?q=expectancy. Accessed Nov 18, 2019.
21. Soil Carbon Center. What is the carbon cycle? Kansas State University. Available at: https://soilcarboncenter.k-state.edu/carbcycle.html. Accessed Nov 18, 2019.
22. Gold T. The effect of peer review on progress: looking back on 50 years in science. J Am Phys Surg 2003;8:80-82. Available at: https://www.jpands.org/vol8no3/gold.pdf. Accessed Nov 18, 2019.
23. Robinson AB, Robinson NE, Soon W. Environmental effects of increased atmospheric carbon dioxide. J Am Phys Surg 2007;12:70-90.
24. Moore P. 12 fake invisible catastrophes and threats of doom. Presented at 37th annual meeting of Doctors for Disaster Preparedness, Tucson, Ariz., July 20, 2019. Available at: https://drive.google.com/file/d/0BGnmn7qC9bcHQmNIM1pGMGZHOWQxM1V4cHctTXJhLXpwMGEQ/view. Accessed Nov 19, 2019.
25. Bastardi J. The Climate Chronicles: Inconvenient Revelations You Won't Hear from Al Gore—and Others. Relentless Thunder Press; 2018.
26. Watts A. Father of global warming Svante Arrhenius: an early false prophet of the 'energy crisis.' Watts Up with That?; Mar 11, 2015. Available at: https://wattsupwiththat.com/2015/03/11/father-of-global-warming-svante-arrhenius-an-early-false-prophet-of-the-energy-crisis/. Accessed Nov 19, 2019.
27. Uppenbrink J. Arrhenius and global warming. Science 1996;272:1122.
28. Connolly R, Connolly M. Balloons in the air: understanding weather and climate. Presented at 37th annual meeting, Doctors for Disaster Preparedness, Tucson, Ariz.; Jul 20, 2019. Available at: https://www.youtube.com/watch?v=XfRBr7PEawY&feature=youtu.be. Accessed Nov 19, 2019.
29. Orient JM. Hide the decline. AAPS News, January 2010. Available at: https://aapsonline.org/newsletters/Jan2010.php. Accessed Nov 19, 2019.
30. Delingpole J. My finest hour: a decade on, the scam I exposed is stronger than ever. Spectator, Nov 9, 2019. Available at: https://www.spectator.co.uk/2019/11/my-finest-hour/. Accessed Nov 19, 2019.
31. Curry J. The legacy of Climategate—10 years later. Climate Etc.; Nov 12, 2019. Available at: https://judithcurry.com/2019/11/12/legacy-of-climategate-10-years-later/. Accessed Nov 19, 2019.
32. Cook J, D. Nuccitelli SA, Green M, et al. Quantifying the consensus on anthropogenic global warming in the scientific literature. Environ Res Lett 2013;8: 024024 (7 pp). doi:0.1088/1748-9326/8/2/024024.
33. Nova J. That's a 0.3% consensus, not 97%. JoNova; Jul 1, 2013. Available at: http://joannenova.com.au/2013/07/thats-a-0-3-consensus-not-97/. Accessed Nov 19, 2019.
34. Freedman A. More than 11,000 scientists from around the world declare a 'climate emergency': study outlines six major steps that 'must' be taken to address the situation. Washington Post, Nov 5, 2019. Available at: https://www.washingtonpost.com/science/2019/11/05/more-than-scientists-around-world-declare-climate-emergency/. Accessed Nov 19, 2019.
35. Ripple WJ, Wolf C, Newsome TM, Barnard P, Moomaw WR. World scientists' warning of a climate emergency. BioScience, Nov 5, 2019. Available at: https://academic.oup.com/bioscience/advance-article/doi/10.1093/biosci/biz088/5610806. Accessed Nov 19, 019.
36. Levant E. 11,000 'scientists' warn of 'untold suffering' from climate change: meet the Canadians who made the list! RebelNews, Nov 7, 2019. Available at: https://www.rebelnews.com/who_were_the_11_000_scientists_warning_of_untold_suffering_from_climate_change. Accessed Nov 19, 2019.
37. Ripple WJ, Wolf C, Newsome TM, Barnard P, Moomaw WR, xxxxx scientist signatories from xxx countries. World scientists' warning of a climate emergency (condensed version). Alliance of World Scientists. Available at: https://scientistswarning.forestry.oregonstate.edu/. Accessed Nov 19, 2019.
38. Lyons L. The Red Decade: the Classic Work on Communism in America during the Thirties (orig. published 1941), Safety Harbor, Fla; Simon Publications; 2001.
39. PSR. Global climate strike calls attention to health emergency. News; Sep 20, 2019. Available at: https://www.psr.org/blog/2019/09/20/global-climate-strike-calls-attention-to-health-emergency/. Accessed Nov 19, 2019.
40. Lindzen R. AZ Quotes. Available at: https://www.azquotes.com/quote/595192. Accessed Nov 21, 2019.
41. Schlanger Z. We need to talk about 'ecoanxiety': climate change is causing PTSD, anxiety, and depression on a mass scale. Quartz; Apr 3, 2017. Available at: https://qz.com/948909/ecoanxiety-the-american-psychological-association-says-climate-change-is-causing-ptsd-anxiety-and-depression-on-a-mass-scale/. Accessed Nov 21, 2019.
42. Williams WE. Scientists: dishonest or afraid? LewRockwell.com; Nov 20, 2010. Available at: https://www.lewrockwell.com/2019/11/walter-e-williams/scientists-dishonest-or-afraid/. Accessed Nov 21, 2019.
43. Lindzen RS. Science in the public square: global climate alarmism and historical precedents. J Am Phys Surg 2003;18:70-73. Available at: https://www.jpands.org/vol18no3/lindzen.pdf. Accessed Nov 21, 2019.
44. Lindzen RS. MIT Professor Richard Lindzen on the corruption of climate science. New Criterion; Apr 25, 2016. Available at: https://www.youtube.com/watch?feature=emb_title&v=RUBrV0VFcbY&time_continue=35&app=desktop. Accessed Nov 21, 2019.

James E. Campbell, M.D.

Distinguished Life Fellow of the American Psychiatric Association

American Board of Psychiatry and Neurology

American Board of Child and Adolescent Psychiatry

American Society for Adolescent Psychiatry Boards

ACKNOWLEDGEMENTS

I wish to thank the following:

Sharon Campbell my best friend and wife who has tolerated my hours of writing, and rewriting, and for her help in the final editing of my books.

Despite occasional digs at the legal profession, I have had the privilege to work with some very fine lawyers over the years, and they have helped me greatly. When one must operate in their arena, however, there is little opportunity to say what might be on your mind.

Despite references to the Pope, I am not anti-Catholic. When the Catholic Church was founded, there were no hospitals. Today, one out of five people in this country receive medical care at a Catholic hospital.

When the Catholic Church was founded, there were no schools. Today, the Catholic Church teaches 3 million students a day, in its more than 250 Catholic Colleges and Universities, in its more than 1200 Catholic High Schools and its more than 5000 Catholic grade schools.

Every day, the Catholic Church feeds, clothes, shelters and educates more people than other organization in the world.

I went to a Catholic Medical School, Saint Louis University, and I have no regrets about that choice.

OTHER BOOKS BY THE AUTHOR

The Manuel: Rapid Relief from Emotional Distress

Book 1 in the Rapid Relief Series: a book for people who suffer: Last revision 2022 Original title Rapid Relief from Emotional Distress. (Co-authored with Gary Emery Ph.D.)

Excerpt:

I have undertaken to rewrite aspects of the original book because, with time, comes further insights. I also wanted to reduce the size of the book, so not only the information, but the book itself would reflect a more rapid event. When I see a book advocating rapid relief and it is over 250 pages long, I think it will take too much time to read it. I have also made a small change in the manner of reporting. It appears socially correct for counselors, therapists, and psychologists to refer to people they work with as clients. The designation seems too commercial, or impersonal, and does not sit well with me, and therefore, when I am referring to individuals I treat, they are referred to by the time-tested designation of patient. The reference to people as patients does not intend to demean, or exalt anyone, but is a reflection of the very special bond doctor and patient have enjoyed since the birth of medicine, and which managed care seems to be doing its best to destroy.

When I entered the real world, I was not prepared by my training to treat patients who needed medicine. I found a form of therapy reducing my need to use medications by nearly half, or more. Currently, I see people being severely over treated for conditions described as metabolic, or medical, which I routinely treat using brief psychotherapy interventions.

In the forty years I have been in practice, I have seen the pendulum swing from one extreme to another; I like neither.

Psychological Therapy in a Pharmacological World

Book 2 in the Rapid Relief Series: a book for doctors, therapists, and those in therapy wanting to speed up the process.

Excerpt:

It has been said doctors go to scientific meetings to learn what colleagues can teach them, and they go to the office to learn what patients can teach them. Simply put, this book is a reflection on some of the lessons I have learned from my patients and other people in my life. What I have learned in brief is that much of what I was taught in my psychiatric residency and child fellowship is cumbersome. I have not come to bury psychiatry, but I hope to wake it up a little.

I chose to become a doctor who would work with the mind when I was five years of age. I did not learn the name psychiatrist until years later. In the small town of Warsaw, Illinois, population of 2000 there were no psychiatrists or psychologists. How the mind worked was a curiosity to me then, and it still intrigues me today.

I have observed professional training bringing about a narrowing of one's perspective, rather than broadening it. I have experienced this when I talk with other colleagues (doctors) about my experience and the points of view I have about treating patients. I get a far narrower response from psychiatrists, therapists, or counselors than when I discuss these ideas with non-professionals. While I was at UCLA for my child fellowship, I tried to present several of these concepts to staff members there. With the blessed exception of Gary Emery Ph.D., I found no one was very interested in my observations. I get letters and calls from patients and non-patients who tell me how Dr. Emery and my book Rapid Relief from Emotional Distress opened an entirely new approach to living for them. However, even in a time when therapy is not being paid for by insurance companies, when there is a shortage of trained professionals, I have a type of therapy which not only works, but is compatible with the typical short appointment times, and most other forms of therapy, I have not been able to mobilize much interest in the medical community.

Parents/Teachers and Mental Health: The art of accurate speech and other ways to help students not become psychiatric patients.

Book 3 in the Rapid Relief Series: a book for teachers and parents.

Excerpt:

Teachers, are you aware children are delusional? You may have had reason to think something is wrong with most children, but you may not have figured out what the "something" was.

In psychiatry, we have a form of thinking referred to as <u>delusional</u>. Webster II New College Dictionary (1999) defines delusion as "Something falsely disseminated or retained-Deception. A false belief held in spite of invalidating evidence especially as a symptom of certain forms of mental illness." I would project a minimum of half of the world is delusional all the time and most likely 98% of the people in the world respond to a situation in a delusional fashion at least once or more during an average day. I will only give a couple of examples here, as this will be a topic for a larger discourse. Children believe others are responsible for their thoughts, feelings and actions. This is not an accurate perception. It is a delusion. Because children grow up, they take this belief system with them into adulthood where they continue to act out this delusion by claiming others are responsible for their thoughts, feelings and actions. Children are taught, by the people who are close to them, to believe and act as if this way of thinking is accurate, and they may eventually end up in prison when segments of society can no longer ignore their behavior. If they escape prison, they are still doomed to a life of conflict and turmoil.

Have you ever wondered (I do) about how prison inmates claim they have done nothing wrong? It is simple; they are delusional. They still believe in the concepts that were a part of the original distorted thinking; if you look at the behavior from within this system of thinking, their behaviors are often logical. If I believe you have the power to make me mad, if I believe you have made me mad, it is logical for me to want to do something to you to impress you to stop your assault (perceived) against me. We do not label this form of delusion a mental illness, although we do often label the behaviors resulting from this form of thinking a mental condition: oppositional defiant disorder, conduct disorder, episodic dyscontrol syndrome, some depressions and some anxiety—the list goes on. Even though we all do it, it is still a delusion; because we all do it, it is not called a delusion. If we called it a delusion, we might try to do something about it. Instead, we ignore it until it reaches an extreme point, and then we punish the person who mistakenly acts out on erroneous beliefs (doing what they feel they should). Teachers <u>could</u> make this right.

Blame and Anger

Book 4 in the Rapid Relief Series

The title speaks for itself. Available only on the internet.

www.ingramcontent.com/pod-product-compliance
Lightning Source LLC
LaVergne TN
LVHW041752060526
838201LV00046B/981